# *From My*
# Kitchen Table

*Abby & thank you for your support!*

*From My*

# Kitchen Table

Mothering in the World
Grounded in the WORD

*Stay grounded! ♡ KeriMae*

KERI MAE LAMAR

A Happy Home Media
KINGSTON, WASHINGTON

Keri Mae Lamar/AHappyHomeMedia.com
P.O. Box 1304
Kingston, WA 98346

Author photograph: Logan Lamar

Links referenced or recommended in this book may be affiliate links, to which the author earns a small commission.

All Scripture is taken from the authorized King James Version.

All dictionary definitions are from Noah Webster's *The American Dictionary of the English Language*, published in 1828.

From My Kitchen Table/Keri Mae Lamar – 1st. ed.
ISBN 978-0-9961100-3-7

10  9  8  7  6  5  4  3  2  1

For Tom:
*That we may tell our children*

and

For our children:
*That their hearts early and honestly
be fixed upon Jesus*

*So we can never give too much attention
to the Bible.*

— James Montgomery Boice

# CONTENTS

Preface ...........xiii

1. A Heart for Study

   Simple Bible Study.................3
   Pick a Word, Any Word.................9
   Lessons from a Character.................17
   Lessons from David and Goliath.................27

2. A Heart for Jesus

   Who Said Bible Study was Boring? .................39
   Ways Worth Considering.................45
   God's Promise and Presence .................53
   Razing the Bar .................59
   Fear of the Lord.................63
   I Choose to Walk Therein.................69
   Prayer: Intreat and Inquire (part 1) .................77
   Prayer: Intreat and Inquire (part 2).................83
   Walking Before God .................91
   Nothing but Manna .................99
   But We See Jesus.................105

3. A Heart for Holiness

   A Gracious Woman .................115
   Look Up, Sister!.................121
   Perfectionism:
      Promise of Peace, Deliverer of Pain.................129

"The Secret" (or...*How to Love the Devil*) ..........137
On Disappointment ...........................143
On Judgment ..............................151
Joy is a Command .........................157
Thoughts on Anger .........................169
Have You Let Go of Your Peace? ..................175
Snickering is a Sin! ...........................181
Oh, to Be a TWIT for God! ...........................193

4.  A Heart for Home

A Simple Life ........................201
No Time for the Lord ......................205
Gadding About ......................211
Quenching My Appetite .....................221
Wanted: a Life of Ease.....................227
Fret Not Thyself ........................233
Grace Like Rain ........................239
Is Motherhood a Calling? ...................243
The Night Watches ......................253
Are You Clingy? .........................259

Epilogue .........................271

Appendix .........................277

Kitchen Table Quickmark ...................283

Other Books By Keri Mae ..................287

Appreciation .........................289

About the Author ......................291

# PREFACE

*Holding forth the word of life....*
– Phil 2:16a

While I was busy raising small children (see photo on the back cover), I kept a blog called "A Happy Home" where I wrote about not only the goings-on in our home and on our hobby farm, but published a number of Bible studies I had done. I did so to encourage other wives, mothers, and homemakers with the Word with the encouragement I had myself received, and to prod others to also look to the Bible for every instruction in righteousness (2 Tim 3:16), for it is a Book that is always current and relevant in all cultures and all times, for all people—even very busy women, tucked in their cozy and sometimes chaotic homes.

This book is a compilation of Bible studies from that blog, and all of the chapters have been edited, rewritten, and updated as necessary. Some of them were previously published in a small booklet, and those, also, have been updated. All of these studies reflect my deepest heart's desire to know God more and to rejoice in Him. I am not a trained theologian, but I trust that as Tyndale's plowboy, I too can glean a morsel of understanding from reading the Bible in my own language, praying, and trusting Him in faith. I am grateful to have the Bible in my own language, and wholeheartedly treasure my copy. I don't take for granted the sacrifices given for it to be so.

My own tools for study are rather simple: my King James Bible, a concordance, and a dictionary. A simple curiosity into a phrase or a word often reveals much about a text. I like to look words up in Noah Webster's 1828

*American Dictionary of the English Language*, but you might like to look into the original Greek or Hebrew, or pull out maps or timelines if you are so inclined; however, I invite you to flip to the appendix to learn more about why I use an English Dictionary when doing a study on Hebrew and Greek words. Nevertheless, you must read the Bible slowly enough and often enough to allow a curiosity about your reading to develop. Then, let your curiosity prod your study.

I am confident that God will continue to teach me through His Word and through His providence, ultimately completing His work in me (Phil 1:6), and that whatsoever lessons I have gleaned, however puny or immature, will be used for His glory. I trust you, dear reader, will, as a Berean, study for yourselves and search the Scriptures, to confirm or deny what you read, no matter the source (Acts 17:10-11). I welcome your loving and thoughtful correction, as my desire is to glorify God and to speak rightly regarding His Word.

# FROM MY KITCHEN TABLE

The title of this book, *From My Kitchen Table*, reflects my earnest desire to be in community with my sisters in Christ, and to welcome them, in essence, to my kitchen table where we might share a cup of coffee or tea, and talk about God's grace and His goodness to us. As iron sharpens iron (Pro 27:17), we might shoulder our struggles together, laugh, or even share a reprimand (Pro 27:6), but all with a heart towards pressing one another on to the prize of the high calling of God in Christ Jesus (Phil 3:14). These things, I hope you and I would do, if you sat at my kitchen table.

The Lord's hand is not too short that it cannot save, nor his ear too heavy that it cannot hear (Isa 59:1). I pray that as you make Bible study the delight of your heart and soul, you will come to know Him more deeply through your studies and prayers, and that your walk with the Good Shepherd would be your greatest joy.

Kingston, Washington
December 2019

# SECTION ONE

# A Heart for Study

*I never saw a useful Christian who was not a student of the Bible.*

— D.L. Moody

# Simple Bible Study

*Neither have I gone back from the commandment of his lips; I have esteemed the words of his mouth more than my necessary food. (Job 23:12)*

If you ask Christians if reading the Bible is important, most will readily agree. What would the answer be if the follow-up question was "How much time do you spend reading it?" or "When did you last read it?" Actions follow true beliefs.

Studying the Bible is not complicated. It doesn't take a seminary degree, just a thirst for the Living Water. Many Christians are parched to the bones and don't realize they've been, as the song goes, "looking for love in all the wrong places." Although there is nothing wrong with study guides, Christian life books, and counseling with other believers, it doesn't take the place of opening up a Bible, praying for the Spirit to open your eyes, and taking a good long drink.

My favorite Bible study tools are a concordance and Noah Webster's *American Dictionary of the English Language,* published in 1828.

Let me give you an example of a study from this passage: "Unto the church of God which is at Corinth, to them that are sanctified in Christ Jesus, called to be saints, with all that in every place call upon the name of Jesus Christ our Lord, both theirs and ours" (1 Cor 1:2).

I took special note of the words *to them that are sanctified in Christ Jesus.* I kept thinking, *are sanctified...are sanctified....* As if it's completed and not in progress? Hmm... I was a bit confused because I know better than anyone I am not fully sanctified by any means, but am a work in progress. I had a decision to make: to either stay confused (not the best plan), think "for myself" (which I am bent to prefer, even though I recognize how often I've been wrong!) or do a little bit of study. There are many ways to study: find a commentary, listen to a sermon on this passage, ask around, or look up the word *sanctify* in the concordance and dictionary.

Do you see the difference? I first want to find out what *God* thinks, not the interpretation of another person or even my own reasoning. And if I'm going to look for further study, for example within a dictionary, it's going to be one written by an author who understands the importance of the Bible as a primary source of information, history and wisdom.

This is what I do. When reading a passage of Scripture, I ask questions, then look up phrases or specific words, and dig deeper.

**Sanctified:** "made holy, consecrated, set apart for sacred services, purified and cleansed from corruption." *(All past tense).*

I popped the word into the concordance, and *wow*, a bunch of stuff came up, including this passage which continued the thread from the original: "And such were some of you: but ye are washed, but ye are sanctified, but ye are justified in the name of the Lord Jesus, and by the Spirit of our God" (1 Cor 6:11).

The same thought crossed my heart and mind: *are* washed, *are* sanctified, *are* justified. But how? "For it is sanctified by the word of God and prayer" (1 Tim 4:5).

*Hmm...by the Word of God...by prayer...*

Sometimes studying the Bible is like embarking on a treasure hunt. Continuing, I read: "Jude, the servant of Jesus Christ, and brother of James, to them that are sanctified by God the Father, and preserved in Jesus Christ, and called" (Jude1:1).

There seemed to be an ongoing theme here, this idea of already *being* sanctified. I begin to wonder if I am already sanctified in God's eyes, but that seemed strange.

What about passages, for example, that seem to say the contrary? Such as: "For the flesh lusteth against the Spirit, and the Spirit against the flesh: and these are contrary the one to the other: so that ye cannot do the things that ye would" (Gal 5:17). And "For that which I do I allow not: for what I would, that do I not; but what I hate, that do I" (Rom 7:15).

Perhaps these passages are speaking of the state I was in before I was saved? My wondering continues, so I read: "For by one offering he hath perfected for ever them that are sanctified" (Heb 10:14). Perfected once and for all, past tense, and yet sanctified, continuously, present tense.

Let your "I'm wondering..." follow the questions you ask. Let yourself stumble and ponder and give yourself time to be curious.

So, continuing then in prayer: *God. I know I'm not perfect, but through Christ, you see me as righteous. I know You are working things out in my life to cause me to realize this more every day. Open my eyes to see myself more and more through Yours. And forgive me for seeing the dirt on other believers instead of marveling how You have cleaned them up as well. Help me to see as You do.*

You can meander through a Bible study even from one sentence! To go deeper, I might also begin looking up the words *justified, washed, preserved,* and *clean.*

Reading the Bible is not hard, but it takes time and thought. You have both; use them wisely. "Jesus answered and said unto them, Ye do err, not knowing the scriptures, nor the power of God" (Matt 22:29).

---

*Are you a student of the Bible, studying to understand?*

# Pick a Word, Any Word

*Thy words were found, and I did eat them; and thy word was unto me the joy and rejoicing of mine heart: for I am called by thy name, O LORD God of hosts. (Jeremiah 15:16)*

Regularly, I keep a journal in which to write scripture, questions, or prayers in response to the chapters I am reading. But now and then, I follow a word or thread of words to gain more insight. Even though it is time consuming, one of my favorite ways to study the Bible is to do a word study. At the end of my study time, I am always blessed and grateful that I dug in a little deeper.

Here is how I did my last word study:

I looked up the word *wisdom* in my concordance. It is a fat, heavy concordance, but since finding the KJV Bible Search online (kjvbible.net), it has been a lot faster and easier. If you want another online version, you can check out BibleGateway.com or use your favorite Bible app.

Two hundred and twenty-two verses popped up on my search. I read them all, albeit not all on the same day. While I read, I jotted down the main ideas and wrote the references. For example, some scripture mentioned where wisdom came from, some mentioned the benefits of wisdom, and some mentioned the follies of trying to live without it.

Being able to group verses into headings is always helpful! For this study, I grouped the verses I found into five headings. Under the heading "Where do we find our wisdom?" I listed: from God Himself (Job 12:12-13, 16; Ps 51:6), from obeying His commands (Deut 4:6), and from a deep abiding reverence for the Lord (Prov 15:33; Job 28:28; Ps 111:10).

Once I got the main ideas, I went back one group at a time and reread the verses. It became clear what God thought about wisdom because the themes repeated, even though different authors wrote these passages over hundreds of years apart. How else could this be if it weren't for the Holy Spirit?

Here are the other headings from my study:

**What is done with wisdom?**

It is spoken and shared (2 Sam 20:22; 1 Kings 4:34; Jas 3:13; Ps 37:30; Ps 49:3; Dan 2:14) with gentleness and kindness (Prov 31:26; Jas 3:17).

It leads to using our time wisely (Ps 90:12), and finds us working wisdom into our days with actions and deeds (1 Kings 2:6; Acts 7:22).

## What are the results of this wisdom?

We will have life! (Eccl 7:12). We will also rely on God's Spirit and power, not our own or another person's (1 Cor 2:4-5). We will have a bright countenance (Eccl 8:1), a pleasant and peaceful soul (Prov 2:10), a godly walk (Prov 15:21), and not only happiness for ourselves (Prov 3:13), but for our households as well (1 Kings 10:8; Prov 29:3). This wisdom will make for peace (1 Kings 5:12; Job 13:5; Prov 11:12) and give us knowledge and proper perception (Prov 1:2), prudence (Prov 8:12), discretion (Prov 3:21), and strength (Eccl 7:19; Prov 8:14).

Naturally, because we'll have no delusions of how we got this wisdom, we'll walk in humility (Prov 11:2; Jer 9:23), and have a hunger for even more godly wisdom (Job 28:18; Prov 8:11; Eccl 2:13).

Lastly, this wisdom will give proper judgment and justice (2 Chron 1:10; Prov 10:31), be evident to others even if they don't like it (1 Kings 10:4-7; Mark 6:2; Acts 6:10; 2 Chron 9:23), deliver what we will find good (Prov 19:8), and be justified by the fruit of our actions (Matt 11:19).

There was nothing in that list I didn't want!

**There was plenty to be said for those who deny or reject God's wisdom:**

They are called fools. "The fool hath said in his heart, There is no God" (Ps 14:1).

They despise wisdom and instruction (Prov 1:7), therefore you ought not bother sharing your pearls (Prov 23:9). They are full of contention and pride (Prov 13:10), aren't liked much (Prov 12:8) and bring about their own suffering

(Prov 10:13; Jer 8:9). God's wisdom is beyond them (Prov 24:7; 1 Cor 3:19; Prov 14:6) because instead of knowing the Lord (Prov 30:3), they listen to their own heart as god (Isa 47:10). Ultimately, they end up destroying good things (Eccl 9:18) and are fooling themselves (Prov 14:8).

For more study on the topic of wisdom, especially on the difference between God's wisdom and the world's wisdom, see 1 Corinthians 1:19-30.

Therefore...

Ask for wisdom and get it (Jas 1:5; Prov 4:5, 7). Embrace God's wisdom (Prov 7:4), and act accordingly (Prov 2:2). Share the gospel with others (Col 1:28 and 4:5; 2 Cor 1:12). Forget crafting a god of your own making (Prov 23:4; Ezek 28:3-7, 17) and work hard now, before it's too late (Eccl 9:10). Do not take counsel from fools or dabble in foolishness (Eccl 10:1-3) and remember to stay in fellowship with believers (Col 3:16).

———————

*Wisdom comes with study. Choose a verse of the Bible and do your own word study.*

# Lessons from a Character

*This book of the law shall not depart out of thy mouth; but thou shalt meditate therein day and night, that thou mayest observe to do according to all that is written therein: for then thou shalt make thy way prosperous, and then thou shalt have good success. (Joshua 1:8)*

I am struck by the people in the Bible.

If someone wanted to make up a religious book that a multitude of people would read and follow, surely its pages would be full of amazingly brilliant and awe-striking people. Instead, we have those such as Noah (got a bit tipsy and slept in the nude), Abraham (lied and allowed his wife into the harem of a pagan king...twice!), Jonah (never repented of his

17

pride), and King David (killed the husband of a woman to have her). These are the people doing God's work???

Well, yes. And thank God, because the open failures and gross unfaithfulnesses give me hope. God can and will use even *me*.

Samson is interesting because, although on the surface it looks like he was a man who let his own desires use him, the story begins further back with his parents.

As told in Judges 13, his mother was barren and received this word from "the angel of the Lord": she would conceive and bear a son, and he was to be set apart and used of the Lord to deliver the Israelites from the oppression of the Philistines. Later, the angel came back to reiterate his words, and both husband and wife not only heard and proved him to be real, but agreed to wholehearted devotion in raising their son to be set apart from the world's ungodly ways.

As Samson grew, the Lord blessed him (Judges 13:24). Two verses later, as a young man, he saw a Philistine woman he wanted for a wife and demanded his parents arrange it for him. Even though the father initially rejects this demand, Samson said, "Get her for me; for she pleaseth me well" (Judges 14:3). There it is, done deal. The parents acquiesced to their son's pull for pleasure at the expense of their primary purpose. Their single-hearted devotion to God gave way to appeasing their child's appetite and set in motion his entire life of error and grief.

The rest of the story is sad. The Lord sent a reminder and warning, but Samson simply pushed them aside. Then, he offered meat to his parents without telling them where it came from, leaving them to wonder if the animal was unclean. There were secrets between child and parents. By verse ten of the same chapter, Samson's father was completely cowed. Even though he was not agreeable to the marriage, he went to get the bride himself.

This bride's true loyalty was never to her husband because she knew nothing of the Lord and His ways for marriage. Instead, she was full of crying, whining, manipulation ["thou dost hate me" (Judges 14:16)], and laying "sore upon him" (Judges 14:17) until Samson finally relented and gave in to her demands to tell her the answer to the riddle that will bring him ruin—and on their wedding night, no less. Inevitably, the boom fell, and when it did, Samson reacted in complete anger (Judges 14:19) instead of showing any semblance of repentance for the mess he had gotten himself into.

After he cooled down, he wanted his wife back. Of course, it was too late by then. The woman's father had now given her to another. Once again, Samson had a temper tantrum and set all the vineyards and crops on fire, which resulted in the death of his wife and father-in-law.

Then this shocking request: "And he was sore athirst, and called on the Lord..." (Judges 15:18).

He never called on God for anything until he had a need for physical comfort. Comfort was one of Samson's idols. And perhaps even more shocking—God responded by giving him water!

It says in verse twenty that Samson judged Israel for twenty years. Did he do this with godly wisdom or from that ornery gut? Because, the next verse says he "saw there an harlot, and went unto her" (Judges 16:1). What?! Then, the whole mess with Delilah happened; she nagged and whined and pouted, and once again, Samson's desires led him astray.

"And it came to pass, when she pressed him daily with her words, and urged him, so that his soul was vexed unto death" (Judges 16:16). It seems like every woman has certain demands her man must meet, or she will vex his life. Oh, the sorrow of my heart to remember all my vexing!

Samson lost his source of godly strength as well as the spirit of the Lord (Judges 16:20). His eyes gouged out, he was mocked and taken as sport for heathen gods. For the first time, there was a prayer of faith from Samson because at this point the Lord's spirit had departed from him. Samson didn't know God's presence anymore, but he had faith God was still there. Prayer became his only lifeline and weapon, and his life is worth sacrificing to alleviate both his wounds and the oppression of the Israelites. God answered his prayer, and Samson died along with his mockers.

There is much fodder for contemplation in every page of the Bible, and Samson's life is no different:

- In what ways has my single-hearted devotion to raise up a godly generation been weakened by caving into appeasing my children's appetites? What does this cost?

- When has God attempted to stop or hinder me from continuing on my destructive path...and I have pushed

Him aside, so to speak, to go the way I want?

- A person's loyalty, if not to the Lord Jesus Christ, is by default their upbringing and their cultural norms. They will be more concerned about what other people think than what is pleasing to God. Or they will focus on meeting their own desires instead of His. In what ways am I grieving the Holy Spirit by my insistence to do what feels right rather than what Scripture teaches?

- In what ways am I "laying sore upon" and "vexing" my husband? What are the demands he must meet to get a cheerful wife?

- Am I calling on God only when I am physically uncomfortable? Am I putting more thought and concern into my body, which is here and gone in a vapor, than in my spirit, which lives for eternity? Am I quicker to pray for my children's healing from illness than for their salvation?

- When the Holy Spirit reproves me, or when circumstances unravel due to my own errors, do I react in anger and vengeance, or do I cry in repentance, my tears upon the Savior's feet?

I am thankful God still works through sinful people. He is gracious to answer prayers for blessings (such as water), and He will always answer any prayer made in faith. My prayer right now is that it will not take the tragedy of pain and blindness for me to see how the Spirit of the Lord has worked within me, and even now gives me the strength to pull down the pillars of ungodliness around and within me.

Can't wait to thank Samson for sharing his messy, sinful life with me.

# LESSONS FROM A CHARACTER

––––––––––

*What ponderings and questions do you have after reading a selection of Scripture? Write them down, even if you are without immediate answers.*

# Lessons from David and Goliath

No matter how well I think I know an event from the Bible, a fresh reading always teaches me anew. Reading God's Word is never boring, never been-there-read-that. Even in the account of David and Goliath, lessons abound:

- "If he be able to fight with me, and to kill me, then will we be your servants: but if I prevail against him, and kill him, then shall ye be our servants, and serve us." (1 Sam 17:9)

  Never make such enslaving agreements and promises with an enemy of the Lord. Why would they hold to their word? "And when the Philistines saw their champion was dead, they fled" (1 Sam 17:51).

- "When Saul and all Israel heard those words of the Philistine, they were dismayed, and greatly afraid." (1 Sam 17:11)

  Dismay and fear ought to be met with faith. "What time I am afraid, I will trust in thee" (Ps 56:3).

- "And David rose up early in the morning, and left the sheep with a keeper, and took, and went, as Jesse had commanded him." (1 Sam 17:20)

  David honored his parents by seeking the welfare of his father's house and in promptly obeying and seeing to his father's needs.

- "And the men of Israel said... that the man who killeth him, the king will enrich him with great riches, and will give him his daughter, and make his father's house free in Israel." (1 Sam 17:25) Irony of ironies, to be promised freedom in Israel. The Israelites *had* been free with the Lord as their ruler and king, but they traded their freedom for purposeful subjection to a man who was goodly, not godly (1 Sam 9:2). In what areas of my life am I trading my freedom in Christ for the slavery of selfishness, comfort, or popularity?

- "And Eliab his eldest brother (said)...Why camest thou down hither? and with whom hast thou left those few sheep in the wilderness? I know thy pride, and the naughtiness of thine heart; for thou art come down that thou mightest see the battle." (1 Sam 17:28)

False accusations abound in response to godly actions or character. Therefore, when others try to slander, it is important we carefully consider our words. It's discouraging, yes, but we need to hear complaints at times. Sometimes there is truth in it, sin we need to repent of. Humility in hearing must happen before discernment and direction.

- "And Saul said to David, Thou art not able to go against this Philistine to fight with him: for thou art but a youth, and he a man of war from his youth." (1 Sam 17:33)

There is a difference between seeing with your physical eyes, and seeing with eyes of faith and truth.

- "And David said unto Saul, Thy servant kept his father's sheep, and there came a lion, and a bear, and took a lamb out of the flock: And I went out after him, and smote him..." (1 Sam 17:34-5)

Reminders of past victories give power to future trials. Don't forget what the Lord has done in the past! And share your testimonies with others; they are powerful! "Thou shalt not be afraid of them: but shalt well remember what the

LORD thy God did unto Pharaoh, and unto all Egypt" (Deut 7:18).

- "And Saul armed David with his armour... And David said unto Saul, I cannot go with these; for I have not proved them. And David put them off him." (1 Sam 17:38-39)

Man's armor, man's provision, will never fit a task of the Lord's size. Feeling overwhelmed? Take off your own trying-to-make-it-work. I certainly wish my own made-up gear weren't tempting me to try on again and again; it never fits!

- "And he took his staff in his hand, and chose him five smooth stones out of the brook, and put them in a shepherd's bag which he had, even in a scrip; and his sling was in his hand: and he drew near to the Philistine." (1 Sam 17:40)

God will use our daily tools. He will even call—and empower—the one with nothing but rocks.

- "And the Philistine said unto David, Am I a dog, that thou comest to me with staves? And the Philistine cursed David by his gods" (1 Sam 17:42-43).

Those of faith will always look foolish and receive mocking or threats. Lamenting this fact won't change anything. We need to get over that and re-read 1 Peter.

- "Then said David to the Philistine, Thou comest to me with a sword, and with a spear, and with a shield: but I come to thee in the name of the LORD of hosts, the God of the armies of Israel, whom thou hast defied." (1 Sam 17:45)

God's armor = His Name.

- "This day will the LORD deliver thee into mine hand...that all the earth may know that there is a God in Israel." (1 Sam 17:46)

  God's purpose = His honor, His glory.

- "And all this assembly shall know that the LORD saveth not with sword and spear: for the battle is the LORD'S, and he will give you into our hands." (1 Sam 17:47)

  The battle is not mine and it's not about me.

- "And it came to pass, when the Philistine arose, and came and drew nigh to meet David, that David hasted, and ran toward the army to meet the Philistine." (1 Sam 17:48)

  We should run in faith to face our fears. We have the Holy Spirit!

- "And when the Philistines saw their champion was dead, they fled." (1 Sam 17:51)

  Do you ever wonder why not a single Philistine stopped to ponder what he had witnessed? God works all around us every day. But most people don't stop to pay attention to those works, or to inquire what those works might mean for their own lives.

- "And Saul said to him, Whose son art thou, thou young man? And David answered, I am the son of thy servant Jesse the Bethlehemite." (1 Sam 17:58)

  Humility is appropriate after victory. David didn't even give his own name because he understood this wasn't about himself.

We all face challenges. Let us be as David, strong in faith even if falsely accused or seen as foolish to the world, using the tools and talents we've been trained in to actively run toward the demons of fear and hopelessness instead of hiding from them and giving them strength. Speak the name of the Lord openly, boldly, and with humility. Give God the glory for the overwhelming challenges your faith enables you to overcome.

"The LORD is my light and my salvation; whom shall I fear? the LORD is the strength of my life; of whom shall I be afraid?" (Ps 27:1)

---

*Take a passage of Scripture and write out the lessons or principles the Lord might have you learn from it. How do you see Jesus in them?*

# A Heart for Jesus

*A truly humble man is sensible of his natural distance from God; of his dependence on Him; of the insufficiency of his own power and wisdom; and that it is by God's power that he is upheld and provided for, and that he needs God's wisdom to lead and guide him, and His might to enable him to do what he ought to do for Him.*

— Jonathan Edwards

# Who Said Bible Study was Boring?

*"Ye shall therefore keep my statutes, and my judgments: which if a man do, he shall live in them: I am the LORD." (Lev 18:5)*

*"And the statutes, and the ordinances, and the law, and the commandment, which he wrote for you, ye shall observe to do for evermore; and ye shall not fear other gods." (2 Kings 17:37)*

When I looked up the word *statutes* (KJV concordance), God was pretty clear we were to *do* them (stated nine times), to walk in them (nineteen times), to observe them (seven), and to keep them (thirty-five). Interestingly enough, only once is it stated we are to *fulfill* those statutes. Now, doesn't that perk the ears?

I can only imagine how many times *commandment* would reveal similar orders.

The word *ordinance* means "a rule established by authority; a permanent rule of action," and it is used in partnership with the word *statute* and *commandment* often.

God gives good reasons for following His ways:

- I am the LORD. (Lev 19:37)

- I am the LORD that healeth thee. (Ex 15:26)

- I am the LORD which sanctify you. (Lev 20:8)

What reasons more could we possibly want?

Alas, God knows those reasons are not enough for us. We need carrots. God's Word says if you diligently hearken, give ear, do what is right... "it may go well with thee, and with thy children after thee, and that thou mayest prolong thy days upon the earth, which the LORD thy God giveth thee, for ever" (Deut 4:40), that thy days may be prolonged (Deut 6:2), that he might preserve us alive (Deut 6:24). Then shalt thou prosper (1 Chron 22:13) and shall surely live (Ezek 18:9). Perhaps the best one of all: "they shall be my people, and I will be their God" (Ezek 11:20).

Even those carrots aren't typically enough to woo us, so there are consequences for not following the Lord's ways. If we do after the manners of the heathen that are round about us (Ezek 11:12), not only will we forfeit the above promises, we can expect curses (Deut 28:15, 45) and vanity (1 Kings 17:15).

Surely now there is enough reason to follow God? Yet, I know I also am tempted to twist scripture to mold it to my own reasoning abilities, my understanding. Much like in Solomon's situation, depending on God *and* myself is impossible: "And Solomon loved the LORD, walking in the statutes of David his father: only he sacrificed and burnt incense in high places" (1 Kings 3:3). The "only" in the verse kind of stings because we are apt to do likewise, but like Solomon, not without consequences. For example, we can't partake in a Bible study on Tuesday only to be watching a lusty TV show on Thursday. We can't praise God on Sunday and keep our lips closed about Him on Wednesday. We can't promise to pray for a friend on Friday only to gossip about her on Monday. I'll follow you, God, in this-this-n-this...only I'll use my own thinking in that-that-n-that.

Following God's precepts doesn't earn our way to heaven, to salvation, or even to His good favor; a good thing, because not one of us is able to do so (and not without subsequent boasting if it were indeed possible). In fact, Jesus abolished the law in his flesh (Eph 2:15) and blotted them all out, nailing them to the cross (Col 2:14). Yet, even as all creation follows God's ordinances (Jer 31:35), it ought to be a delight to approach God and to seek Him daily (Isa 58:2). Even though we have all strayed as the sheep we are (Isa 53:6), God still hopes in our return (Mal 3:7). In fact, the only observances commanded today are baptism and partaking of the Lord's supper (Heb 9). Still, Jesus promises paradise for repentant sinners even without those sacraments. The thief on the cross near Jesus certainly did not get baptized. Take the time to read Hebrews 9:8-14.

The choice is still ours today: blessing if we hearken unto the voice of the Lord, cursing if we don't. "See, I have set before thee this day life and good, and death and evil" (Deut 30:15). How we are going to walk is always our choice. His ways are not hidden. "But the word is very nigh unto thee, in thy mouth, and in thy heart, that thou mayest do it" (Deut 30:14). He is willing and able to teach us if we keep humble hearts toward Him: "Teach me, O LORD, the way of thy statutes; and I shall keep it unto the end" (Ps 119:33).

Let us seek wholeheartedly God's paths, running upon them with joyful abandon:

"I call heaven and earth to record this day against you, that I have set before you life and death, blessing and cursing: therefore choose life, that both thou and thy seed may live. That thou mayest love the LORD thy God, and that thou mayest obey his voice, and that thou mayest cleave unto him: for he is thy life, and the length of thy days: that thou mayest dwell in the land which the LORD sware unto thy fathers, to Abraham, to Isaac, and to Jacob, to give them." (Deut 30:19-20)

"Let your heart therefore be perfect with the LORD our God, to walk in his statutes, and to keep his commandments, as at this day." (1 Kings 8:61)

———

*What keeps you from doing His ordinances, or following in His ways?*

# Ways Worth Considering

The book of Haggai has been a great encouragement and exhortation. It was written after the Jewish people returned from captivity, laid the foundation for the temple of the Lord, and then gave up the task because of adversity from surrounding nations. God spoke to Haggai and said, "This people say, The time is not come, the time that the LORD'S house should be built. Is it time for you, O ye, to dwell in your cieled houses, and this house lie waste?" (Hag 1:2,4)

These are the words I use and hear used a lot: *"It's not a good time...."* The work to be done doesn't matter, whether cleaning the bathroom floor, reading a book to a toddler, or forgiving a family member; there is always a reason, even a seemingly proper and understandable one, that the time is not quite right. Do the words *"in a minute"* sound familiar?

In the meantime, what really gets accomplished? Sometimes, God's commandment to love one another is put aside to make room for self-indulgences, or the Bible is buried under the stack of other more urgent reading. God sees our weak spiritual condition and says the following words:

> Now therefore thus saith the LORD of hosts; Consider your ways.

> Ye have sown much, and bring in little; ye eat, but ye have not enough; ye drink, but ye are not filled with drink; ye clothe you, but there is none warm; and he that earneth wages earneth wages to put it into a bag with holes.

> Thus saith the LORD of hosts; Consider your ways. (Hag 1:5-7)

Consider your ways. Webster (1828) defines *consider* in this way: "to sit by or close to, or to set the mind or the eye to; to view or examine with attention." In other words, stop, look, and listen, and do it with focus. Are we seeing good fruit and godly results from current priorities? Or are we simply making excuses?

When the people of Israel returned to Jerusalem from captivity, they were excited to rebuild the temple to the Lord. The foundation was laid; the prayers were long and beautiful, the celebration joyful. But then, the heathen nations around them wanted to help because, in their own words: "Let us build with you: for we seek your God, as ye do" (Ezra 4:2). In other words, *"We're just like you! We pray to the same God! C'mon, let's join hands and work on this thing together!"*

The chief priests replied with words we still need to hear today: "Ye have nothing to do with us to build an house unto our God; but we ourselves together will build unto the LORD God of Israel" (Ezra 4:3). The Jewish leaders recognized the weakening effect of these other people and called them on it: *"No, you can't build our temple. No, you don't know our Lord. No, and we aren't even going to pretend."*

The response was (and aren't we surprised): "Then the people of the land weakened the hands of the people of Judah, and troubled them in building. And hired counsellors against them, to frustrate their purpose" (Ezra 4:4-5).

They even took the whole matter to the king himself and "wrote they unto him an accusation" (Ezra 4:6), which led to the "commandment to cause these men to cease, and that this city be not builded, until another commandment shall be given from me" (Ezra 4:21).

Who says the Bible is not current or relevant? Don't we see this exact scenario playing out today in all matters Christian? People who do not know the Lord, who do not follow Him or hear His words to heed them, still want to participate in Christian sacraments or traditions. And Christians who are bold enough to stand and say "no" are then subjected to trouble, adversity, frustrations, and yes, even lawsuits.

It is interesting to see the Lord's response to all this nonsense. The word after He says "consider your ways" is *go*. "Go up to the mountain, and bring wood, and build the house" (Hag 1:8).

In other words, *"Yes, I see what is happening. Yes, I know your excuses. Yes, I understand how hard it is. Yes, I know people will press you to give up if you don't bend to them. Now, go. Go do the work I gave you to do."*

The people listened. And obeyed. "Then spake Haggai the LORD'S messenger in the LORD'S message unto the people, saying, I am with you, saith the LORD" (Hag 1:13). *That* was enough to get the gloves back on and the tools clinking on stones again. Nothing else had changed in their circumstances; all they had (as if that was such a light thing!) was the *word of the Lord.*

Where have I not followed through on foundations I have begun? Where have I allowed the mores of the culture and people around me to dictate the work I should be doing? Where have I received a clear word from God and answered Him, *"The time is not come...not yet...in a minute...later...."* And, perhaps most importantly, is the Word of the Lord enough for me?

We can all do the work the Lord has given to us (Titus 2:4-5, for starters). It is a matter of seeing the Lord's priorities and of resting upon His promises, regardless of clamor around you. The time is come, and it is now.

"Not by might, nor by power, but by my spirit, saith the LORD of hosts." (Zech 4:6)

"Yet now be strong, O Zerubbabel, saith the LORD; and be strong, O Joshua, son of Josedech, the high priest; and be strong, all ye people of the land, saith the LORD, and work: for I am with you, saith the LORD of hosts." (Hag 2:4)

———————

*Have you in any way read a clear word from the Lord and answered Him "not yet"?*

# God's Promise and Presence

*"I am with you saith the Lord. And the Lord stirred up the spirit." (Hag 1:13c-14a)*

Once the people of Israel heard the word of the Lord, they did not waste time getting back to work on the labor God planned for them. They revered God enough to promptly return to His priorities and received not only the promise of His presence, but also His equipping power stirring up their spirits.

Many of us have a need to feel ready to do God's work. Once the word of the Lord comes (through Bible reading), it passes through a multitude of filters, including frameworks built on feminist, evolutionist, and humanistic-secular worldviews. For example, if we do not have a "work of faith, labour of love, and patience of hope in our Lord Jesus Christ," (1 Thess 1:3) then I wonder, why? Why do we not have these things? Could it be we do not believe God? Because if we truly believed He was speaking to us about our relationships and our homes, there would not only be a joyful partaking in His work, there would be sweet communion with Him.

Anyone can find a variety of excuses to discount the Bible, but what response ought Christians, born again by the blood of Jesus Christ, have regarding His Word or the work set out for us to do? It is the same response I require of my own children: honor, obedience, and an attitude of trust.

Instead, the response from us all, children included, is often debate or excuse, reasons to not do what is required. Bless our enemies? Forgive our debtors? Pray without ceasing? Meditate on His law day *and* night? Not let the sun go down on our anger? Respect our husbands? Receive children as a blessing? Take care of widows and orphans? Tithe? Love the "LORD thy God with all thine heart, and with all thy soul, and with all thy might" (Deut 6:5)? It seems an impossible list.

But what if God proclaimed children a blessing and we believed Him (Psalm 127:3-5)? What if in God's sight a meek and quiet spirit was truly of a great price (1 Peter 3:4)? What if we revered our husbands (Eph 5:33)? Would our families look different? Would there truly be the peace surpassing all understanding? Do we even believe there *is* such a thing?

God didn't part the sea until the Moses hit it with his staff . He didn't part the river Jordan until the feet of the priests stepped into it. If we are waiting to feel like it's a "good time" to jump in, forgive, love, etc., it may never happen. If we are waiting to feel like reading the Bible, praying, seeking the Lord while He may be found, it may never happen. God has spoken enough, created enough, and done enough. It is up to us to respond in faith to His Word and His work, despite our feelings.

What does our humble response and work of faith bring? His promise and His presence: "I am with you, saith the Lord. And the Lord stirred up the spirit" (Hag 1:13c-14a). What more could anyone possibly want? "Glory and honour are in his presence; strength and gladness are in his place" (1 Chron 16:27). Who doesn't want glory and honor? Strength and gladness? It isn't going to come from ourselves, no matter how hard we try.

We do not need to wait for convincing; we need only to step out in faith and trust. God will empower and equip us to do His work, whatever it is. As it is said, "God doesn't call the equipped; God equips the called."

It's time to get to work, friend—or back to work—on the things of the Lord.

"That thou mayest love the LORD thy God, and that thou mayest obey his voice, and that thou mayest cleave unto him: for he is thy life, and the length of thy days" (Deut 30:20).

---

*What work needs doing that you are avoiding?*

# Razing the Bar

Do you ever feel other people set the bar a little too high for you? For me, it is a struggle to meet the standard in how I spend money. For example, most times I feel fine shopping for clothing at consignment stores and happy with both the amount of clothing I buy and the money I save. Other times, I look at well-dressed people and begin to have the nagging thought I must not love my family enough to give them "the very best." I am looking up at a mountain of expectations of what is proper and good to buy, but my pudgy fingers are jiggling the humble coins in my pocket.

God dealt with me. He didn't beat me up for my discontentment. He also didn't smooth my feathers and tell me my life was going to be cheery and bright with promises of treasures to come. Instead He in essence took my cheeks in His hands and said, "Hey, look at *Me*."

"And there ye shall eat before the LORD your God, and ye shall rejoice in all that ye put your hand unto, ye and your households, wherein the LORD thy God hath blessed thee. Ye shall not do after all the things that we do here this day, every man whatsoever is right in his own eyes." (Deut 12:7-8)

Those bars may or may not be imaginary, set by my own insecurities. They don't matter because I am supposed to rejoice—to experience joy and gladness in a high degree— in all I put my hand unto, whether it is cleaning my way, schooling my way, spending my way, or whatever else. Who needs a bar when Jesus gives His perfect peace?

"Are ye so foolish? having begun in the Spirit, are ye now made perfect by the flesh?" (Gal 3:3). Frequently, I am easily muddled by whose expectations I am trying to meet. But praise be to God, He is always there to remind me of who I am, and He's provided His Spirit to give me contentment today, and strength to raze the bars when necessary.

"My soul, wait thou only upon God; for my expectation is from him" (Ps 62:5).

———————

*Are you trying to reach a standard outside of God's will and provision?*

# Fear of the Lord

*"And now, Israel, what doth the LORD thy God require of thee, but to fear the LORD thy God, to walk in all his ways, and to love him, and to serve the LORD thy God with all thy heart and with all thy soul, To keep the commandments of the LORD, and his statutes, which I command thee this day for thy good?" (Deut 10:12-13)*

I've got quite the list of projects I'd like to tackle. That's on top of the other lists getting shoved underneath piles of other papers also too urgent to put away or file. I'm great at making lists (and apparently, piles of papers). Checking those lists off, however, is another matter altogether.

Often my lists get plain overwhelming. Let's see...there's creating, preparing, serving, and cleaning up after healthy, homemade meals; organizing, buying, cleaning, and sorting through clothing for myself and my husband and for many growing children; ditto for shoes; managing the housework through chores (governed by lists); and, of course, I must read my Bible, plan and implement schoolwork, meet my husband's needs, answer letters, phone calls, and cries ranging from boo-boo's to various other needs arising mostly around three in the morning. And blog. And, on occasion, get around to washing my own hair.

*God, could You stop the world for a bit, so I can catch up?*

"What doth the LORD thy God require of thee?" He gently asks (Deut 10:12).

*All of the above, Lord, plus 15,438 other items to check off during my day. I have a list. Or two.*

"What doth the LORD thy God require of thee?"

*I give up. You better tell me again. Because I think I forgot. Again.*

Stop the world, indeed. Nothing stops the world faster than opening His Word and drinking from the pure spring. Therefore, I slowly began to read from the scripture above, savoring His voice.

"But to fear the LORD thy God...."

*Fear God? Pshawww. Done deal. Check. Next?*

"But to fear the LORD thy God...."

*Why am I stumbling here? Waddaya mean "fear"? Don't you mean "revere"? I got it already.*

"But to fear the LORD thy God...."

*Ok. I'll look.*

I looked up "fear the Lord" and found it thirty times in the King James Bible. It does mean to revere God, but it is *much more*. It also means to seek Him, serve Him, bless Him, praise Him, glorify Him, stand in awe of Him, confess Him, cleave to Him, swear by His name, obey His voice, and depart from evil. Even more, how we're to do these is in sincerity and truth (Josh 24:14), and to punctuate that point even further—*with all of our hearts.*

"Only fear the LORD, and serve him in truth with all your heart: for consider how great things he hath done for you" (1 Sam 12:24). *All my heart? Wholeheartedly?* Most days, my heart seeks after my own wants first. Even during the evening hours, I halfheartedly put the kids to bed, wanting my own time. Recently, I wanted to throw in the towel when the whining began over schoolwork.

*"Yes,"* I responded with less patience than I would have liked, *"you do have to write in your journal today. Yes, do the whole page of math. Yes, help your sister make her letters."* I didn't realize my lack of wholeheartedness wasn't exactly

blessing the Lord. It stemmed from a lack of fear.

The fear of the Lord must be learned: "Then one of the priests whom they had carried away from Samaria came and dwelt in Bethel, and taught them how they should fear the LORD" (2 Kings 17:28).

We *learn* how to fear the Lord by hearing, learning, and observing God's Word (Deut 31:12). We also learn by reading and copying scripture (Deut 17:18-19). Other good teachers: gratefully living where the Lord places you, and tithing (Deut 14:23). Well, I am thankful He doesn't pass out dunce caps to poor learners!

As we learn to properly and wholeheartedly fear the Lord, we will see bountiful results in our lives: no want (Ps 34:9), God as our help and shield (Ps 115:11), blessings both small and great (Ps 115:13), prayers heard (Jer 26:19), and a grateful acknowledgment of His provisions (Jer 5:24).

I need to pray for wholeheartedness in the tasks *du jour,* even through all those lists, because I can't just buck up and be wholehearted. I also need to spend more time in His Word. These are the first of my goals every year. Are they yours?

As we grow in the fear of the Lord, the needs of our family and other commitments and responsibilities will become less overwhelming.

"But seek ye first the kingdom of God, and his righteousness; and all these things shall be added unto you" (Matt 6:33).

———

*Do you need to grow in your fear of the Lord? How will you do so?*

# I Choose to Walk Therein

In our day and culture, a promotion is more apt to be praised than a pregnancy, so it doesn't come as a surprise that sometimes we shy from sharing the celebration of another baby with others.

How sad.

"Speak unto the children of Israel, and say unto them, I am the LORD your God. After the doings of the land of Egypt, wherein ye dwelt, shall ye not do: and after the doings of the land of Canaan, whither I bring you, shall ye not do: neither shall ye walk in their ordinances. Ye shall do my judgments, and keep mine ordinances, to walk therein: I am the LORD your God. Ye shall therefore keep my statutes, and my judgments: which if a man do, he shall live in them: I am the LORD" (Lev 18:2-5).

In this text, God reminded Israel: "I am the Lord your God." That was reason enough not to follow practices from the culture they had left (past) or the practices of the land where they were going (tomorrow). No other reason to obey can possibly be greater than "I am the Lord your God."

Why should we be mindful of His judgments, keep His ordinances, walk therein, and keep His statutes? Because "he shall live in them." Life flourishes for the believer under the care of the Master.

The word judge comes from the Latin *judex*, which is combined from *jus*, meaning law or right, and *dico*, meaning to pronounce. When God plainly and graciously gave Israel His judgments, Israel promised to keep them.

"And Moses came and told the people all the words of the LORD, and all the judgments:

and all the people answered with one voice, and said, All the words which the LORD hath said will we do" (Ex 24:3).

Well, we all know how those promises went: out the window like our own! Although it is impossible to be holy as God is holy, it doesn't excuse us from the standard God has set.

Many lessons were learned upon study of the word "judgement":

I ought not to depart from them (2 Sam 22:23), and if I walk in His ways, I will prosper in all I do (1 Kings 2:3; 1 Chron 22:13). God's judgments are no secret; there is no excuse for being ignorant of them; they are in all the earth (1 Chron 16:1; Ps 105:17). God exhorts me to "be strong, and of good courage; dread not, nor be dismayed" (1 Chron 22:13) regarding His judgments because "the fear of the LORD is clean, enduring for ever: the judgments of the LORD are true and righteous altogether" (Ps 19:9).

They are also as a great deep (Ps 36:6), good (Ps 119:39), righteous (Ps 119:62), right (Ps 119:75), and upright (Ps 119:137). Furthermore, gladness comes about because of them (Ps 48:11) along with rejoicing (Ps 97:8), hope (Ps 119:43), comfort (Ps 119:52), and a holy reverence (Ps 119:120). Who doesn't want more rejoicing, hope, and comfort?

Even though God has graciously revealed His expectations and desires for how we are to walk in holiness, preparation of the heart is still necessary (Ezra 7:10). And, if you break from His directions, although there are painful consequences, God says, "Nevertheless my lovingkindness will I not utterly take from him, nor suffer my faithfulness to fail" (Ps 89:33). How many times have we been disappointed or hurt by others yet have responded with "nevertheless, I will continue in lovingkindness to them"?

What am I to do? Before I can "not depart" from the good and godly paths the Lord has planned for my life, I need to choose the way of truth (Ps 119:30) and then declare it (Ps 119:13; Jer 1:16). As an example, I have not kept secret about my desire to have fullness in childbearing, although brows will raise (at best) with each pregnancy.

There are, as I mentioned, consequences for not following God's judgments. There are consequences for scoffers: "Judgments are prepared for scorners, and stripes for the back of fools" (Prov 19:29). There are consequences for God's people, too, if they follow the ways of the ungodly: "Therefore thus saith the Lord GOD; Because ye multiplied more than the nations that are round about you, and have not walked in my statutes, neither have kept my judgments, neither have done according to the judgments of the nations that are round about you; Therefore thus saith the Lord GOD; Behold, I, even I, am against thee, and will execute judgments in the midst of thee in the sight of the nations" (Ezek 5:7-8). No one is exempt from facing judgment, as we have all sinned and fallen short of the glory of God (Rom 3:23).

"We have sinned, and have committed iniquity, and have done wickedly, and have rebelled, even by departing from thy precepts and from thy judgments" (Dan 9:5). We are not Israel, but the principles remain.

Yet God's goodness and desire for relationship is seen repeatedly throughout history. In Ezekiel 20, God teaches about His statutes...then the people rebel and despise them, their hearts going after idols...then God tries again with their children...then the children rebel....

It may seem hopeless, trying to follow God's ways, even if the desire is there at the outset. And, truly, without the Holy Spirit, it *is* hopeless. But praise be to God, Jesus lived as I ought to and died as I earned to, so in the mystery of the ages, I am a grateful recipient of God's Holy Spirit. "And I will put my spirit within you, and cause you to walk in my statutes, and ye shall keep my judgments, and do them" (Ezek 36:27).

"Who shall not fear thee, O Lord, and glorify thy name? for thou only art holy" (Rev 15:4). As we face ridicule or downright hostility in areas we decline cultural norms and expectations, let us remember these words. There is truly none better than the ways of the Lord.

———

*Have you compromised your walk with the Lord in any area in order to fit in with your own country or cultural norms?*

# Prayer: Intreat and Inquire
## (part 1)

*"And Isaac intreated the LORD for his wife, because she was barren: and the LORD was intreated of him, and Rebekah his wife conceived. And the children struggled together within her; and she said, If it be so, why am I thus? And she went to enquire of the LORD." (Gen 25:21)*

Isaac and Rebekah had been married for twenty years before we're told that Isaac intreated the Lord for his wife. Was this the first time Isaac intreated the Lord? What does *intreat* mean?

**Entreaty, n.:** Urgent prayer; earnest petition; pressing solicitation; supplication.

**Urgent, a.:** 1. Pressing with importunity (Exod 12). 2. Pressing with necessity; violent; vehement; as an urgent case or occasion.

**Earnest, a.:** 1. Ardent in the pursuit of an object; eager to obtain; having a longing desire; warmly engaged or incited.

**Pressing, ppr.:** Urging with force or weight; squeezing; constraining; crowding; embracing; distressing; forcing into service; rolling in a press.

Back to our verse, we can now see this was no flippant prayer, sort of tossed up to the Father in a "take it or leave it" manner. It's unlikely Isaac asked for a child only once and then forgot the matter. In fact, he knew of the promise given to his father, Abraham, of being made into a great nation, and was probably distraught that twenty years had passed in barrenness. Perhaps he remembered his father had been in the same situation. Perhaps he recalled the consequences of Abraham "solving" the problem on his own with another woman. Whatever Isaac was thinking, it brought him urgently to his knees, where, with great longing, he pressed the Lord in pursuit of seeing God fulfill His promises.

Today, God's promises to us overflow within the covers of the Bible, promises of being partakers of the divine nature (2 Pet 1:4), of life which is in Christ Jesus (2 Tim 1:1), of His coming (2 Pet 3:4), of eternal life (1 John 2:25). I wonder, do we ever intreat the Lord over these? If we don't have life in Jesus, what is life but a bumbling through? And if we have His life, are we lazy about watching when the Lord shall come? Or do we look around and urgently and earnestly pray to see Him return? Do we pray as such for our children's salvation? "For the promise is unto you, and to your children, and to all that are afar off, even as many as the Lord our God shall call" (Acts 2:39).

Scripture records many instances of people intreating the Lord:

- "And Moses went out from Pharaoh, and intreated the LORD." (Exod 8:30)

- "Then Manoah intreated the LORD, and said, O my Lord, let the man of God which thou didst send come again unto us, and teach us what we shall do unto the child that shall be born." (Judg 13:8)

- "And David built there an altar unto the LORD, and offered burnt offerings and peace offerings. So the LORD was intreated for the land, and the plague was stayed from Israel." (2 Sam 24:25)

- "And the king answered and said unto the man of God, intreat now the face of the LORD thy God, and pray for me, that my hand may be restored me again. And the man of God besought the LORD, and the king's hand was restored him again, and became as it was before." (1 Kings 13:6)

- "And they were helped against them, and the Hagarites were delivered into their hand, and all that were with them: for they cried to God in the battle, and he was intreated of them; because they put their trust in him." (1 Chron 5:20)

- "And prayed unto him: and he was intreated of him, and heard his supplication, and brought him again to Jerusalem into his kingdom. Then Manasseh knew that the LORD he was God." (2 Chron 33:13)

Thankfully, we worship a God whose wisdom is "first pure, then peaceable, gentle, and easy to be intreated, full of mercy and good fruits, without partiality, and without hypocrisy" (Jas 3:17). And even when we are defamed, "Being defamed, we intreat: we are made as the filth of the world, and are the offscouring of all things unto this day" (1 Cor 4:13).

Prayer is how we communicate with God, the source of all light and wisdom. Are we sending Him lazy, flippant, or demanding prayers? If so, we need to repent, for a prayer that intreats is a prayer that God seems to enjoy hearing and answering.

———————

*How often do you sincerely, urgently press the Lord for His promises to you?*

# Prayer: Intreat and Inquire
## (part 2)

*"And the children struggled together within her; and she said, If it be so, why am I thus? And she went to inquire of the Lord."* (Gen 25:22)

In regard to both entreaty and inquiring, it seems most of my prayers are rather lackluster. Why is that? I'm not speaking about trying to make my words flowery or plenteous, which the Lord warns about; but in the simplicity of my speaking with God, I wonder how hot desire burns within me to see those prayers answered. Must there be a looming catastrophe for fervency to be stoked? Have I gotten too comfortable? I don't know. But it has been on my mind, this entreaty and inquiring business. My praying so deeply to God about *anything* requires me to be moved to do so because of a negative situation. What a shame I cannot meet Him in joyous times just as deeply.

The word inquire comes from *in* (into) and *quoero* (to seek). God's Word tells us we should be seeking His face when we have a question, a wonderment, a decision to make. Underline the word "seek" in each verse below.

- "And they that know thy name will put their trust in thee: for thou, LORD, hast not forsaken them that seek thee." (Ps 9:10)

- "One thing have I desired of the LORD, that will I seek after; that I may dwell in the house of the LORD all the days of my life, to behold the beauty of the LORD, and to inquire in his temple." (Ps 27:4)

- "When thou saidst, seek ye my face; my heart said unto thee, Thy face, LORD, will I seek." (Ps 27:8)

- "Let all those that seek thee rejoice and be glad in thee: let such as love thy salvation say continually, The LORD be magnified." (Ps 40:16)

- "O God, thou art my God; early will I seek thee: my soul thirsteth for thee, my flesh longeth for thee in a dry and thirsty land, where no water is." (Ps 63:1)

- "Let all those that seek thee rejoice and be glad in thee: and let such as love thy salvation say continually, Let God be magnified." (Ps 70:4)

- "Seek the LORD, and his strength: seek his face evermore." (Ps 105:4)

- "Blessed are they that keep his testimonies, and that seek him with the whole heart." (Ps 119:2)

- "Evil men understand not judgment: but they that seek the LORD understand all things." (Prov 28:5)

- "Seek ye the LORD while he may be found, call ye upon him while he is near." (Isa 55:6)

The sad words we read, even after *knowing* what—*who*—we should be seeking, are these: "There is none that understandeth, there is none that seeketh after God" (Rom 3:11). Do you see how using a concordance can be helpful in study?

Too many times, we struggle for years with what we should do in a particular situation, we look for answers everywhere *except* the Word of God.

In many matters, seemingly too specific or too small to take to the Lord, we rely on our own wisdom and on the collective wisdom of advisors, the library, the internet, the telephone. At least this is true of me: Keri Mae, a woman who lives and blooms and fades within a vapor of time, knows better than the Lord about what it is worth bothering Him for. How foolish.

# PRAYER: INTREAT AND INQUIRE (PART 2)

Not only is God clear about to Whom we are to direct our inquiries, He is clear about how to go about it: read the Bible and seek. "Seek ye out of the book of the LORD, and read: no one of these shall fail, none shall want her mate: for my mouth it hath commanded, and his spirit it hath gathered them" (Isa 34:16).

Too often, we Christians wonder what God wants, what He desires and commands. We wish He would boom His voice from the clouds and say, "Turn here...go hither...stop," while not understanding how frightening such an event would be! But God says truly, "I have not spoken in secret, in a dark place of the earth: I said not unto the seed of Jacob, seek ye me in vain: I the LORD speak righteousness, I declare things that are right" (Isaiah 45:19). The Lord is not hiding from us, nor does He delight to keep us in confusion as the devil does. His purpose, no matter how small or great the questions slushing about in our minds, is for us to *seek* Him.

How do we go about this seeking business?

- Daily and with delight:

  "Yet they seek me daily, and delight to know my ways, as a nation that did righteousness, and forsook not the ordinance of their God: they ask of me the ordinances of justice; they take delight in approaching to God." (Isa 58:2)

- With our whole hearts:

  "And ye shall seek me, and find me, when ye shall search for me with all your heart." (Jer 29:13)

- With a desire to know the LORD's will:

  "For all seek their own, not the things which are Jesus Christ's." (Phil 2:21)

- With soberness:

  "And I set my face unto the Lord God, to seek by prayer and supplications, with fasting, and sackcloth, and ashes." (Dan 9:3)

- By faith and with diligence:

> "But without faith it is impossible to please him: for he that cometh to God must believe that he is, and that he is a rewarder of them that diligently seek him." (Heb 11:6)

- With a focus on eternity:
  > "If ye then be risen with Christ, seek those things which are above, where Christ sitteth on the right hand of God." (Col 3:1)

God promises in our seeking Him, He will reward us with Himself (Isa 55:6), with life (Amos 5:4), and with "all these things" that truly matter (Matt 6:33). Let us seek, let us inquire of the Lord, and let us rejoice in the answers and treasures we shall find. "Ask, and it shall be given you; seek, and ye shall find; knock, and it shall be opened unto you" (Matt 7:7).

---

*Are there areas of struggle in your life in which you have yet to inquire of the Lord?*

# Walking Before God

*"And when Abram was ninety years old and nine, the LORD appeared to Abram, and said unto him, I am the Almighty God; walk before me, and be thou perfect." (Gen 17:1)*

I continue to be amazed at how God uses His Word to speak to my heart. It doesn't matter how many times I read a passage, without fail I will see something I completely passed over before. For example, after Noah got into the ark, a whole seven days passed before God closed the door, giving everyone who heard Noah's saving message an opportunity to get onboard. This was a revelation to me. God saved whomever got onto the ark at His invitation to "come." My husband said it is the same today; the offer stands, the ark awaits, but soon, the door will shut.

By the time the Lord appeared to Abram in Genesis 17:1, thirteen years had passed from the time of Ishmael's birth. You might remember Abram's wife Sarah took it upon herself to provide a way for her husband to have the son God had promised to her. She reasoned he should impregnate another woman. After all, Abram was seventy-five years old when God promised him a son, and that's a lot of years of waiting without any baby showing up. Therefore, Ishmael was conceived with a servant woman, and grew up, well on his way to becoming the "wild man" whose hand will be against every man (Gen 16:12).

What struck me in Genesis 17:1 were God's words, "I am the Almighty God; walk before me, and be thou perfect." This verse can be broken into three parts: the identity (I am), the command (walk before me), and the result (be thou perfect). Perhaps we read that verse and think God is saying *to be* perfect. That is, to manifest perfection only God Himself embodies. My curiosity led me to study further.

When God speaks of "walking before" in other verses, it is usually tied to a promise. These promises are not necessarily for us as individuals today, but you can still glean that God desires a people who walk in His ways. Look up these verses and see: 1 Sam 2:30, 1 Sam 2:35, 1 Kings 2:4, 1 Kings 8:23, 1 Kings 8:25, 1 Kings 9:4-5, 2 Chron 6:14, 2 Chron 7:17, Ps 56:13, Eccl 6:8.

In light of all of those promises, isn't Psalm 116:9 our heart's cry? "I will walk before the LORD in the land of the living."

What does it mean to "walk before" the Lord? To walk, in scripture, is "to live and act or behave; to pursue a particular course of life" (Webster, 1828).

There are many ways to walk:

- To walk with God, to live in obedience to his commands, and have communion with him (Gen 5)

- To walk in darkness, to live in ignorance, error and sin, without comfort (1 John 1)

- To walk in the light, to live in the practice of religion, and to enjoy its consolations (1 John 1)

- To walk by faith, to live in the firm belief of the gospel and its promises, and to rely on Christ for salvation (2 Cor 5)

- To walk through the fire, to be exercised with severe afflictions (Is 43)

- To walk after the flesh, to indulge sensual appetites, and to live in sin (Rom 8)

- To walk after the Spirit, to be guided by the counsels and influences of the Spirit and by the Word of God, and to live a life of holy deportment (Gal 5:16)

- To walk in the flesh, to live this natural life, which is subject to infirmities and calamities (2 Cor 10)

Using as guide the dictionary's definition of *before*, I conclude that to "walk before the Lord," means to be "in presence of, with the idea of power, authority, respect, in sight of; as before the face."

When God used these two little words, "walk before," He wasn't saying to walk ahead of Him and in this case, not necessarily to "follow" Him. If He did, wouldn't He have only said "follow"? We have many promises about His presence. Wouldn't that include His walking *with* us? Popping open the dictionary illuminates words and meaning.

But going back to our original verse, "I am the Almighty God; walk before me, and be thou perfect." What does the word *perfect* mean? The word comes from the Latin *perfectus*, and it means "to complete." Does the following verse sound familiar? "When Jesus

95

therefore had received the vinegar, he said, It is finished: and he bowed his head, and gave up the ghost" (John 19:30).

You don't have to be perfect because God has does it for you. He has perfected you in Christ Jesus, and the job is finished. When God sees you, He sees nothing defective, a perfect likeness to His Son, someone complete. When we see *ourselves*, we see sin, the *im*perfections, the mistakes, the weaknesses, the failings. God is indeed gracious, and merciful.

God, the only wise and glorious Father and Creator of all, is commanding us to live and act as one of His own, walking in obedience to his commands, having communion with him, in the light, by faith, after the Spirit and by the Word of God. *He* is our completion and perfection.

"And Abram fell on his face..." (Gen 17:3). As we walk before God, may our hearts have the same response.

---

*Where are you striving to achieve perfection? Can you trust God to grow you in holiness, even when you stumble?*

# Nothing But Manna

My husband broke rule #2 tonight: under no circumstances is Daddy allowed to be ill at the same time as Mommy. (Rule #1 is, of course, Mom will not get sick, especially if any of the little ones are already ill). Alas, Husband came home, stumbled around for a couple of hours, and hit the sheets early.

I wish I could say I was loving and sensitive toward this, but truly, after dragging around all day, waiting for my rescuer to arrive, all I could muster was lame sympathy. He'd jilted me from my own evening rest time. So, I bathed and put the children to bed, handwashed the dishes, dealt with little feet running upstairs, put the turkey stock in the freezer, folded the day's laundry, consoled and re-put the baby back to sleep, set out tomorrow's beans to soak...and grumbled between my own coughs and gags.

"And when the people complained, it displeased the LORD: and the LORD heard it; and his anger was kindled" (Num 11:1). I read this not even a week ago. In Hebrew, the word *displeased* here means "it was evil in the ears of." Many times, I have felt sorrow over the Hebrews continual griping; yet here I was doing the same.

"But now our soul is dried away: there is nothing at all, beside this manna, before our eyes" (Num 11:6). Nothing but manna? Nothing but the *bread of life?* How easily I become entangled when I focus on the hardships of daily life and forget the soft mercies of God falling upon me every morning. If all were to be gone tomorrow, I would still have manna. Why isn't that enough? Shame on me to hunger and lust for more than the good Lord sees fit to provide. And tonight, He provided my husband with a good meal, a clean bed, and an opportunity to recover. Where was my gratitude?

There is a "no whining" sign on my kitchen cabinet, the curl of its paper giving away its age. A visitor pointed at it and asked, "Does that work well for the kids?"

I explained, "No, no, no. That isn't for the kids. It's for *me*," and we both laughed.

How I wish it were as simple as:
Step one—decide not to whine.
Step two—whining disintegrates.

And who is the poor soul within earshot of my griping? My husband? My kids? My God?

"I am not able to bear all this people alone, because it is too heavy for me. And if thou deal thus with me, kill me, I pray thee, out of hand, if I have found favour in thy sight" (Num 11:14-15). Oh, Moses, Moses, Moses. He understood what it was to hear, *"Oh poor me, I can't have/get/make what I want, wah wah wah."* Poor guy would rather be killed than deal with the nagging. I wonder if our dear husbands ever feel the same!

"A complaining spirit is a heavy burden upon the ears of another. It is utterly displeasing to the Lord" (Num 11:20). This includes not only our words, but also the stony silence, the rolling eyes, slumping shoulders, and dragging feet. It also includes those little barbs thrown into a conversation to remind so-n-so of dissatisfaction due to inattention to the demands.

A woman once admitted to me she nags because, in the end, she gets what she wants, so I ought to do it, too. What I worry about more is this: what if I get what I want? What if I'd shown hot displeasure tonight, and my hubby had decided to play the hero and help me with the evening chores? What would I have gained? Another ninety minutes to rest (can you rest and feel guilty at the same time?) and probably a man who would be far worse tomorrow morning and unable or unwilling to go back to work. Occasionally, the Lord gives what we nag for, but do not assume because whining "worked," it is God-blessed and without consequences.

"And while the flesh was yet between their teeth, ere it was chewed, the wrath of the LORD was kindled against the people, and the LORD smote the people with a very great plague. And he called the name of that place Kibrothhattaavah: because there they buried the people that lusted" (Num 11:33-34).

*Lord, forgive us for wanting different meat, different circumstances, when You have blessed us so richly with your manna. And thank You for the strength You give us to get through the tough days.*

"Now all these things happened unto them for ensamples: and they are written for our admonition." (1 Cor 10:11)

———————

*In every hardship, there is always enough manna for the day. Copy and post a Bible verse to remind you of His all sufficient provision and grace.*

.

# But We See Jesus

*"But we see Jesus, who was made a little lower than the angels for the suffering of death, crowned with glory and honour; that he by the grace of God should taste death for every man." (Heb 2:9)*

The phrase "but we see Jesus" keeps coming back to me. This little four-word phrase implies a lot. Let's dissect it, using the 1828 Webster's Dictionary.

> **But:** "alternatively, in comparison to, on the outside, separated, excepted."

At times, I struggle with feeling alien around other people. I understand the Bible says this world is not my true home, but alternatively, my heart wants better than to be merely tolerated. It wants me to be accepted by each person I meet. This is, of course, ludicrous because to be embraced by one person would necessarily repel another due to differing values. So I try to love each person, my "neighbor," each made in the image of God, in goodwill, prayer, and in deed. This may be as simple as sharing treats with a hardhearted neighbor or graciously allowing a gentleman to hold the door open for me. There are a multitude of simple ways to act differently, alternatively, and separated, with respect and kindness, apart from the mainstream demands of unity at any price.

> **We**: "the brethren, closely united resembling another, kinsman by blood."

"We" are all my brothers and sisters in Christ, all who have believed on the Lord Jesus Christ and have been rescued from the burdens of sin and have received the joy of the Holy Spirit. "We" means I may not be home yet, but at least I have a family here who understands I am not out of my mind or living in a make-believe spiritual dreamland. They see Jesus, too!

**See:** "to perceive by the eye, to have knowledge of the existence and apparent qualities of objects (or people) by the organs of sight, to behold, to observe, to note or notice, to know, to regard or look to, to discover, to understand, to converse with, to visit as to call and see a friend, to attend, to feel, to experience, to know, to learn, to comprehend, to know by revelation, to enjoy, to have fruition of."

Wow! Look at all those verbs! And if we read the next part of the verse, we *see* who we are talking about: Jesus!

I can answer questions about who I am, what I do, what I believe, what I hope to become, and why I have such joy inside with these four little words: but we see Jesus. There are trials and painful situations, heartbreaks, and mocking. But we see Jesus. There before me are presented my own failings and shortcomings, the temptation to despair and react. But we see Jesus. It is He who has overcome, and in Him, I do the same. Why? Because I see Jesus.

What is my response to this? I read all the definitions of *see* and ponder, *So what?* The Word tells me "so what." How lovely I don't have to figure things out on my own: "Thou hast loved righteousness, and hated iniquity; therefore God, even thy God, hath anointed thee with the oil of gladness above thy fellows" (Heb 1:9).

Well, I'm anointed and covered with the oil of gladness. Pour it on, Lord, because often I can't make myself glad for anything. "The Spirit of the Lord GOD is upon me; because the LORD hath anointed me to preach good tidings unto the meek; he hath sent me to bind up the brokenhearted, to proclaim liberty to the captives, and the opening of the prison to them that are bound" (Isa 61:1).

What music to my ears! Thank You for preaching good words to me, for binding up my broken heart, for setting me free! And wow... Now, I have His spirit; therefore, I may do the same. What privilege!

"Saying, I will declare thy name unto my brethren, in the midst of the church will I sing praise unto thee" (Heb 2:12). I will speak of You to my brothers and sisters, reminding them of Your goodness. I will belong to Your church and sing praises to You, even from my kitchen. "And again, I will put my trust in him. And again, Behold I and the children which God hath given me" (Heb 2:13). I will put my trust in You, especially when I seem to have misplaced it! And I will receive the children you give to me and teach them to trust You as well.

Take a moment to read Hebrews 3:6-19.

If you are unsaved, departing from the living God brings the hardening of your heart, which causes the restlessness of searching and seeking and sealing your fate to not only wander in the wilderness, but to die in your sins.

If you have been saved, verses six and fourteen are for you and I: to hold fast our confidence, to rejoice in the hope firm to the end, to be steadfast.

Following, are two steps to make it plainer:

**1) Enter into His rest, via belief.**
>"And they said, believe on the Lord Jesus Christ, and thou shalt be saved, and thy house" (Acts 16:31). It isn't complicated, no rote and proper sinner's prayers or ceremony or whatnot. Simply, come to Him as a child, repent of your sins, and trust Jesus Christ for your salvation.

**2) Stay there.**
>"Abide in me, and I in you. As the branch cannot bear fruit of itself, except it abide in the vine; no more can ye, except ye abide in me. I am the vine, ye are the branches: He that abideth in me, and I in him, the same bringeth forth much fruit: for

without me ye can do nothing" (John 15:4-5). This means to stay close to His Word, to be near in prayer, and to not forsake His teachings, even when it is difficult.

---

*When have you sought the approval of others at the expense of your Christian witness? Seeing Jesus as He is meets your heart's desire to be truly known and loved.*

# A Heart for Holiness

*There is nothing destroyed by sanctification but that which would destroy us.*

— William Jenkyn

# A Gracious Woman

Grace is one of the character traits I desire to live out and be remembered by. In our time, there are many women who are strong (as coffee can be strong...and bitter) yet short on lovingkindness. They are lacking in grace.

> **Grace:** "favor, good will, kindness, a disposition to oblige another...the free unmerited love and favor of God, the spring and source of all the benefits men receive from him." (Webster, 1828)

What is lacking today is the "free unmerited love and favor" streaming from an inward kindness to oblige and serve a person who hasn't earned it. Others ought to be treated kindly and graciously because they are made in the image of God, deserving of dignity simply because they are human. We all want grace. But it's hard to give it.

I don't want my hackles raised when I'm wronged. I don't want the cynic in me to prove how people never change. What I really want is to grow as a woman of grace, one who is known and will be remembered as a gracious woman.

God's Word is good; He has much to say about anything you desire to know, so I look to the Bible for a clear picture of graciousness.

The word *gracious* is found in the King James Version thirty-four times, and of those, there were certain words that came along with it. Fourteen times graciousness was paired with *mercy*, six times with *compassion*, and five times with *slow to anger*. The Lord also paired these traits: righteousness, great kindness, truthfulness, longsuffering, forgiveness, wisdom, and goodness. Do we want grace? If so, it comes with the other traits as well.

**Mercy**: "that benevolence, mildness or tenderness of heart which disposes a person to overlook injuries, or to treat an offender better than he deserves."

It is what we cry out for ourselves even as we demand justice for others.

**Compassion**: "a sensation of sorrow excited by the distress or misfortunes of another; pity."

It is the opposite of indifference or, worse, satisfaction of someone's downfall.

**Slow to anger**: a slowness "to take vengeance, or to obtain satisfaction from the offending party."

Do you share in my conviction? We have trouble meeting even *one* of these character traits on any given day!

But the Lord says, "Follow me," and so let us walk with Him. As His adopted children, we can run after Him in joy, knowing He will model and teach us even as we struggle in how we should respond to challenges that grow us in grace.

When I am tempted to anger, He will remind me to show mercy, to be gracious: "Hath God forgotten to be gracious? hath he in anger shut up his tender mercies" (Ps 77:9)?

He will teach me to forgive the sins of others, to put away my anger: "But he, being full of compassion, forgave their iniquity, and destroyed them not: yea, many a time turned he his anger away, and did not stir up all his wrath" (Ps 78:38).

He will promise me that in giving mercy, I shall find it: "Blessed are the merciful: for they shall obtain mercy" (Matt 5:7).

Grace is nothing we can work into ourselves any more than flour and water can knead itself into bread. Rather, the Lord will hear our cries to become women of grace, and He will send us lessons and testings to fulfill His purpose, so we may reflect the image of His Son. My hope is I will remember I have tasted that the Lord is gracious, and because of that, I indeed have the Holy Spirit's power to lay aside grievances hindering my growth in grace.

May we reflect His image more and more, that we may decrease, and that He with *His grace* may increase in us!

"A gracious woman retaineth honour." (Prov 11:16)

————

*Growing in grace requires a willing student of the Word. Are you studying well?*

# Look Up, Sister!

There are times when the downward spiral into despair feels as a vortex pulling you to the earth, pressing your spirit and defying even the waft of a breeze that might brush the hair from your brow.

The reasons for your position may be all too clear: Your home chokes with the smog of bitterness, or your husband has left you either physically or emotionally. Your children are diseased with foul character, or your health swings from discomfort to agony. Worse, as you lie splayed and frozen in spirit, remembrance of your sins taunts and teases you, and your will to overcome has gone. You are as Ezra, claiming, "O my God, I am ashamed and blush to lift up my face to thee, my God: for our iniquities are increased over our head, and our trespass is grown up unto the heavens" (Ezra 9:6).

121

The devil has gleefully claimed victory, and your flesh may not even care, but there is a way out, and it's the same way you were saved before: looking upon Jesus in belief. Use whatever semblance of fraying faith is left upon the fibers of your spirit, then move your sight to Him: "I will lift up mine eyes unto the hills, from whence cometh my help" (Ps 121:1).

Do you remember when the people of Israel were falling by the waysides from serpent bites? What did the Lord ask of them in the midst of their deathly agony and pain? Did He demand the inflicted get themselves up?

"And the LORD said unto Moses, Make thee a fiery serpent, and set it upon a pole: and it shall come to pass, that every one that is bitten, when he looketh upon it, shall live. And Moses made a serpent of brass, and put it upon a pole, and it came to pass, that if a serpent had bitten any man, when he beheld the serpent of brass, he lived." (Num 21:8-9)

"And as Moses lifted up the serpent in the wilderness, even so must the Son of man be lifted up." (John 3:14)

In the same way the Israelites needed to look upon the pole to live, we need to look upon the cross.

There is a landslide of Christian self-help books, and a lot of people offering counsel. They even have degrees or a robust social media following to prove their abilities to help you up. But none of this even comes close to what you need to do first: see Christ and Him crucified. When the devil uses your circumstances to cultivate confusion, teasing you to doubt the goodness of God, the remedy is to look upon Jesus.

"But I fear, lest by any means, as the serpent beguiled Eve through his subtlety, so your minds should be corrupted from the simplicity that is in Christ" (2 Cor 11:3). "Humble yourselves in the sight of the Lord, and he shall lift you up" (Jas 4:10).

Do you believe Him? He sits there with you in the dust, loving eyes upon you, waiting for you to stop wallowing in self-condemnation of your own shortcomings, offering you broken bread and wine. He is not waiting for you to come out of misery to admonish you for being miserable; He is waiting for you to look up.

Maybe you've read 2 Corinthians 12:9, many times, which says, "And he said unto me, My grace is sufficient for thee: for my strength is made perfect in weakness. Most gladly therefore will I rather glory in my infirmities, that the power of Christ may rest upon me."

God has not failed you, and you have not failed God. Perhaps you have given ear to deception, the world, or your own expectations of perfectionism, or given in to your heart's desire to be happy in this life instead of being made into the image of holiness. Or God has gifted you with these afflictions to refine you and deliver you from clinging to this present world. Either way, these troubles look tremendous and insurmountable but are neither.

Rather, they are an opportunity to awaken to you a longing for something everlasting and immensely more satisfying than whatever has discouraged you. "The godly have some good in them, therefore the devil afflicts them; and some evil in them, therefore God afflicts them" (Thomas Watson).

Start right now, before another minute passes. Lift up your eyes and seek first the Lord's face, His kingdom, and His righteousness (Matt 6:19-33). May you feel His loving hand upon your chin to lift your head, to bring you face-to-face with His compassionate loving gaze. "But thou, O LORD, art a shield for me; my glory, and the lifter up of mine head" (Ps 3:3).

Then you will be enabled to take each thought captive to obedience to Christ (2 Cor 10:5), and you will be given the opportunity to examine yourself for wrong attitudes, thoughts, and motives (1 John 1:5-10) and to repent. You can forget about trying to create and lean on your own pieced-together understanding (Prov 3:5-7). Perhaps more importantly, you will remember in Christ you have been given victory over the devil and his schemes, and you can resist the devil, and he will flee from you. "Submit yourselves therefore to God. Resist the devil, and he will flee from you" (Jas 4:7).

My sweet sister, my only fervent prayer and plea for you during this time in your life is this: lift up your eyes!

*If I look at myself, I am depressed.*
*If I look at those around me, I am often disappointed.*
*If I look at my circumstances, I am discouraged.*
*But if I look at Jesus, I am constantly, consistently, and eternally fulfilled!*

(author unknown)

# LOOK UP, SISTER!

---

*In what situation do you need to stop, look up at the cross, and listen to His Word?*

# Perfectionism: Promise of Peace, Deliverer of Pain

I once read a terrific blog post that struck me—specifically a phrase in it about when my family gets in the way of my service to my family. That led to some thought! I tend to be task oriented and can ignore people's needs in the midst of accomplishing those tasks. Call me Martha.

Many years ago, I began my journey as a "flybaby." Flylady (flylady.net) is a blogger who helps women regain control of their homes and learn to take care of themselves while doing it. I've enjoyed using her ideas and look forward to my daily "missions," whether it is cleaning out my purse or chucking the old rags from under the kitchen sink.

She's a big fan of using a timer ("you can do anything for fifteen minutes," she says). Thus, when the daily task was to wipe down the shower wall, I obediently set my timer and went to work. The timer went off...and I went back to the shower wall. For another ninety minutes! The children woke from naps. I scrubbed the shower. They finished watching the video I set before them. I still scrubbed. I fed them crackers...and still scrubbed. I got out the toothbrush and scrubbed every inch of grout. I also, after using the gritty stuff and the window cleaner, brought out Tom's car wax and polished away, albeit at this point not loving myself *or* my shower. My fifteen-minute task morphed into a huge project I wasn't ready for, all because I thought I could do the job perfectly. My children ended up exasperated, and truth be told, I wasn't happy with how my shower looked when I finished!

There is much vanity in trying to reach perfection, as if we could attain it, and as if we could enjoy our lonely little mountain peak once we've arrived, anyway.

## PERFECTIONISM: PROMISE OF PEACE, DELIVERER OF PAIN

In search of answers about where true perfection lies, I turned to my Bible. God alone is perfect: in works (Deut 32:4), in His ways (2 Sam 22:31; Ps 18:30), in knowledge (Job 36:4), in law (Ps 19:7), in beauty (Ps 50:2), in faithfulness (Isa 25:1), in His will (Rom 12:2), in power (2 Cor 12:9), in gifts (Jas 1:17), and in love (1 John 4:18). Furthermore, Jesus alone is the Lamb without blemish (1 Pet 1:9). All the scrubbing, learning, wishing, counseling, reading, works, grooming, and efforts will never get me close to anything perfect. In fact, all our righteousnesses are as filthy rags (Isa 64:6).

Jesus is the Master Cleaner. One lesson I gleaned through my study is that He alone makes my home beautiful (Num 24:5) and makes me lovely (Song of Sol 4:7). Through Christ, I am no longer imperfect in God's eyes. When we become depressed or discouraged with how imperfectly a job we are doing, as if we could attain perfection, we are questioning God's words about where our worth comes from and how it is measured. For example, "Now ye are clean through the word which I have spoken unto you" (John 15:3). I am clean because Jesus has cleansed me, not because of who I am or anything I have done. And what a relief to know what He has begun, He will complete (Phil 1:6).

So, what to do? Jesus Himself gives us a few pointers when we ask (Prov 3:5-6). Meet God in your daily routine, either for an unbreakable appointment or throughout your day, for a little focused Bible study and prayer. In the grand scheme of chores and duties, only one task is necessary, and it is taking the time to sit at the feet of your Lord. See Luke 10:38-42. God says we can assure our hearts before him (1 John 3:19).

Another lesson He taught me was through my child's violin lessons. While my five-year-old daughter was playing, I asked a host of questions such as, "Is she playing in the right place? Is it supposed to sound like that? Should it be louder?"

# PERFECTIONISM: PROMISE OF PEACE, DELIVERER OF PAIN

And what her teacher lovingly told me was, "Look for what is right, and I will take care of what is wrong."

*Hmm.*

"I know that there is no good in them, but for a man to rejoice, and to do good in his life. And also that every man should eat and drink, and enjoy the good of all his labour, it is the gift of God" (Eccl 3:12-13). There is nothing better than doing good—not perfect—and seeing the good in the labor you and I do.

When I was a teacher, I used to mark my students' spelling tests +8 rather than -2. I need to do the same for myself and my family and celebrate what is good rather than focus obsessively on dirty grout lines. Instead of dwelling on negatives, I can choose to dwell on "whatsoever things are true, whatsoever things are honest, whatsoever things are just, whatsoever things are pure, whatsoever things are lovely, whatsoever things are of good report; if there be any virtue, and if there be any praise, think on these things" (Phil 4:8). I can dwell in peace even as I am cleaning or doing other chores.

If you are frustrated or overwhelmed with trying to attain a standard of perfection, might I encourage you to seek wisdom in whatever area you are having trouble? "If any of you lack wisdom, let him ask of God, that giveth to all men liberally, and upbraideth not; and it shall be given him" (Jas 1:5). Is there an older woman you could ask for advice? She could be very encouraging (see Titus 2:4). You don't have to reinvent the wheel. Women have been caring for homes and families since Eve walked the earth. We don't often want to admit we need help, but consider that attitude may stem from pride and a need to be seen as self-sufficient.

I do still set my timer on occasion. Even if I am not following Flylady's methods *perfectly*, my home and my heart is recovering from perfectionism, and I am learning a lot in the process. Thankfully, Jesus is waiting to say, "Well done, thou good and faithful servant," (Matt 25:21) and *not,* "Well done, thou perfect woman." He wants to say the same to you.

———————

*Are you angry or agitated when your family steps on or messes up your house, meal, plans, budget, schedule, or ...? Our job is to be faithful in our work, not perfect by the results of it.*

# "The Secret"
## (or...How to Love the Devil)

*"Beloved, believe not every spirit, but try the spirits whether they are of God: because many false prophets are gone out into the world." (1 John 4:1)*

The book of Leviticus is sobering. If anyone had any sort of inclination to believe God was a big teddy bear or cosmic Santa Claus, Leviticus's laws and expectations of holy living along with the finality of judgments for sin would straighten those fallacies in an instant.

I watched a few snippets of the film *The Secret*. To the backdrop of uplifting and exciting images, sincere yet misguided people filled the screen, imploring and counseling others to be the creator of themselves. Truthfully, I was troubled by the film's message: a person got what they deserved.

What they deserved, of course, was whatever their thought processes attracted, including money falling out of the sky (one of the scenes), cancer, and disease. How utterly cruel.

We all know people who have lost the battle for their lives...they wanted that? Several friends have buried children. They attracted this? What about children who fill the wards of hospitals, waiting for miracles? Did they secretly hope for such things? Worse, did their parents? What foolishness. What deceitfulness! To believe that whatever befalls you, good or bad, is a result of your own law of attraction is fodder for the most prideful of attitudes at best, and a recipe for the drowning sorrow of depression and suicide at worst. You have only to read the journals of Anne Frank to know this fifteen-year-old's thought life is not what led to her death.

This sort of mentality sounds like the devil's mouthpiece: you are the masterpiece of your own thoughts; you deserve what you get by virtue of your thoughts; your failure, disease, and hardships are your fault; you are god, creator of your own destiny. Want money? Say out loud what you require, demanding it. Want health? Claim full health. Want the exuberance of "faith"? Say you *are* faithful, all good favors will come to you. It sounds like fallacious name-it-and-claim-it heresies running amuck in Christian-like circles, and millions are emotionally attracted to it out of greed, loneliness, or desperation. Ultimately, it is based on a false understanding of who God is.

Oh, the shackles that come from such thinking! God's word is clear in matters such as this: "Love not the world, neither the things that are in the world. If any man love the world, the love of the Father is not in him. For all that is in the world, the lust of the flesh, and the lust of the eyes, and the pride of life, is not of the Father, but is of the world. And the world passeth away, and the lust thereof: but he that doeth the will of God abideth for ever" (1 John 2:15-17).

No one wants to suffer. No one wants negative consequences, nor to be at the wrong place at the wrong time. No, you did *not* "draw to you" a car accident, nor can you call out of the sky a million dollars. The truth is, life isn't easy. It is not free of hardship. It is not free of struggles and pain, because we live in a fallen world. God uses all these struggles and sufferings for His glory, and if you are in Christ, for your sanctification. Suffering, ultimately, is not pointless.

The devil's ploy, however, says, *"If you are in the doctor's office, if you have a disease, if your kid broke his arm, if your business failed, you are nothing. You brought it on yourself. You thought wrong thoughts. You deserve every poor outcome because you asked for it."*

Whenever exhortations of this nature attempt to lead you astray, go back to Jesus and what He says in His Word, both in times of peace and in trial. Only there can you find reason to exude gratefulness for pleasures and rejoice in suffering (Rom 5:2-5), and to rest in

## "THE SECRET"
## (OR...HOW TO LOVE THE DEVIL)

the knowledge that the trials or blessings in life, in general, are not about you. This sort of all-about-you "secret" imprisons people in both mind and spirit. Thankfully, with repentance and a reliance on Him and His character, that prisoner can trust God will mercifully set him free.

"And ye shall know the truth, and the truth shall make you free." (John 8:32)

————————

*What is the current wildly popular Christian teacher, book, movie, or movement? Is he, she, or it Biblical?*

# On Disappointment

At ten years old, I was a military brat living in England. I played with half a dozen friends who lived close by, and they were the closest to thing I had to America other than going to McDonald's in London.

An argument erupted one day, and all the shouting prompted one of the fathers to come out and admonish us to solve our problems and to remember we were, in essence, a family and needed to behave in respect for each other. About this time, my own father came home from work, and I ran to greet him.

When I returned to the group a few minutes later, the thirteen-year-old boy—the one on whom I had an immense crush—folded his arms and, as if speaking on behalf of the group, said to me, "We've decided we need to be a family...except for you." I cast a horrified glance at my best friend, who was in the thick of this revelation, but she kept her eyes glued to a random blade of grass. I went home in quiet tears, pretending not to care.

"And God shall wipe away all tears from their eyes; and there shall be no more death, neither sorrow, nor crying, neither shall there be any more pain: for the former things are passed away" (Rev 21:4). Therein lies the only real hope I have. I am never presented with promises of a painless life, only to eventually being made whole again, minus the wounds. It almost sounds trite—I can simply forget about the pain and tears. Yet the Lord doesn't say I will forget them. He simply says He will wipe them from my eyes, which confirms He knows I will shed them.

Disappointment has visited me in many ways: unmet expectations, plans unraveling, and people ignoring my attempts at a relationship. And there are many potholes in the road of disappointment. One danger is the desire to give up and not care anymore. I am sorry to admit I have at times been consumed by bitterness and squelched my desire to love others, then allowed my zeal for the Lord to fizzle. It saddens me to remember how, during those times, I've let heartache steal my joy.

I want you to know how far-reaching Jesus is. We can speak to Him about our disappointments and can also look to His life for guidance. Hoping for wisdom, I've mulled over those three ways I have experienced disappointment.

### 1) Unmet expectations

Jesus was always realistic about His plans, other people, and His ability to minister to them. He perhaps wanted Peter to walk to Him across the water and the rich young ruler to follow Him, but I question whether He expected them to do so. When He needed reassurance, He went off by Himself to pray: "And when He had sent the multitudes away, He went up into a mountain apart to pray" (Matt 14:23). When He was in despair, He prayed earnestly to His Father to change circumstances: "O my Father, if it be possible, let this cup pass from me" (Matt 26:39). However, like David at the end of the most heart-wrenching psalm, He found himself strengthened in hope and trust, not invested in personal expectations: "Nevertheless not as I will, but as thou wilt" (Matt 26:39b).

## 2) Unraveled plans

Jesus always focused on God's will. When as a boy, He was found at the temple teaching, but He still obeyed His parents by returning home (Luke 2:51). His ultimate purpose was to glorify His Father in every moment, not follow a schedule. And indeed, all was accomplished exactly on time, exactly as it was meant to be.

### 3) Unreturned investment

> Jesus loved Judas, even though He knew Judas was going to be betray Him. In fact, none of the disciples had a clue which disciple Jesus was speaking of before the betrayal! Jesus served others but did not depend on receiving affirmation from others; He didn't need to. "For I know whence I came, and whither I go" (John 8:14b). Though He called His disciples friends, ultimately His sense of self-worth was not connected to them but rather by his relationship to his Father. "They shall not be ashamed that wait for me" (Isa 49:23).

Those are a few lessons I gleaned from Jesus. Now, they minister to me in the face of disappointments, whether small or large. Going off by myself to pray brings me closer to my Father, who affirms me and fills me anew with His joy and His love. I can continue to love and invest in and serve others, which is

God's primary mission for me. Also, my ultimate purpose is to glorify God, and it happens when by faith I believe Him and choose to act in ways within His perfect will, even if it seems counterintuitive. He strengthens me with hope and genuine trust. I believe He is good, faithful, and all-wise. I can choose to walk with grace even in my disappointments.

Making plans, caring about others, having dreams: all are tricky business because we can only hope they will turn out well, and a lot of times they may not. Being open to disappointment takes courage, and it requires vulnerability. But we can press toward the mark for the prize (Phil 3:14) because God says hope maketh not ashamed (Rom 5:5).

Your greatest disappointments can bring the biggest returns. Take them to the Lord and trust Him to continue the work He has begun. "They cried unto thee, and were delivered: they trusted in thee, and were not confounded" (Ps 22:5).

# ON DISAPPOINTMENT

---

*In what ways has God drawn you closer to Him through your disappointments?*

# On Judgment

I do most of my reading while nursing a baby, which works only if he or she is content to nurse and keeps those little hands from grabbing the pages. My nursing time allowed me to finish reading *Feminine Appeal* by Carolyn Mahaney, and it was as good as I was told.

There is no end to books carving out meaning from Titus 2, but Mrs. Mahaney brings fresh insight into the whole matter of loving your family and what it means to serve the Lord in any circumstance. I especially liked her section on "hindrances to kindness," where she laid out the big three: anger, bitterness, and judging. She is right on! As I think of all the times I have been unkind, I can definitely see those roots.

I took special interest in her thoughts on judging as well as this definition from Ken Sande: "looking for others' faults and, without valid and sufficient reason, forming unfavorable opinions of their qualities, words, actions, or motives. In simple terms, it means looking for the worst in others." Talk about hitting the nail on the head.

I have been guilty of presuming to know what the person is going to say before she opens her mouth. It's true that over time people create their own drumbeats, but where is the room for grace, for the opportunity to love them despite it all? If my mind is already set on my expectation due to past history, then I am expecting the worst instead of judging with right judgment (John 7:24). There is a difference between hearing rotten words from their lips in the moment, and presuming you're going to hear it.

It's always humbling to admit I was wrong, especially in assuming motives. Discern means to "see or understand the difference; to make distinction; as, to discern between good and evil, truth and falsehood" (Webster, 1828). In other words, it means having enough knowledge to judge righteously, which is a virtue.

Where do we get proper discernment, a righteous judgment? From God, of course, from Whom every good gift comes:

- "And he hath filled him with the spirit of God, in wisdom, in understanding, and in knowledge, and in all manner of workmanship." (Exod 35:31)

- "And God gave Solomon wisdom and understanding exceeding much, and largeness of heart, even as the sand that is on the sea shore." (1 Kings 4:29)

- "The fear of the LORD is the beginning of wisdom: a good understanding have all they that do his commandments: his praise endureth for ever." (Ps 111:10)

- "The fear of the LORD is the beginning of knowledge: but fools despise wisdom and instruction." (Prov 1:7)

- "The fear of the LORD is the beginning of wisdom: and the knowledge of the holy is understanding." (Prov 9:10)

- "And they shall teach my people the difference between the holy and profane, and cause them to discern between the unclean and the clean." (Ezek 44:23)

We should want to know wisdom and instruction, to perceive words of understanding and justice (Prov 1:2-3). We are exhorted to seek wisdom. "Wisdom is the principal thing; therefore get wisdom: and with all thy getting get understanding" (Prov 4:7). And our cry for righteous discernment and wise judgment should be as Solomon said: "Give therefore thy servant an understanding heart to judge thy people, that I may discern between good and bad: for who is able to judge this thy so great a people?" (1 Kings 3:9).

And with the wisdom we receive, we ought not to judge others in thinking the worst of them, but instead speak righteously (Ps 37:30), with wisdom and an understanding heart (Ps 49:3), departing from evil ways (Job 28:28), and instead keep the Lord's commandments. In doing so, we'll find peace in what we discern, regardless of any bitterness or anger coming from calling out the truth. "Whoso keepeth the commandment shall feel no evil thing: and a wise man's heart discerneth both time and judgment" (Eccl 8:5).

Lastly, you and I both know when we have stepped over the bounds of righteous judgment. Wisdom from God will never fail this test: "But the wisdom that is from above is first pure, then peaceable, gentle, and easy to be intreated, full of mercy and good fruits, without partiality, and without hypocrisy" (Jas 3:17).

If we are living with hypocrisy or harshness, not allowing even the benefit of the doubt in what we perceive as maleficent motivations, then seeking God's ways and wisdom would seem a reasonable place to begin. In any case, here is another reason I don't get through many books while I'm nursing. I chew on good Christian teaching a long time.

———

*Do you give people the benefit of the doubt before discerning what might be their motives?*

# Joy is a Command

*"Joy is a delight of the mind, from the consideration of the present or assured approaching possession of a good." (Webster, 1828)*

My mind is often full of tasks to do, errands to run, meals to prepare, calls to return, and on-the-spot training issues for children. "Delight of the mind" seems far removed, a dream perhaps arriving on the day when I am sitting on a chaise lounge, my feet digging into warm sand, my gaze stretching out over turquoise waters into a fiery sunset.

And yet, after doing a word study on *joy* in the Bible, I have realized joy does not equate to happiness or a life of ease, but rather it is expected from the hearts of God's children because of what He has done for us. It stems from a thankful spirit. No thankful spirit, no joy. No understanding of who God is and what He has done, no thankful spirit.

When I am feeling joyless, it is my own fault because not only have I been focused on myself, I have been misled by an inaccurate definition of *joy*.

First, and perhaps most surprising, is that joy is a command, stated as such in many passages of scripture. The command is: "be glad in the Lord, and rejoice ye righteous; and shout for joy all ye that are upright in heart" (Ps 32:11). This to be expected from the Lord's people, regardless of circumstances.

Other scripture says:

- "Let them shout for joy and be glad" (Ps 35:27). "Them" being those who..."Trust in the Lord" (Ps 40:3).

- "Make a joyful noise unto God." (Ps 66:1; 98:4; 100:1)

- "Sing aloud unto God our strength." (Ps 81:1)

- "Rejoice in Him who made him." (Ps 149:2)

- "Eat and drink with joy" Why? Because... for God "now accepteth thy works" (Eccl 9:7).

- "With joy draw water out of the wells of salvation" (Isa 12:3). Yet how many times do we seek joy from other means?

- "Sing and be joyful" Why? Because..."the Lord hath comforted his people, and will have mercy upon his afflicted" (Isa 49:13).

- "Rejoice and leap for joy when persecuted." (Luke 6:23)

There are no conditions given, simply the command to sing, to rejoice, to be joyful. We are to be joyful not only when we are prospering, but when persecuted as well (Ps 35:27, Eccl 7:14).

This all sounds an impossibility. How can we possibly rejoice when our minds are flat with the mundaneness of laundry sorting or when we're too sad to be joyful?

According to God's Word, here is what joy looks like on the outside:

- Singing, dancing, and playing with instruments (1 Sam 18:6; Ps 27:6; 98:6, 8; 149:5, Isa 52:9)

- Willing offerings to the Lord (1 Chron 29:9, 17)

- Keeping the house of God (Ezra 6:16)

- Keeping your head above enemies around you (Ps 27:6)

- The beauty of creation (Ps 65:13; 96:12)

- Shouting for joy (Ps 132:9)

- Enjoying wise children (Prov 23:24)

- Humility (Isa 29:19)

- Peace (Isa 55:12)

- Likemindedness in Christ (Phil 2:2)

- The words of my mouth (Prov 15:23)

Joy is associated with much of what the world chases after and wants, but cannot attain without the Holy Spirit (Acts 13:52): peace (Prov 12:20), light, gladness, and honor (Esther 8:16), thanksgiving (Ps 95:2), gladness (Isa 35:10), reverence (Matt 28:8), worship (Luke 24:52), hope [through the power of the Holy Spirit] (Rom 15:13), boldness of speech, humility and comfort (2 Cor 7:4), prayer (Phil 1:4), and children walking with the Lord (3 John 1:4).

True joy comes from only *one* source—God Himself, our exceeding joy (Ps 43:4). *For the Lord had made them joyful, and in turn, strengthened their hands (Ezra 6:22).* God made them rejoice with great joy (Neh 12:43). Joy comes from God's presence (Ps 16:11) and salvation (Ps 21:1; 132:16), and He brings His people forth with His own joy and gladness (Ps 105:43). He alone makes mothers joyful (Ps 113:9), gives joy in the work we do (Eccl 2:24), and gives wisdom and knowledge along with it(Eccl 2:26). Joy comes from Jesus' words (John 17:13) and loving and believing Him (1 Peter 1:8). He gives joy in response to prayer and sacrifice (Isa 56:7) via His Holy Spirit (1 Thess 1:6), and it is possible to have full and fulfilled joy (John 16:24; 17:13) solely by asking.

The fact is, if we are not joyful, something is greatly amiss and needs to be dealt with because Scripture says that indeed we *shall* be joyful (Ps 35:9). And for whom are we to be joyful? Repeatedly, I read "unto God," "unto

God our strength," "unto the God of Jacob," and to "the Lord."

For what is there to be joyful?

Victories over our enemies (Ps 27:6), God's morning mercies (Ps 30:5), His trading our ashes for beauty and the garment of praise for our spirits of heaviness (Isa 61:3), His garments of salvation and righteousness (Isa 61:10), His redemption (Isa 52:9), his atonement (Rom 5:11), His defense (Ps 5:11) and the utter and complete hope we have in Him and in His returning (Isa 66:5), and the amazing joy of seeing His face (Job 33:26). We should be joyful for having the Bible (Jer 15:16), for living on this side of the birth of Jesus (Luke 1:14), and for even one sinner who repents (Luke 15:10).

And truly, who can have more reason to be joyful than this: "The LORD thy God in the midst of thee is mighty; he will save, he will rejoice over thee with joy; he will rest in his love, he will joy over thee with singing" (Zeph 3:17)?

Unfortunately, there are severe consequences of joylessness extending to even our children. Read this sobering one: "Thou shalt beget sons and daughters, but thou shalt not enjoy them; for they shall go into captivity...Because thou servedst not the LORD thy God with joyfulness, and with gladness of heart, for the abundance of all things" (Deut 28:41, 47). How sad to be robbed of enjoying our children through our joylessness.

Alternatively, we can have not only what joy is associated with, but also great results from it, such as: others hearing of it (1 Kings 1:40), contagious joy (Neh 12:43), conversions (Esther 8:17), healing (Ps 51:8), restoration (Ps 51:12), a satisfied soul and praising lips (Ps 63:5), walking in light of His face (Ps 89:15), sorrow which through hope turns to joy (Ps 126:5), justice (Prov 21:15), comfort and refreshment (2 Cor 7:13), strengthening unto all patience and longsuffering (Col 1:11). And here's an eye opener for all of us homemakers: hands will be strengthened in the work He gives us (Ezra 6:22).

But what about those people who are not believers, who seem happy, or even claim they are? Why would they look for this God from whom true joy supposedly comes? As I mentioned, there is a real difference between happiness and joy. This happiness does not come from wisdom and, ultimately, results in complete folly(Prov 15:21). It comes from appealing circumstances and material goods, not from the Lord, from whom even in deep poverty we have joy (2 Cor 8:2). For example, you might find a nation or family growing, but no joy (as noted above in the results list, Isaiah 9:3); prosperity and economic growth but no trust in the Lord's provisions (1 Tim 6:17), hedonism and seeking every comfort (Isa 22:13) but not in the Holy Spirit (Rom 14:17; Heb 11:25), security in the past (Isa 23:7) and in idolatry (Hosea 9:1), but not in refusing or enduring temptation (Jas 1:2). Biblical joy comes from enduring mocking or insults in His name (Luke 6:23) and in persevering through current sorrows because of the hope we have in seeing Him again. (John 16:20, 22; 1 Thess 2:19; 1 Peter 4:13).

The antidote to joylessness is to look to our good Shepherd Jesus Christ and to continue our work, knowing each day is holy unto our Lord. There is no reason to be sorry for our circumstances or for ourselves when we not only think on and remember all we have to be joyful about, but we also remember from Whom our joy comes. We need to be glad *in* the Lord. If we are tired or ill, we can still sing aloud upon our beds (Ps 149:5)!

This verse speaks volumes: "Then he said unto them, Go your way, eat the fat, and drink the sweet, and send portions unto them for whom nothing is prepared: for this day is holy unto our Lord: neither be ye sorry; for the joy of the LORD is your strength" (Neh 8:10).

And the exhortation for me and for you is this: "O come, let us sing unto the LORD: let us make a joyful noise to the rock of our salvation.

Let us come before his presence with thanksgiving, and make a joyful noise unto him with psalms" (Ps 95:1-2).

I long to be filled with *His* joy and am thankful He continues to teach me what it means to be His child. Lord, may this be true about all of your children: "Yet I will rejoice in the LORD, I will joy in the God of my salvation" (Hab 3:18).

---

*Have you allowed anything to rob your joy or hinder you from expressing it?*

# Thoughts on Anger

*"He who angers you conquers you."*

— *Elizabeth Kenny*

I blew it with my toddler yesterday. I was in the rocking chair nursing my baby when I noticed my little girl trying to traipse around with her pajama pants stuck around her ankles.

*"Sweetie? You need to sit down right now."*

I don't remember what she said, but I do remember worrying about the stairs nearby and listening to her become frustrated in her tangled-up clothing. I tried to reason with her about why she needed to stop. *Ha!* As some wise person once said, trying to reason with a toddler is like trying to reason with the wind!

*"Honey. Sit down. Now. I don't want you to fall down the stairs."* Meanwhile, the baby was still contentedly nursing, his tussled curls in the crook of my arm. My toddler began to move more quickly and began to whine loudly about her pajamas. After about the third or fourth time, I found my deep belly voice and angrily and loudly commanded, *"SIT DOWN!!"*

Babe paused, looked quizzically up at me and then continued suckling. Toddler stopped, looked up at me, miraculously sat (thank you, Jesus), and angrily replied, "Mama...that hurt ears!"

I'd failed. In my head I'd heard how important it is to train your toddler, how important it is to be consistent, how important it is never to lose your temper. I'd taken a huge hit in the war on obedience training. Toddler scores one. Mama scores zippo.

At this point I thought, *God, why do you keep giving me toddlers?* Then I thanked Him for those calming nursing hormones to go along with those toddlers, took a deep breath, and tried again.

*"Baby, stand up."* I worked up a smile.

She stood up. (Oh, praise God!)

*"Good job! You stood up! Oops. Your pants are tangled. Now sit down again."* At that point, my smile was ridiculous. An aren't-we-having-a-great-time kind of smile. Inside, I felt wretched.

We played the sit-down/stand-up game a few more times, and then I called her to me. *"Baby, I am sorry I yelled. Mama's sorry."*

"Sorry you," she responded, which means, "Sorry...[I forgive] you."

I thought, *Well, at least she's got the "I forgive you" part down.*

Anger is loss of the control over events or people we think we should have. It is tragic because we never own that sort of power in the first place, but when the only other reasonable emotion is anxiety, we'd rather be angry! It doesn't seem as weak. What doesn't come to my own mind are thoughts such as put the baby down and deal with it softly, plan obedience boot camp for the morning, and don't lose my sense of humor.

And why does this not come to mind? Because I can be lazy in consistency, lazy in training, and lazy in cultivating the heart-to-heart relationship that might guarantee my toddler would always *want* to obey me. In the short run, it is more pleasant to seek the easy road and to ignore the disobedience. But from there, I can see the long road stretching ahead from parents who have traveled that journey. They've disengaged with their children either physically ("I can't wait to send them off to school") or mentally ("That's expected behavior because she's *that* age") or emotionally ("I love my children, but I don't like them").

# THOUGHTS ON ANGER

I am still learning to be a mother of grace, patience, and persistence. I am thankful my Father is a far better parent than I, and as a shepherd, He leads me. I have taken to heart this scripture, thinking of how my toddler might say this to me: "O LORD, rebuke me not in thine anger, neither chasten me in thy hot displeasure" (Ps 6:1). Hot displeasure is one thing, but rebuking in anger is altogether another ball of wax. And this is good, also: "Be not hasty in thy spirit to be angry: for anger resteth in the bosom of fools" (Eccl 7:9). *Ouch.*

Let's leave the yelling for emergencies and fools. Next time I hope I remember these verses and to choose the "weak" route of uncertainty, and to use it as an opportunity to pray for clarity, wisdom, strength, and grace. Perhaps in declining to travel the lazy road, that angry-yelling road, the road that inevitably leads to hurting wee ears and hearts, there will be hope for me, and even for the toddlers in my life yet to come. And praise the Lord for toddlers short on memory and long on "sorry yous."

"Be careful for nothing; but in every thing by prayer and supplication with thanksgiving let your requests be made known unto God." (Phil 4:6)

---

*What makes you angry? Why? Is your anger a God-righteousness anger?*

# Have You Let Go of Your Peace?

*"And Aaron held his peace." (Lev 10:3)*

In the book of Leviticus, much effort is expended in explaining how to properly prepare for the coming glory of the Lord, from the materials to be used in worship and sacrifice, to the colors of the garments the priests were to wear. After Moses explained how it was all to be done, Aaron and his sons took over the rites.

The first time these men took care in these matters, all the congregation stood without the tabernacle, waiting. As the offerings were completed, "there came a fire out from before the LORD, and consumed upon the altar the burnt offering and the fat: which when all the people saw, they shouted, and fell on their faces" (Lev 9:24).

No doubt! I think most of the people were milling around, enjoying the spiritual stuff of the hour, and feeling their emotions stimulated. But once fire from heaven fell: "Oh!" Reality set in quick!

I wonder then, at the next verse, in which Aaron's sons decided to offer strange fire before the Lord, which He commanded them not to do. One minute they witnessed fire falling from the sky, and the next they felt they needed to add to their worship experience in selecting their own methods of meeting God. Well, they met God all right: "And there went out fire from the LORD, and devoured them, and they died before the LORD" (Lev 10:2). Approaching God was done His way or no way at all. It's the same today: His way or not at all.

Moses immediately spoke to Aaron regarding the matter, and it says Aaron held his peace. He did? How did he do that? Both of his sons were judged, found wanting, and destroyed...and Aaron held his peace?

I think what strikes me most is that Aaron's peace was really God's peace given to him, and it was his to do with as he pleased. God had already consecrated him, forgiven him, and given him a special duty. Aaron understood the ways of God to the best of his ability; he was witness to God's workings; and he had been spared despite his own gross sins. As sorrowful as he must have been, he actively and willfully chose to hold on to the peace God had given him.

If you belong to the Lord, you too have His peace. It's not hiding underneath religious sacraments or platitudes, and it's not waiting to be unfolded after hours of Bible study. You have it already, even if your experience or your feelings betray the matter and try to tell you otherwise. It is yours to do with what you wish.

"For the mountains shall depart, and the hills be removed; but my kindness shall not depart from thee, neither shall the covenant of my peace be removed, saith the LORD that hath mercy on thee." (Isa 54:10)

"Peace I leave with you, my peace I give unto you: not as the world giveth, give I unto you. Let not your heart be troubled, neither let it be afraid." (John 14:27)

I want to challenge us to hold onto our peace. Irritations will come. Pain will come. Cups will be spilled, and diapers will be gross. People will disappoint, and at times, household chores will be cumbersome. But the Prince of Peace is come into our hearts. Let us not offer Him the strange fire of doubt and discouragement, and instead choose to accept His sweet gifts of the heart.

"The LORD will give strength unto his people; the LORD will bless his people with peace." (Ps 29:11)

# HAVE YOU LET GO OF YOUR PEACE?

---

*Have you let go of your peace in any area?*

# Snickering is Sin!

It is grievous the amount of chortling going on at the expense of our sisters at Christian seminars, on the internet, and even in person. Typically, the speaker will list out a multitude of activities, assuming them to be an impossibility for "real" women: early Bible study, baking homemade bread, sewing their own clothes, and so forth. This means, of course, the woman who actually *does* these things is not only being unreal, but is actually all too pious for everyone else.

Let us go to the standard for our measuring tools, however. What does God, in His perfect Word, have to say about our activities and manner?

"I beseech you therefore, brethren, by the mercies of God, that ye present your bodies a living sacrifice, holy, acceptable unto God, which is your reasonable service" (Rom 12:1). Presenting our bodies through service and gratitude is an offering unto God, an act of worship. We ought not chide our sisters for lengthy prayer times, covering their heads, or for eschewing junk food, simply because we may not do those things ourselves. Why should those women be mocked?

Women who are attempting to serve God should not be focused on how someone else's own walk with the Lord is going—they are simply struggling through (and at times gaining victory over) their own challenges and goals. If we look down upon one another even for great accomplishments, we are casting stumbling stones to make ourselves feel better for our own failures, and trying to shame others for daring to accomplish what we secretly wish we could do ourselves.

"And be not conformed to this world: but be ye transformed by the renewing of your mind, that ye may prove what is that good, and acceptable, and perfect, will of God." (Rom 12:2)

Let's look at an example of rising early, say daybreak, to greet the Lord and study the Word. Yes, I've heard snippy comments about women who do this practice. As we ought to know, renewing the mind occurs through reading and studying the Bible. So why might we snort at our sisters who get up in the wee hours of the morning to drink from the Living Waters? In fact, we ought to simply search the word *morning* in the Bible and see:

"My voice shalt thou hear in the morning, O LORD; in the morning will I direct my prayer unto thee, and will look up." (Ps 5:3)

"Evening, and morning, and at noon, will I pray, and cry aloud: and he shall hear my voice." (Ps 55:17)

"But I will sing of thy power; yea, I will sing aloud of thy mercy in the morning: for thou hast been my defence and refuge in the day of my trouble." (Ps 59:16)

I understand the difficulties involved with waking in the morning. I, too, have spent time nursing through the night and/or have been exhausted from the day. But all of this does not negate the importance of God's Word. I know He is merciful to me and gives me sleep, but even when I cannot rise after difficult nights, it is still God's best for me I do it.

And let us be rather frank here as well. Most of us see nothing wrong with staying up to blog, read, scroll on our smartphones, work on projects, and watch TV. Staying up too late may indeed be our own discipline issue! The fact that another woman rises early for prayer and study may be a matter of conviction and priority for her, and when we tease her about it, it only shows our own lack of sobriety for the things of God.

"For I say, through the grace given unto me, to every man that is among you, not to think of himself more highly than he ought to think; but to think soberly, according as God hath dealt to every man the measure of faith." (Rom 12:3)

**Soberly:** "without excess, with moderation, calmly and seriously."

When scoffers point out another woman's good deeds and good habits as if these were impossibly unattainable "in the real world," they are thinking of themselves more highly than they ought. They are exaggerating the facts to elevate themselves, perhaps someone to whom another struggler can relate. It is a common tactic in our culture to step on the heads of others to raise ourselves over them.

"For as we have many members in one body, and all members have not the same office: So we, being many, are one body in Christ, and every one members one of another." (Rom 12:4-5)

We ought to be ashamed of any mocking tones in our speech. We belong to one another, even though by design we have different gifts, talents, treasures, personality traits, habits, and patterns. My Christian sister, who does a far better job of exercising her body than I do (for example), belongs to me, and I should not be expecting her to do anything other than what she has been taught of the Lord. If anything, I should be asking her for encouragement, guidance, and wisdom!

What else ought we to be doing?

"Let love be without dissimulation. Abhor that which is evil; cleave to that which is good." (Rom 12:9)

"Blessed is the man that walketh not in the counsel of the ungodly, nor standeth in the way of sinners, nor sitteth in the seat of the scornful. But his delight is in the law of the LORD; and in his law doth he meditate day and night." (Ps 1:1-2)

Scorning: bad.

Delighting in God's law: good.

If we are snickering over a sister's good walk, we are in sin, plain and simple. "Be kindly affectioned one to another with brotherly love; in honour preferring one another" (Rom 12:10). "Thou shalt not go up and down as a talebearer among thy people: neither shalt thou stand against the blood of thy neighbour: I am the LORD" (Lev 19:16). It is not kindly affectioned to cause mischief by cutting another person down, to listen to and chuckle with the talebearer at the expense of another. Even though the victim may not hear of it, the Lord your God does.

"But God commendeth his love toward us, in that, while we were yet sinners, Christ died for us" (Rom 5:8). Even if our sisters are sinning by bragging about their good works, we still ought to be tying the towel round our waists, filling the basins, and washing their feet. We are not to be comparing our walk with theirs but with that of Jesus and the Father. Truly, we need to see ourselves as less than others because we are to compare ourselves to God's standard, not to man's.

"Not slothful in business; fervent in spirit; serving the Lord" (Rom 12:11). What a lovely picture of a godly woman's *modus operandi*. She ought to be emulated, not ridiculed.

"Rejoicing in hope; patient in tribulation; continuing instant in prayer" (Rom 12:12). We rejoice in our own failures, even the delay of having a home in order, even as we pray for patience in the chaos of trying to organize a schedule. Our hindrances and troubles ought to cause us to pray without ceasing for a godly, joyful, peace-filled home.

"Distributing to the necessity of saints; given to hospitality" (Rom 12:13). Some women have the gift of hospitality. Instead of excusing ourselves from hospitality because we aren't as perfect or well organized as those women, we ought to humble ourselves and learn from them! This is not about personality traits or "just how I am." It's about taking responsibility for the areas in our walk that God may be trying to speak to us about. Yes, even through the examples of these other women that may cause pinches of envy.

"Bless them which persecute you: bless, and curse not" (Rom 12:14). Even if you are sure there are ladies lording over you, you are to *bless* them. Otherwise, you are acting in retaliation for the hurt you feel.

"Rejoice with them that do rejoice, and weep with them that weep" (Rom 12:15). Praise God for His working in your sisters' lives! If someone is accomplishing more than you are in an area, rejoice! And then, encourage and edify the sisters who are struggling in areas in which the Lord has strengthened you. When we are struggling with failures, what we do not need is a pat on the head accompanied by the line, "This is as good as it gets." God will help us do whatever He has called us to do, and we can reassure one another in that.

And what has He called us to do?

"I will therefore that the younger women marry, bear children, guide the house, give none occasion to the adversary to speak reproachfully" (1 Tim 5:14). "Be of the same mind one toward another. Mind not high things, but condescend to men of low estate. Be not wise in your own conceits" (Rom 12:16).

Sometimes we shy from offering help because we believe it makes us appear haughty. And asking for help makes us appear lame. The fear of (wo)man over our desire to grow closer to Jesus causes us to fail to exhort one another or to ask for help. Can we see how ridiculous this is? So, are we instead to rejoice in our ineptitudes to gain fellowship with other mockers? Are we to hide the tools given to us by the Lord to gain popularity?

Mocking, scoffing, chortling, snorting, and disrespecting is unbecoming of a woman of God and does not give peace. See your sisters as ones with whom you belong to Christ, successes and failures alike. Let us uplift and rejoice in one another's accomplishments and look to the Lord who calls us all higher and provides us the unity of sisterhood to cheer us all on.

"If it be possible, as much as lieth in you, live peaceably with all men." (Rom 12:18)

---

*Whom do you need to forgive for snickering against you? Of whom do you need to ask forgiveness?*

# Oh, to Be a TWIT for God!

Long ago I decided to be a TWIT for God. This is my acronym for Titus Woman in Training. I find it humorously in keeping with how the world defines *foolishness*. Here is the passage I am referring to:

> "The aged women likewise, that they be in behaviour as becometh holiness, not false accusers, not given to much wine, teachers of good things; That they may teach the young women to be sober, to love their husbands, to love their children, To be discreet, chaste, keepers at home, good, obedient to their own husbands, that the word of God be not blasphemed." (Titus 2:3-5)

My job is to forsake self-pity and annoyance at the perceived failings of other people. Instead, God wants me to trust Him to use this time to mold me into the Titus 2 woman He wants me to be, to pay attention to what He is teaching me through every hardship or difficulty.

There are many studies about this passage, but I want to look at the word *teach*. The first time the word appears in the Bible it is from the Lord after He has chastised Moses for his whiny excuse of not being equipped to do the task he has been given. Boy, do I relate to Moses here!

"Now therefore go, and I will be with thy mouth, and teach thee what thou shalt say." (Ex 4:12)

Is the Lord saying the same thing to us now? *Now therefore go!* God gave us the amazing task of parenting and leading tender children into His truth, liberating them from slavery and bondage. We do not have to feel sorry about our task. We do not have to make excuses for our perceived or very real inadequacies. And we do not have to behave poorly to attract pity for every difficulty we experience along the way.

God Himself will shepherd us, even if we feel all alone, missing aged women who are supposed to be leading and teaching us.

Here is His promise: "He shall feed his flock like a shepherd: he shall gather the lambs with his arm, and carry them in his bosom, and shall gently lead those that are with young" (Isa 40:11).

But I know many of us have cried out, *"Where are the Titus 2 women? Where are my mentors?"* We grieve their absence, but instead of spending all of our energy lamenting MIA Titus women, we need to allow the Lord to train us into them. The next time you attend church, take a good look around. All those sweet, young girls growing up need encouragement. Show them a model of someone worth emulating. *Become* the mentor you wish you had.

That young mom with her first or even her second child is thirsty for the big picture of Living Water. Give a word of blessing. Invite her and her children over for lunch. Provide her family with a freezer meal for those extra trying days.

As for any older women who do not edify or perhaps speak outright disheartening words, forgive and bless them. They raised their children in an era of blooming radical militant feminism, and even if they loved being a mother, there was tremendous pressure to downplay it or abandon it altogether. Perhaps many of them are pained by their own mistakes, and the devil plays on their regrets. Others may feel like mothering failures, or they did not have the intact family that you do, and they feel envious. If you are a joyful wife and mother, it may be a befuddlement to one and a shame to another. So, bless them. Ask about their grandchildren, hobbies, jobs, lives.

When they pat you on the arm and say, "Oh, you poor thing with all those kids!" you can hug them in return and proclaim in truth how *good* God is, even in the thick of mothering. You do not have to agree you are a poor thing!

Let us raise up our eyes above disillusionment and joyfully commit to becoming these Titus 2 women for the generation ahead. God is with us; He will shepherd us; and He will be there to bless and encourage us. Forsake the foolishness of the world in regard to motherhood and become a TWIT for God, instead.

———————

*Imagine yourself twenty years older than you are. Write to the woman you are today. What encouragement and blessing can you give?*

# A Heart for Home

*I have no faith in that woman who talks of grace and glory abroad, and uses no soap and water at home. Let the buttons be on the shirts, let the children's socks be mended, let the roast mutton be done to a turn, let the house be as neat as a new pin, and the home be as happy as home can be.*
— Charles Spurgeon

# A Simple Life

It is finally rest time, and I am drained from the morning's work. I thought about all my sister mamas out there today as I picked up the vacuum wand. I could almost hear a multitude of rotating bristle brushes beating the rug fibers in many homes, muted only by the muffled roar of my own motor. I wondered if you were also reaching down, tossing toys aside, and if you also ventured underneath beds and desks, that dark abyss known as Dust Bunny Haven. I admit my mind wondered, *When will I get to stop redoing it all? When will the day come when the table stays clean for more than one meal? When will the dryer remain silent for longer than a day? Ack!* The tantalizing aroma of more time for me, me, me....

I wonder how the mamas in yesteryear did it all. They not only had laundry, they had to do it all by hand. They not only had chicken dumplings, they had to choose and kill a hen. With an axe. With their bare hands. They not only had smudgy noses, dirty toes, and stringy matted hair to deal with, they had to clean up the children with a single tub, with water they first had to fetch and heat up. On a stove they had to chop wood for and feed into an oven. Chores were much more complex back then, and let us remember that it is still this way today for millions of people. It is a wonder we dare to call it the *simple life*.

What is the simple life? Is it parting with rugs to be free of the vacuum? Is it paring down clothing to be free of mountains of laundry? Regretfully, my own selfishness and distaste for sacrifice too often feeds that longing for a simple life, but mostly I desire a slice of heaven in my home, a lightness, a place for easy laughter and a safe place to shed tears. Don't I have that already?

Yes, yes I do. I see those things in my children. Squeals of raucous laughter, shouts of injustice, pleadings for forgiveness, stompings of tantrums, and anger uninhibited. All in the mix of toys to trip over, books to repair, and paint splotches to prayerfully lift from the rugs that my vacuum cleaner is running over.

It is exasperating, excruciating, exhausting work to be a mother. But all things considered, it is a simple life: love God, love your husband, love your children, keep the home. This is a full-enough life, and anything else only threatens and steals precious emotional, mental, and physical strength from our short lives. Someday, perhaps, my great-great-granddaughter will wipe her brow, put the children to nap, and wonder about me, about how I did it. I will tell her, "Not as well as I wanted, nor as much as I had hoped, but Jesus walked with me through it all, and it was more than enough."

———

*In what areas do you long for a simpler life? Why?*

# No Time for the Lord

*Neither will we say any more to the work of our hands, Ye are our gods: for in thee the fatherless findeth mercy." (Hosea 14:3b)*

Work around here is never-ending. As soon as the laundry is complete, dirty shirts and socks find their way (I hope!) into the empty baskets. As soon as the evening meal is finished, the dishes await washing. And boo-boos, bumps, and bruises from outside play mingled with dirty patches on little elbows and knees call for bath time. Often the work feels circular, as if the work feeds upon itself to no end, but it isn't. It is more a tide, with ebbs and flows that feel monotonous but have the purpose of keeping the home fresh and alive through its movement. Work is not purposeless.

Misunderstanding this has led me at times to an all-out drive to complete as much as I can in as small of a time-space as possible. As eventide commences, I have a need to see order, such as the kitchen readied for morning. My craving to do a good job keeps my feet moving, my hands busy, my mind mentally addressing and planning and contemplating multitudes of issues at a time. On occasion, I will lament the loss of a lazy afternoon on a swing set, but that reverie is soon lost in more mental checklists.

I contemplated these things as I read the verse above from Hosea because I find much of my time walking and talking with the Lord during my work: "Sure, let's talk, Lord...while I fold laundry. Sure, I'll pray...while I cook the meal."

Is that so bad? Maybe not, but is it enough?

The best food for my heart has always been in the quiet morning, alone with my Bible and journal. Alas, I often do not rush to get up to meet with God because my nights have been long. He does not press me, unlike the need to get dressed, get breakfast, get going.

Has the work of my hands become my god? Does my sense of satisfaction and purpose lie in my work? Do I expect to find goodness and mercy in these accomplishments? If so, then imagine my disappointments in picking up broken glasses, cleaning urine off the floor, and wiping smudges off the walls. Imagine my defeat, looping in a never-ending workload. Where is my gold star?

"I will be as the dew unto Israel: he shall grow as the lily, and cast forth his roots as Lebanon. His branches shall spread, and his beauty shall be as the olive tree, and his smell as Lebanon. They that dwell under his shadow shall return; they shall revive as the corn, and grow as the vine: the scent thereof shall be as the wine of Lebanon." (Hosea 14:5-7)

Dew does not fall on anything constantly in motion. We must stop and sit with a Bible opened. Stop and put aside the list of the tides of work to be done. In other words, stop and allow the dew to collect. Only then will we grow to be more beautiful, branches spreading in love and our children reviving and growing under our care. The scent of our homes will be an atmosphere of sweet wine, pleasant and good. It will not come from running about from sunup to sundown and beyond; it will only truly come from the Lord. "From me is thy fruit found" (Hosea 14:8b).

We do not need to "make time for the Lord". He has already made time. Give it back to Him and let Him multiply the fruit in His own mysterious way. Allow the dew of God's grace to have a place to settle a little more, allowing the day's work to take its rightful place in the ebb and flow of our lives. Work may be neverending, but pausing to drink in His Word won't leave us thirsty when we get back to our labor.

"Who is wise, and he shall understand these things? prudent, and he shall know them? for the ways of the LORD are right, and the just shall walk in them." (Hosea 14:9)

"Abide in me, and I in you. As the branch cannot bear fruit of itself, except it abide in the vine; no more can ye, except ye abide in me." (John 15:4)

———————

*Do you at any part of the day give God your full attention?*

# Gadding About

*"And withal they learn to be idle, wandering about from house to house; and not only idle, but tattlers also and busybodies, speaking things which they ought not." (1 Tim 5:13)*

The Lord convicted me regarding my time spent on the computer. I began to notice bloggers I much admire dropping out of the blogosphere, and my snickity attitude was, "Too bad they can't manage their time better."

Well, apparently, I suffered the same problem! Isn't it interesting how other people's most pestersome sins are reflective of the same we carry ourselves?

Don't get me wrong. I worked hard to plan and implement a schedule in my home. It worked fairly well, and I enjoyed a lot of free time, such as when the children were napping or resting. My problem? I was spending most of my free time on the computer. My cookie jar stayed empty. My quilt border stayed unfinished. My pantry remained unorganized. My books gathered dust. All for what?

It dawned on me everything I did on a blog was made up of airspace. Maybe all I had written would be saved in a format for my children, but truthfully, if the internet crashed, all of it would —poof!— be gone.

As I was thinking of this with verse above, I looked up several of the words to get a better understanding:

**Idle**

Idleness is not laziness, but it can be the effect of it. According to Webster's 1828 Dictionary, it means, "Not employed; unoccupied with business; inactive; doing nothing; slothful; given to rest and ease; averse to labor or employment.

"Idle differs from lazy; the latter implying constitutional or habitual aversion or indisposition to labor or action, sluggishness; whereas idle, in its proper sense, denotes merely unemployed. An industrious man may be idle, but he cannot be lazy."

Perhaps staring at a computer screen and letting my fingers do the talking isn't exactly laborious. It is educational, informational, and entertaining, but it doesn't get my hands dirty or the laundry folded. It's not *bad*, but it keeps my engines running (idling) without stepping on the gas and moving forward. "By much slothfulness the building decayeth; and through idleness of the hands the house droppeth through" (Eccl 10:18).

**Tattler**

One of its definitions is "an idle talker." Unlike propping the phone on my shoulder when I'm washing dishes, I'm not moving when I'm on the computer.

Tattles: "To prate; to talk idly; to use many words with little meaning." And what does prate mean, anyhow? "To talk much and without weight, or to little purpose; to be loquacious; as the vulgar express it, to run on." In other words, *blah blah blah blah blah*. That was me!

I'd read a blog, feel compelled to comment, and *click!* be elsewhere. Repeat: read, comment, *click!* *Ad nauseum.*

**Busybodies**

This word only occurs twice in the KJV Bible. Once in the scripture at the top of this piece and once in 2 Thessalonians 3:11: "For we hear that there are some which walk among you disorderly, working not at all, but are busybodies."

See how the Bible defines itself? Busybodies are those who are disorderly and not working. I was feeling pretty good from the definition of idle because I learned I was "simply" idle and not lazy. But doesn't "working not at all" sound like laziness to you?

**Wandering**

"Roving; rambling; deviating from duty; traveling without a settled course [blog-hopping anyone?], aberration; mistaken way; deviation from rectitude; as a wandering from duty; A roving of the mind or thoughts from the point or business in which one ought to be engaged."

That last line was me in all my splendor —my mind wandering to what I wanted to write and what websites I wanted to visit, hoping I had comments waiting for me and neglecting what was truly important.

These were some of the changes I made:

1) I stopped maintaining a list of other blogs for my readers. It's not that I didn't want to share other blogs, but I felt compelled not to be party to the gadding about. I then used Pinterest to store links to helpful sites, but found over time that all I was doing was adding to a resource library that I rarely needed. I was saving images just for the sake of saving images. Now I simply share relevant links in the context of individual blog posts.

2) I set the timer. One hour a day for computer use: checking and answering email, writing blogs, doing necessary research, and otherwise putzing around. An hour was a painful weaning, and as it turned out, I didn't have time to blog as much anymore. The push in my head to write-share-write-share quieted. As my children got older I found more

time to write but the increased pull to internet-hop has been tamed.

3) I became a lurker. Reducing likes and comments left on other blogs and social media lessened my compulsion to give advice and opinions at every opportunity. I dropped my subscription load to two blogs: one because I liked his writing, and the other because her art made me smile. I've added a couple more since then, on the topics of weaving. A handful of subscriptions is manageable.

4) I turned off my comments feature for a season. Why? Because if I received an encouraging or funny comment, it made my day! Guess what a discouraging comment did? I needed to concentrate on what the *Lord* thought of me and to seek *His* favor and not get wrapped up in the hope and worry of who will leave me a comment and what it will say. Since then, I've turned it back

on, and check on it once or twice a week. I love hearing from my readers, but do not base my mood on what is, or isn't, left for me.

With regards to blogging, I now find myself enjoying mini-blogging on Instagram and connecting with others there. I don't have any notifications turned on for emails and social media at all, and I try to keep my Instagram "follow" list around 100, deleting when it starts to creep up. Otherwise, I'd spend too much time scrolling not to miss anyone's feed.

I feel I've found a better balance, and you can read more about how in my book, *PRESENT*. I still read comments, email, and reviews on my book and podcast. It's not hard to find me, but I feel untethered to the call of gadding about, of being distracted from what I consider the priorities in my life. Since writing *PRESENT* and overcoming my internet and blogging addictions, I've noticed that moms today are far more likely to be gadding about through their smartphones. Is this you? Oh, that we would be wise and redeem the time!

A quote which helps prod me into taking action when I am convicted is: "Resolved, whenever my feelings begin to appear in the least out of order, when I am conscious of the least uneasiness within, or the least irregularity without, I will then subject myself to the strictest examination" (Jonathan Edwards). Do you need any self-examination in gadding about? Perhaps ask your spouse and your children for honest and more objective opinions on this matter. (Do you dare to ask?)

"She looketh well to the ways of her household, and eateth not the bread of idleness." (Prov 31:27)

———

*In what areas might you be eating the bread of idleness? Are you willing to trade the payoff of those areas for a deeper and richer life, even if that life becomes mostly undocumented and only for your family and God to see?*

# Quenching My Appetite

*"All the Labour of a man is for his mouth, and yet the appetite is not filled." (Eccl 6:7)*

The children and I had a race. Whoever got their room cleaned up first won a quarter.

They had clothing to pick up, toys to get off the floor, books sprawled everywhere and enough small Legos and doodads underfoot to make a midnight run to the bathroom a perilous undertaking.

Me? I had worse problems. On my kitchen counters, I had piles of mail, toys needing a fix, bills to file, receipts, homeschool papers, torn-out recipes, ValPak coupons, books on bunny care, birthday streamers, magazines, and a half-finished model airplane. I know the adage "don't put it down, put it away," but I can't seem to follow it when I've got meals to make, Band-Aids to put on, and diapers to change. All paper multiplies when I am away, creating more piles. On the plus side, it absolves me of dusting!

So, the children were thumping about furiously upstairs, running hither and thither to put their toys away whilst trying not to knock heads in the process. I was trying to stay focused on the task at hand.

*Coupons...where do I put the coupons? Oh, look! Concrete borders. How interesting! Oh, and pizza for ten dollars! What am I making for supper again...?*

Finally, most of the piles were put either in their proper places or, better yet, into the circular file underneath the kitchen sink. I still had a small stack on my kitchen desk to go through "later". I thought about the verse from Ecclesiastes that says labor will never satisfy my appetite for a perfectly clean and orderly home because, after all, the morning mail was yet to come!

Labour, from the verse above: "work done, or to be done; that which requires wearisome exertion."

Truth! And then, my eye wandered to where the word *originated*, and I laughed out loud! It was from the Latin *labo*, which means "to fail." To fail? To *fail?!* What do you mean to *fail?* What kind of word is that?! All wearisome exertion is ultimately a failure?

And what's the "appetite" all about? It means "a strong desire, eagerness or longing, natural such as hunger or thirst, or artificial such as ice cream or new shoes, desire of pleasure or good."

My artificial appetite for a crispy clean home led to fun and games for us all for the moment, but in reality, once the next day ensued, all that labour would vanish. I had to be reminded any appetite for a perfectly spotless home was going to leave my stomach wrenching in hunger and my children starved for a happy home. As I *oohed* and *aahed* over clean rooms and doled out the quarters, their chirpy voices filled my evening. Even though tomorrow it would seem our labour "failed," none of it was done in vain in the Lord's eyes.

"Therefore, my beloved brethren, be ye stedfast, unmoveable, always abounding in the work of the Lord, forasmuch as ye know that your labour is not in vain in the Lord." (1 Cor 15:58)

Although my desires for an orderly home are not bad, having a spotless one does not satisfy. Neither does a multitude of other important tasks at hand. Satisfaction comes from going to the Source and from sitting at His feet. It is better to read a Bible story and to share His wisdom in the midst of stray socks than to put it off until the last barrette is picked up and put away. "For wisdom is better than rubies; and all the things that may be desired are not to be compared to it" (Prov 8:11).

Lastly, I was reminded of this verse: "Delight thyself also in the LORD; and he shall give thee the desires of thine heart" (Ps 37:4). To me, this verse is circular. If I find my delight in the Lord, then His desires for me will become my own, part of which is more of Him. And if I have more of Him, even plowing through the piles of stuff growing overnight will be more fun than a horse race.

———

*Is your primary daily business a delightful fellowship with the Lord? Where are you allowing your labor to feed an appetite that does not satisfy?*

# WANTED: a Life of Ease

*"We give thanks to God always for you all, making mention of you in our prayers; remembering without ceasing your work of faith, and labour of love, and patience of hope in our Lord Jesus Christ, in the sight of God and our Father." (1 Thess 1:2-3)*

What does Paul, without ceasing and with the upmost gratitude, remember about the Thessalonians? He remembers a lifestyle which brings forth the fruit of thanksgiving to God. A few key phrases in this passage are: work of faith, labour of love, and patience of hope. To help us bring about practical application, here are several of those words as defined by Noah Webster's 1828 *American Dictionary of the English Language*:

**Work:** "To be in action or motion, as the working of the heart; to obtain by diligence, to influence by acting upon, to mold or shape."

Of: "From or out of, proceeding from as the cause, source, means, author or agent bestowing."

Faith: "From the Latin *fido*, which means 'to trust'; an entire confidence or trust in God's character and declarations, and in the character and doctrines of Christ." And from J. Harnes, we read, "Faith is an affectionate practical confidence in the testimony of God."

Here, we have physical, diligent motion working to mold or shape something, proceeding from the source of a trust in God's character and words. If we claim to trust the Lord, there is no room for carelessness in our work, whether it is housework or raising children. Rolling up shirt sleeves is a response to simply believing God, not an act of trying to gain His favor. Galatians 5:6 says, "For in Jesus Christ neither circumcision availeth any thing, nor uncircumcision; but faith which worketh by love."

Labour:"To act or move with painful effort; to take pains, to be burdened; to move with difficulty, to be pressed; to move irregularly with little progress." The last being my personal, very applicable favorite.

Love: "A strong attachment springing from good will and esteem."

Well, who would want to labor? Look at the adjectives: painful, effort, pains, burdened, difficulty, pressed. And to get what? Little progress! My flesh cries out to give me the life of ease! Can you relate? We work hard to learn, read, commit, and then embark on creating a cozy, sweet home, and it can all fall apart in an instant with broken dishes, snotty noses, sour attitudes, and clumps of dirt tracked on a newly cleaned carpet. Sometimes, it feels the whole day was spent pushing wrought iron cannon balls uphill, only to have them roll back to the bottom. But we see the reason here for the labor. It is not progress per se; it is love.

"The love of God is the first duty of man, and this springs from just views of his attributes or excellencies of character, which afford the highest delight to the sanctified heart. Esteem and reverence constitute ingredients in this affection, and a fear of offending him is its inseparable effect." (Webster, 1828)

Labor flows from a love of God. Aren't you glad when you are wanting to give up on your work, God doesn't give up on His?

Patience: "From the Latin root 'to suffer.' The sufferings of afflictions, pain, toil, calamity, provocation or other evil, with a calm, unruffled temper; endurance without murmuring or fretfulness." I want a calmer, more unruffled temper. Alas, it will not be granted unless paired with suffering.

**Hope:** "To place confidence in; to trust in with confident expectation of good." I want the joy that hope gives; it is more sure, unlike a desire or wish.

My flesh inclines to forsake painful toil. Many times, I would rather not cook the meal, do the laundry, weed the garden, deal with a whiny child. These tasks can require terrific effort, but because I do trust God, I do love Jesus, and I do have confidence in Him, I continue steadfast in the work He has given me to do, knowing He sees the big picture and has only my good in mind.

How ought I to work? The answer is: by His Word, in His power, in the Holy Ghost, and with much assurance (1 Thes 1:4-5). As you can see, nowhere in there does it say, *"Hey, you're on your own. Buck up, figure it out, and get to it."* Thank you, Jesus; I am not alone in this work You have given me!

Lastly, in First Thessalonians, chapter one, verses seven and eight (after reading verse six:

"in much affliction, with joy"), we see why we should snub laziness and instead work hard: to be an example to others, spurring them on and motivating them, with the purpose of my faith spread abroad, a lively reflection of a living, loving God who desires to empower others to not only press on in the daily work, but to do it with a heart full of gratitude and thanksgiving.

Shall we get to work?

"Take heed to the ministry which thou hast received in the Lord, that thou fulfill it." (Col 4:17)

—————

*What is your most difficult work? How does the Scripture encourage you?*

# Fret Not Thyself

I regretfully read base comments on a blog discussing the topic of modesty. It saddened me to see venom directed toward the lovely and pure. I wondered what was so horrible about modesty that it caused such hatred to spew out, and I remembered it is, indeed, a wretchedly fallen and wicked world in which we live.

Then I read another blog (whose stated purpose is to protect children) regarding a contemptible man whose sole drive in life is to have a "relationship" with as many boys as he desires, and he is continuing to fight for this "right" by publishing books and contacting lawyers.

It does not take much effort to find our eyes opened unto the filth, whether via the internet, talk radio, or the evening news, does it? And yet we desire to know about it, and look to be informed. Why do we need to incessantly know about such fallen people? "Their feet run to evil, and they make haste to shed innocent blood: their thoughts are thoughts of iniquity; wasting and destruction are in their paths" (Isa 59:7).

How much better it would be to eat of the tree of life instead of the knowledge of good and evil! Yet the draw is to read or hear about wicked and foolish people, to know what evil report is out there. Sometimes, we desire to know in order to engage in legal or cultural debates. Or it might be to answer their sin with well-thought-out arguments and logical presentations to hopefully bring them to their knees in repentance and save them from perishing forever. I fear, however, there is an element of demanding justice to be done through the anger of our own responsive keystrokes, and as we know, "the wrath of man worketh not the righteousness of God" (Jas 1:20).

Perhaps I excuse imbibing the world's woes by saying I simply need to know what is going on in the world. Then I ask myself, "Why? Will it equip me to train my children? Will it help me create a healthier meal or happier home for my family? Will this information help me better understand how to live by faith? Will it draw me to rest in God more?" Maybe...and yet maybe not. The daily news is presented with a sense of urgency or with a lot of yelling, and the result inevitably feeds fear, depression, and anxiety. This should not surprise any Christian, but do we have to go looking for it?

My primary focus should be to serve my Lord Jesus Christ and do the work He sent me to do. If I fast from or forgo the news of the world, this does not mean I am somehow not fulfilling the Great Commission or hiding my light under a bushel. No, God wants me to carry my own burden (Gal 6:5) and not take on additional sacks of mental and emotional weight to fluster or frighten me, causing me to miss the peace, harmony, and joy He desires for me.

We should not concern ourselves if we choose to refrain from TV and internet hopping. Don't we have enough trouble with following after righteousness, godliness, faith, love, patience, and meekness (1 Tim 6:11)? Why make pursuing holiness more difficult?

If you are feeling a little ignorant about the world at large these days, especially if you are eschewing media news, count it as a blessing and do not chase after gaining knowledge in exchange for your peaceful life. You don't need to partake in the daily newscasts of chaos and confusion. Be content in the sphere you have been given.

"Behold, I send you forth as sheep in the midst of wolves: be ye therefore wise as serpents, and harmless as doves." (Matt 10:16)

---

*For further encouragement, please read Psalm 37 and slowly pick out the verbs related to what we should be doing in the midst of a wicked and perverse generation.*

# Grace Like Rain

Rain falls and pings,
sending echoes into the
staunch black wooden stove
while muted musical drops thump on the rooftop
rolling into sheets off the shingles;
It cascades through the downspouts
and dribbles downwards on the windows,
creeping one onto another;
A wonder...this water from heaven
Cleansing, replenishing, renewing.

*He watereth the hills from his chambers:*
*the earth is satisfied with the fruit of*
*thy works.*

I hear God's voice in the rhythm
wrapping my heart in its soothing melody
of falling mercies, new with the day.
His scent lingers in the air
Warmth permeating in pockets

# FROM MY KITCHEN TABLE

Of chill, becoming a shawl of embrace.

*And, behold, the glory of the God of Israel*
*came from the way of the east:*
*and His voice was like a noise of many waters:*
*and the earth shined with His glory.*

Outside the evergreen boughs
float their limbs in the moving breeze;
They drink silently from the hidden rivers,
nourishing their swelling roots.

*And the LORD shall guide thee continually,*
*and satisfy thy soul in drought, and make fat thy bones:*
*and thou shalt be like a watered garden, and like a*
*spring of water, whose waters fail not.*

In their dependence,
the trees are strengthened;
Cedars become arrows,
drawing their tips to the heavens,
brushing the sky in sweet caress,
trusting in the secure foundation far below.
Limbs move as multiple conductors
creating whispers of grand symphonies,

# GRACE LIKE RAIN

harmonious hymns of honor and praise.

*Let us draw near with a true heart in full assurance of*
*faith, having our hearts sprinkled from an evil conscience,*
*and our bodies washed with pure water.*

Morning breaks,
diffusing horizon gray light
through the pregnant clouds;
the pattering softens and soothes,
and peace beckons as a lullaby.

*And he said unto me, It is done.*
*I am Alpha and Omega, the beginning and the end.*
*I will give unto him that is athirst*
*of the fountain of the water of life*
*freely.*

Freely all nature receives life giving water
poured by grace from heaven,
and opens thirsty roots by design.
Our own hearts naturally cry out
for quenching; and I am reminded
as the rain stops,
as silence ensues,

241

I, too, must drink of the Living Water,
and raise my hands to the heavens,
giving glory to the Father,
who feeds my every need.

*Jesus answered and said unto her,*
*Whosoever drinketh of this water shall thirst again:*
*But whosoever drinketh of the water*
*that I shall give him shall never thirst;*
*but the water that I shall give him*
*shall be in him a well of water*
*springing up into everlasting life.*

(Scripture from: Psalm 104:13; Ezekiel 43:2; Isaiah 58:11; Hebrews 10:22; Revelation 21:6; John 4:13-14)

————

*Try writing a poem with your favorite scripture or doing a piece or art or handwork to reflect your meditations.*

# Is Motherhood
# a Calling?

**Calling:** *a Divine summons, vocation, or invitation.*

This is an interesting question because various people emphatically tell me motherhood is a "calling," to which my response has been one of skepticism. Given that the definition of *calling* begins with the adjective *Divine*, pondering this question is important. If we miss our calling, we miss the invitation to partake in God's best for us.

We must begin with the foundation: searching the Bible to learn what a calling is, to find examples of people who have been called, and to see if there are any specific callings to women in general. Obviously, a person's foundation may be different, and thus, that person may come to different conclusions, but this is how a Bible-believer should approach the matter.

As scripture states, it is the "weak" and "foolish" (by the world's standards) whom God calls to be His. "For ye see your calling, brethren, how that not many wise men after the flesh, not many mighty, not many noble, are called: But God hath chosen the foolish things of the world to confound the wise; and God hath chosen the weak things of the world to confound the things which are mighty" (1 Cor 1:26-27).

God does not seek people who have decent morals, consider themselves to be good, and have no need for the Healer. "When Jesus heard it, he saith unto them, They that are whole have no need of the physician, but they that are sick: I came not to call the righteous, but sinners to repentance" (Mark 2:17). If any woman told me she felt complete and total assurance and confidence in her abilities to either become or be a mother, I would wonder how she arrived at such conviction. God, in His wisdom, chose Sarah who was barren and elderly, Elizabeth who was barren, Hannah who was barren, Mary who was a young betrothed teen. None had confidence in their bodies or in their circumstances, yet it could be argued they were called to carry those babies at a time of God's choosing. And it would seem foolhardy timing to every witness.

A calling in the Bible is synonymous with gifting. "For the gifts and calling of God are without repentance" (Rom 11:29). There are many gifts specifically named in the Bible: prophecy, ministry, teaching, exhortation, giving, ruling, mercy (Rom 12:6-8), wisdom, knowledge, miracles, discernment, faith, healing, helps, governments, diversities of tongues and interpretations (1 Cor 12:8-10). I am not sure motherhood is a calling in this sense, as it is not included in these lists.

I think we mistake *calling* with the idea of feeling equipped. That is, if I am fairly confident of my abilities, my finances, my health, and my own desires to nurse a babe once again, then I could say with confidence I was called to do so. But what if I have none of these? Would God ever call a person to do what is, in our eyes, completely senseless?

"By faith Noah, being warned of God of things not seen as yet, moved with fear, prepared an ark to the saving of his house; by the which he condemned the world, and became heir of the righteousness which is by faith. By faith Abraham, when he was called to go out into a place which he should after receive for an inheritance, obeyed; and he went out, not knowing whither he went." (Heb 11:7-8)

Senseless, the entire chapter of Hebrews 11. None of these saints felt ready to do God's work or even saw the results of it. In a similar way, many of today's believers suffer cruelly, and even so, steadfastly walk in faith, knowing Him to be true to His promises. And besides, "without faith it is impossible to please him: for he that cometh to God must believe that he is, and that he is a rewarder of them that diligently seek him" (Heb 11:6).

Feeling ready to do anything—whether embracing motherhood, respecting one's husband, or learning to cheerfully work in the home—is the antipathy of walking by faith. It is relying on our own provisions instead of God's promises. Relying on God's promises may look unintelligent, especially in our culture, but we are either in the ark, or we are getting wet.

"For the preaching of the cross is to them that perish foolishness; but unto us which are saved it is the power of God. For it is written, I will destroy the wisdom of the wise, and will bring to nothing the understanding of the prudent. Where is the wise? where is the scribe? where is the disputer of this world? hath not God made foolish the wisdom of this world? For after that in the wisdom of God the world by wisdom knew not God, it pleased God by the foolishness of preaching to save them that believe." (1 Cor 1:18-21)

So then, is each married woman called to the "foolishness" of motherhood? I wonder about Sarah's heart and if she lamented her barrenness because God did not give her the blessing of a child, or if she was sorrowful because others considered her cursed in a time when children were treasures (how far we've fallen!). To answer this question, it is fair to look at scripture regarding married women and where their hearts ought to be:

"That they may teach the young women to be sober, to love their husbands, to love their children." (Titus 2:4-5)

"I will therefore that the younger women marry, bear children, guide the house, give none occasion to the adversary to speak reproachfully." (1 Tim 5:14)

"And did not he make one? Yet had he the residue of the spirit. And wherefore one? That he might seek a godly seed. Therefore take heed to your spirit, and let none deal treacherously against the wife of his youth." (Mal 2:15)

"Her children arise up, and call her blessed; her husband also, and he praiseth her." (Prov 31:28)

If we know the Lord and sincerely desire to please Him, we must take these verses to heart by faith (see Heb 11:6 again). Clearly, married women normally have children.

But how many? What about birth control? I would encourage you to seek your heart for the reasons behind your decisions. It is good to dig deeply into why we think what we think, and to test those thoughts against scripture. "And be not conformed to this world: but be ye transformed by the renewing of your mind, that ye may prove what is that good, and acceptable, and perfect, will of God." (Rom 12:2)

I also am not sure if a married man is "dealing treacherously" (Mal 2:15) if he withholds the possibility of a godly seed, although you'd think Onan should give pause for thought (Gen 38:9-10). However, God is completely able to open and close the womb at His will:

- All the wombs of the house of Abimelech (Gen 20:18)

- Leah (Gen 29:31)

- Rachel (Gen 30:2, 22)

- Blessings to Joseph (Gen 49:25)

- Blessings to Israel (Deut 7:13)

- Hannah (1 Sam 1:6)

- As a heritage and reward (Ps 127:3)

- The barren woman (Ps 113:9)

"Shall I bring to the birth, and not cause to bring forth? saith the LORD: shall I cause to bring forth, and shut the womb? saith thy God." (Isa 66:9)

If we shut our wombs on our own because of "me time," financial savings, or even our vehicle size and vacation plans, God may allow us to suffer negative consequences. But I am also sure He uses a lot of ways to say "enough" to close the womb. It is definitely a matter between husband and wife and the Lord, but I caution against relying on "personal peace" because the devil himself can promise you that. What is needed is great soberness with much prayer, a great wealth of scripture, and godly council. This is not to make a law where none exists, but rather to walk circumspectly.

Motherhood may or may not be a calling, but trusting God with your womb may be an act of faith. Our weakness in confidence, provision, and abilities are simply seeds for prayers to bring about an even sweeter dependence upon the Lord, whose grace is always sufficient for every need.

———————

*Do you think motherhood is a special calling? Why or why not?*

# The Night Watches

*"Her candle goeth not out by night." (Prov 31:18)*

I overdid it with the toddler, busy all day and into the evening, and as the lights went out, she began covering her ears, crying. Her low-level cold had backed up into her wee ears and was now causing painful pressure. She was exhausted from the events of the day in addition to missing a decent nap, so she alternated between thrashing like a codfish pulled from the deep and sleeping in short fits of time.

I quickly administered the usual course of treatment: garlic oil in the ear, remedies on the tongue, and chamomile in her water. Unfortunately, she was too wound up and could not relax, even in our bed. Hubby took to the store and around 11:00 p.m. came home with a pain-relieving drug we hoped would mellow her out enough to fall asleep. It did, and she slept between us.

I woke from each cough, wheezy snore, knobby knee, and rolling head. Her little hand would plop onto my face. I would bunker down into my covers only to get them kicked off. I don't remember when I fell asleep, but I do remember hearing the baby cry, as if through a fog, and got up to feed and quiet her. Twice. My snippets of sleep served mostly as a tease.

Doesn't this just characterize motherhood? Part of embracing it is receiving the night watches. It does not have to be a time of bitterness. Any mother with babe in arms can soak in these verses when the sky is dressed in stars:

- "Thou hast proved mine heart; thou hast visited me in the night; thou hast tried me, and shalt find nothing; I am purposed that my mouth shall not transgress." (Ps 17:3)

Isn't it wonderful God Himself will visit us in the night? I don't want to look up and, as Peter, find the Lord looking at me as I show my own true heart: bitterness because a wee one is keeping me up.

- "Yet the LORD will command his lovingkindness in the daytime, and in the night his song shall be with me, and my prayer unto the God of my life." (Ps 42:8)

If we are following Jesus, we are to do what He does: command our lovingkindness to our children in the daytime and sing our songs to them in the night.

- "O LORD God of my salvation, I have cried day and night before thee." (Ps 88:1)

Can you imagine if God had working hours? Our hurting children should not come across the Closed sign after dark on our bedroom doors.

- "To shew forth thy lovingkindness in the morning, and thy faithfulness every night." (Ps 92:2)

Let us do likewise.

- "I prevented the dawning of the morning, and cried: I hoped in thy word." (Ps 119:147)

Cry if you need to but do not lose hope in His words to you. Open to a psalm and read.

- "Behold, he that keepeth Israel shall neither slumber nor sleep." (Ps 121:4)

Well, praise the Lord. Unlike me, He does not need this kind of repose and rest. Thus, I can draw upon Him for the strength and clear-headedness I am desperately needing.

- "Therefore let us not sleep, as do others; but let us watch and be sober." (1 Thess 5:6)

Let us not spend our time and energies in anger over lost sleep. Let us comfort our children in their angst and use the time to commune with our Lord. Let us go 'round the world in prayer, lift up our friends and enemies, and do neglected spiritual housekeeping.

- "It is of the LORD'S mercies that we are not consumed, because his compassions fail not. They are new every morning: great is thy faithfulness. The LORD is my portion, saith my soul; therefore will I hope in him. The LORD is good unto them that wait for him, to the soul that seeketh him." (Lam 3:22-25)

May the Lord bless our night watches, and may we be found faithful in them.

---

*On a card, write a verse or set of verses you find edifying, then put it close to your night-watch station, to encourage you and lighten your load when you need it.*

# Are You Clingy?

Inevitably, babies grow into toddlers, marking the beginning of an awareness "Mommy is not completely connected to me." Games such as *peekaboo* work because for a split moment, you truly are gone!

Some children at this point in their development are content to simply make eye contact on a regular basis or play with ears tuned to Mama's voice. Other children, however, need extra cuddle time, extra lap time, and even extra "pick me up and carry me" time.

This awareness of being separate from mom is a blessing in disguise. This is an opportunity to build a wholesome and steadfast relationship, and if it is not squandered, you will plant seeds of trust and reassurance into his little heart, resulting in self-confidence. His self-confidence will not be built on him*self*, it will be built on a present mama to uphold him and give him a foundation from which to flap his wings.

As usual, this paints a picture of our need for God. In essence, I am the toddler in His eye. At times, I exude a sweet and loving attitude; other times, tantrums are thrown. But at all times, whether I want to admit it or not, I have a need for God.

Aren't you a bit amused when your toddler fights to get into a piece of clothing, charging to do it "m'*self!*"? Of course, he can and will learn to put on his shirt, but the proper response is to offer help and speak words of encouragement. It is not put him away from you and leave him to figure it out. One way builds a relationship; the other builds a cold heart. He still needs you.

Look at your toddler's eyes and hear his heart as he reaches for you, even it if is for the morning's hundredth time. Listen to his heart say to you: "Thou art my hiding place and my shield...hold thou me up, and I shall be safe." (Ps 119:114, 119)

He desires communion with you. He is beginning to realize he is separate from the one he has known every moment from conception, and it frightens him. He wants the reassurance of your lap, your arms, your smell. A toy, a blankie, a thumb will not suffice. Even another person is but a poor substitute.

Thankfully, our heavenly Father serves as a beautiful example of how to handle this incessant need. Observe how He responds to us when we stretch up our arms and cry out for a lap to sit on:

- "Let him take hold of my strength, that he may make peace with me; and he shall make peace with me." (Isa 27:5)

- "For I the Lord thy God will hold thy right hand, saying unto thee, Fear not; I will help thee." (Isa 41:13)

- "The Lord is good, a stronghold in the day of trouble; and he knoweth them that trust in him." (Nah 1:7)

God offers His strength and security, His peace, His right hand, His comfort and reassurance, and His goodness. Why, then, do we believe our response to our clingy toddlers should be any different? Instead, we might pat them on the head and push them away, frustrated with the exhausting needs threatening to rob us of our free time, our rest, ourselves. The world says your child needs to learn to become independent. Jesus says, "Let the little children come to me." (Luke 18:16)

Whom are you going to heed? "For laying aside the commandment of God, ye hold the tradition of men." (Mark 7:8) Or… "A new commandment I give unto you, That ye love one another; as I have loved you, that ye also love one another." (John 13:34)

Choose to follow your heavenly Father's example in three ways:

# ARE YOU CLINGY?

## 1) Lean

"Casting all your care upon him; for he careth for you." (1 Pet 5:7)

Twice, John mentions (John 13:25, 21:20) he was leaning on Jesus at the last supper. It was a gentle Jesus he was leaning on for his identity, and he called himself "the disciple whom Jesus loved" (John 21:20). Do you consider yourself "the mommy whom Jesus loves"? Where do you go when you need encouragement, help, a steady hand?

Jesus will never put you off, put you out, or deny His shoulder to your anxious head. Your child looks to you in the same way; your shoulder is his sweetest place of refuge.

## 2) Listen

"I love the Lord, because he hath heard my voice and my supplications. Because he hath inclined his ear upon me,

263

therefore will I call upon him as long as I live." (Ps 116:1-2)

"Bow down thine ear, O Lord, hear me: for I am poor and needy." (Ps 86:1)

"In my distress I cried unto the Lord, and he heard me." (Ps 120:1)

Your toddler will hold fast what he has been taught. Will you be a mama who hears his needy voice? Will you bend down your ear? If not, eventually, he will know you are tuning him out, and he will stop trying to talk with you. Is it any wonder children tune out their parents when they are older? When he wants your attention, get down to eye level and listen to him. Look into his little eyes. Try to understand his frustration and speak sound words of life and love back into his heart. Words he will remember and hold on to.

"Hold fast the form of sound words, which thou hast heard of me, in faith and love which is in Christ Jesus." (2 Tim 1:13)

**3) Lead**

"He found him in a desert land, and in the waste howling wilderness; he led him about, he instructed him, he kept him as the apple of his eye. As an eagle stirreth up her nest, fluttereth over her young, spreadeth abroad her wings, taketh them, beareth them on her wings: So the Lord alone did lead him, and there was no strange god with him." (Deut 32:10-12)

It is not simply enough for your toddler to know you exist when it is convenient for you to appear. Your presence breathes life and security into his little soul. Your presence cannot be bought with gifts, playmates, or babysitters. It doesn't matter how effectual a mother you believe you are, and it doesn't make a difference to the child what your life circumstances are. All your toddler wants to know is your presence and to become your little shadow for a season. And yes, even twenty-four hours a day!

"Lead me in thy truth, and teach me: for thou art the God of my salvation; on thee do I wait *all the day*." (Ps 25:5, emphasis mine)

"Mine eyes are *ever* toward the Lord." (Ps 25:15, emphasis mine)

Your toddler cannot follow what you feel is best for him if you are not there to lead him. In similar fashion, God cannot lead you if you do not follow Him.

Your toddler's clinginess is a blessing. He is showing you he loves you, he needs you, he wants you. He is trying to teach you what it is to be dependent and to have needs, and you are in a tremendous place and time to meet these simple needs in his life. All he wants is you.

We are not super-mommies. We have needs, too. Learn to lean on, listen to, and follow the lead of our heavenly Father. Hear him now:

He shall feed his flock like a shepherd: he shall gather the lambs with his arm, and carry them in his bosom, and shall gently lead those that are with young.

Lift up your eyes on high, and behold who hath created these things, that bringeth out their host by number: he calleth them all by names by the greatness of his might, for that he is strong in power; not one faileth.

Why sayest thou, O Jacob, and speakest, O Israel, My way is hid from the LORD, and my judgment is passed over from my God? Hast thou not known? hast thou not heard, that the everlasting God, the LORD, the Creator of the ends of the earth, fainteth not, neither is weary? there is no searching of his understanding.

He giveth power to the faint; and to them that have no might he increaseth strength. Even the youths shall faint and be weary, and the young men shall utterly fall: But they that wait upon the LORD shall renew their strength; they shall mount up with wings as eagles; they shall run, and not be weary; and they shall walk, and not faint. (Isa 40:11, 40:26-31)

Being clingy is a blessing. May you clearly see how God is using your circumstances to draw you to Him, and may you in turn open your heart to drawing your toddler closer to you in these short, needy hours.

# ARE YOU CLINGY?

---

*In what ways might you draw your child closer to you? Have you been pushing your child away? Have you declared your own independence from God in any area?*

# EPILOGUE

*But this I say, brethren, the time is short...*
– 1 Corinthians 7:29

Thank you for reading this book. I pray it was helpful to you, not simply in peering over my shoulder to glean lessons I have been learning, but also in encouraging you to do your own Bible reading and study. God always knows exactly what we need and when we need it. I urge you to not neglect this most important practice and to joyfully make it a priority in your day.

To help you get started or to encourage in the way, I've added some ideas below that may be profitable to you.

And, if you are willing, I would love to read a study *you've* done, so that I might have the pleasure and blessing of peering over your shoulder as well.

Because of Jesus,

# EPILOGUE

---

- Get up early in the morning and read.

- Read a psalm when you sit down to nurse.

- Put a Bible or passage of scripture behind your cookbook holder in the kitchen. Even a hymn book is nice there.

- Read a couple of lines here and there while you work.

- Listen to it as you vacuum or do laundry. Try the Bible.is app.

- Commit to not reading anything else until your eyes have feasted on the Word first.

- Read a chapter of Proverbs, aligning with the day of the month. For example, today is the eighteenth; read Proverbs 18.

- Listen to an sermon based on the reading you are on. (This is, of course, not a substitution for attending your local church).

- Copy a short passage onto an index card. The simple act of copying gives the words contemplative power. Tape a card wherever you are the most; for me, it's the kitchen.

- Call up a friend and, while you are talking, ask her to read a verse or passage from the Bible to you.

- Read from a short book, such as Ruth or Philippians. You'll get through it quickly and it may provide the momentum you need to keep going.

- Read from the fast-moving gospel of Mark.

- Get the multitude of Bibles off your shelves and put them all over the house instead: by your bathtub, on the coffee table, next to your sewing machine.

- Before starting a project or reading your novel, give yourself a sip of the Word.
- Join a Bible study where there is accountability and homework. Occasionally, we need the added social pressure to make it happen.

- Start off your homeschooling day with Bible study. Read to your children from the Bible or Bible storybooks. Talk about what the passage is saying about God and what it is saying about people. Focusing on those two aspects will teach a lot!

- Are you hungry for a particular fruit? Choose patience or kindness or faithfulness and look it up in a concordance. Then read the passages you may find relating to those. You can copy your favorite passage onto an index card.

- Commit to reading through the whole Bible and start at the beginning. Or in the middle. Or in Matthew. But read the entire Bible, over and over again.
- Read a psalm before turning out the lamp for the night. I enjoy reading the psalm matching the date and then adding thirty until the end. If today were the fourth day of the month, my reading would include Psalms 4, 34, 64, 94, and 124.

Of all the challenges we face during the day, the challenge of making time to read our Bibles is one worth taking on. You will be blessed!

# APPENDIX

*Reading the Bible is not where*
*your engagement with the Bible ends.*
*It's where it begins.*

– Michael Heiser

## Why do you use an English Dictionary to do study on Hebrew and Greek words?

The short answer is: *that is what I had.*

I did not grow up in a Christian home, did not go to Bible college, did not have a mentor to disciple me, and had no idea which study tools and books in the local Christian bookstore were safe and which ones were borderline, or truly, heretical.

But as I have thought this through more, I have other reasons why using an unabridged English dictionary (published prior to 1960 due to changes in pronunciation guides and overreaching political influences) alongside a King James Version of the Bible is still a very useful and profitable practice, even as I now know of, and use, other helpful tools.

I trust the KJV for many reasons. Fifty-four gifted translators worked on this version for over four years, and built on the passion and work (and intellectual brilliance) of William Tyndale. As I am a native English-speaking woman, and so much blood (literally), sweat and tears were poured into the work of providing me the Word in my own language, I see no real reason to be hindered from study simply because I do not have training or education in the Greek and Hebrew languages. I trust the translators' extraordinary and thorough education in those languages. Sure, I can study Greek and Hebrew...but I do not need to.

Also, the Bible is not a mystery with hidden passages, clues, or additional revelation that somehow I am missing by only using English. I find the Bible pretty clear to study and understand when I take the time to treat it as the Holy Word of God (which it is), and expect it to speak to my spirit and life (which it does). The Bible is a fascinating living book that transcends time and culture, and explains and reveals Jesus in every single book. Exercising the time in daily reading and meditation is what leads to good fruit and life application. I find that the Bible explains itself and defines its own words (here a concordance is another helpful tool, but you must have one that matches the Bible version you choose to use), so if all I have is a Bible, a Bible is all I need.

In studying to show ourselves approved (that is, saved), we need to beware of other Bible teachers, devotionals, and books that appeal, especially to women, to emotionalism, how things "feel" (especially "to YOU") and try to bring about a "new" or "evolving" understanding using worldly systems and logic. That is another reason I prefer the KJV: over four hundred years of faithful use. We need to be mindful of chronological arrogance and thinking that those scholars from yesteryear were, well, so yesteryear. This doesn't mean new evidence isn't considered when it appears, but with the downgrading of the English language both in print and in speech even within our own lifetimes, it does mean being extra, extra slow to introduce yet another translation.

I sometimes find that there is more confusion and contention when we choose our translations based on our own comfort or cultural worldview. It's sad to have a congregation of people who can't all memorize and speak aloud the same text, and instead we hear stumbling in disunity over different words. The KJV translators took into account cadence, alliteration, sound, and rhythm. Do we really need another translation to understand the Scripture more? Or do we need, rather, a more earnest desire to understand the text, and to take the time to study it in context to the chapter, book and the Bible as a whole? Too often, our readings are used as a rote checklist to get done, so we seek the "easier" translations so we can get on with our day. It is an error to think the KJV is too difficult to read or understand, and I find that many translations today either substitute cultural or general ideas for pointed and plain teachings, or substitute plain-understanding words for more academic-speaking words, making it even more difficult for everyone, including children, to comprehend. For example, the "thee"s and the "thine"s actually had, and continue to have, a clarifying purpose in the text.

Lastly, before I was saved, I liked reading the proverbs for pithy quotes to use in my snail mail, but they had no real power. If you are finding that reading the Bible is difficult whether in practice or in motivation, I would urge you to examine yourself to see if you are truly in the faith. For the Bible is like manna, a daily food, and strengthens and equips the believer for every good work. We ought to have a real hunger for it. An attitude of shrugging off study of the Word ought to be repented of and corrected immediately. With prayer and with deep gratitude, reading the Bible with a dependance on the Holy Spirit to teach and correct will result in personal growth in holiness and a deeper love for Jesus Christ.

May we all purpose to use what we have, for His glory, and to exercise ourselves unto godliness.

# KITCHEN TABLE QUICKMARK

*I have esteemed the words of his mouth more than my necessary food.*

– Job 23:12

Thank you for your interest in, and purchase of, *From My Kitchen Table.* I pray this book was a blessing to you, not only as a devotional read, but as an exhortation for you to do your own Bible reading and study.

To assist you further, I've created a combination bookmark / action guide to walk you through the checklist I take myself through when doing a Word study. You can download it for free (no email required) here:

AHappyHomeMedia.com/KitchenTableQuickmark

Sadly, there seems to be a dearth of Bible knowledge and understanding not only in our homes, but in our nations. My brothers and sisters, this ought not to be, as saints freely blessed with personal copies of the Word written in our own plain languages.

I understand the challenge of study while in the trenches with littles, a house to keep, and a husband to love and honor. I wrote the chapters in this book when I was a younger mother with many little hands to nurture and while pregnant and nursing and grabbing little snippets of sleep for years at a time. But I will tell you that every minute I spent in God's Word, even if it were only minutes at a time, was a rich feast that encouraged me, taught me, corrected me, and nurtured me as only God can do. Truly, He understands all of the thoughts and intents of the heart (Heb 4:12) and leads gently those with young (Isa 40:11).

But you have to commit to showing up. Manna is manna, even in small doses. May you be encouraged from my own personal studies, and come to Jesus in prayer with an earnest desire to sit at His feet, and learn from His Word, generously and lovingly gifted to you.

# OTHER BOOKS by Keri Mae

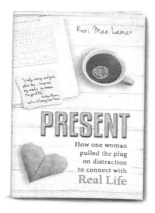

*PRESENT: How one woman pulled the plug on distraction to connect with Real Life*

AHappyHomeMedia.com/Present

*PRACTICES: Morning and Evening – helping moms have happier homes*

AHappyHomeMedia.com/Practices

Available at Amazon.com and other online book sellers.

# APPRECIATION

*That I may publish with the voice of thanksgiving,*
*and tell of all thy wondrous works.*

– Psalm 26:7

Thank you...

- to my blog readers, some of whom have become lasting friends.

- to our patrons, for believing in our ministry and making it possible to be a light in the media world.

- to Celeste, Mary and Karen, willing and encouraging first readers.

- to April Gardner, a most careful and gracious editor.

- to Karen Lewis, a very patient and competent web design helper (and fixer!).

- to Meela, for our quick and fabulous cover design.

- to Daesha, for her cheerleading and willingness to model for the book cover.

- to my family, for making room for me to disappear into Bible Study and writing.

- to Jesus, for everything and beyond everything, and for more than I can ever know.

# ABOUT THE AUTHOR

Keri Mae Lamar is a homemaking mama committed to Jesus and to her husband, Tom.

She was saved at the age of 26 and still stands in awe that Jesus would care about her, much less die and suffer God's wrath on her behalf. She loves to delight in His creation, His work, and His people, and enjoys nothing more than spending time quietly in the Word of God and seeking application from it for all of life.

She serves her community in a variety of ways, including practicing herbalism and running a longstanding book club.

She and Tom met the first day of college. They are currently raising and homeschooling nine children, and run a full and well-loved chiropractic business. They also serve their community together as chapter leaders for the Weston A. Price Foundation, and enjoy getting behind the microphones to podcast about topics such as Down syndrome, downsizing, and slow schooling.

You can contact Keri Mae or learn more about her at the following:
Email: kerimae@ahappyhomemedia.com
Website: ahappyhomemedia.com
Instagram: @ahappyhomemedia

But she loves snail mail the most:
PO Box 1304
Kingston WA 98346

# NOTES

# FROM MY KITCHEN TABLE

# NOTES

# FROM MY KITCHEN TABLE

# NOTES

A Happy Home Media

*Happy is that people, that is in such a case:*
*yea, happy is that people, whose God is the Lord.*

– Psalm 144:15

Made in the USA
Lexington, KY
30 November 2019

# Life Strategy

HOW TO DESIGN A LIFE OF
PERMANENT SATISFACTION

Felipe Rivera

# Table of Content

Introduction .................................................................7

1. The Fundamentals .......................................13

    The Purpose of Life ...................................14

    The Principles ..............................................24

    Resources .......................................................31

    Internal Resources ....................................33

    External Resources ...................................40

    The Process ...................................................45

2. Step 1: Where are you? ...........................53

    Temperament ..............................................54

    Core Values ...................................................58

    Strengths and Weaknesses ...................67

    Opportunities and Obstacles ..............72

3. Step 2: Where are you going? ...............79

    The 9 Areas of Life ...................................80

    Personal Growth ........................................81

    Health ..............................................................88

Work                                                      93

Finances                                                 103

Tools and Places                                         115

Romance                                                  121

Family                                                   130

Social Relationships                                     134

Recreation                                               138

How to Set Goals                                         143

4. Step 3: What will you do?                             151

Planning                                                 153

Tasks                                                    157

Habits                                                   164

Reflexion                                                172

Epilogue                                                 179

Likely obstacles                                         182

Final Recommendations                                    184

References                                               193

# Introduction

There is an essential knowledge that all humans need but that is rarely taught in a systematic way. That is the knowledge on how to live. Throughout formal education we learn about a huge number of subjects such as the location of a river from a different country or how to use dozens of arithmetical equations but there is something that even though is really important for all people isn't taught with that same intensity and that is how to live.

There are several elements that the lives of all people have in common and those elements allow us to understand it so we can make better decisions that give us true well-being.

We all have certain characteristics that make us act, think and feel in a different way and it is necessary to be conscious of those characteristics to know ourselves better and to choose the most appropriate roads for us.

We also count with many basic and universal resources but very few times we learn how to use them efficiently and that's the reason why we spend our life always stuck in the same place without much growth or progress.

There are certain areas of life that affect all people and at the same time interact with one another which is why knowing them, understanding them, and knowing how to integrate them in our life is essential so that the goals we set really have the potential to make us feel good.

Lastly, we people have several internal blocks that keep us from getting our goals and don't let us act as we'd like and therefore it is important to learn how to manage them if we really want to have a good life.

Since we don't find this knowledge in formal education, we depend on the luck of having people in our lives that guide us or teach us about these concepts or if we are curious enough it is possible that we can research about these concepts ourselves. The problem is that when we start to research about these elements we don't know exactly what is it that we should learn and that implies a constant trial and error that in some cases can make us make catastrophic decisions in our lives or simply it can delay our development unnecessarily.

Researching and reflecting about each one of these subjects has been my main motor throughout all my life. I've felt a strong motivation to understand each of the aspects that make up human life not for the simple fact of knowing them but to develop a model that allows us all to make better decisions and gain more control in our lives. I haven't limit myself to learn about these subjects but I've also applied this knowledge into my own life and thanks to it I've been able to acquired a development in many areas that makes me feel good and at the same time allows me to keep growing and trying to reach bigger goals.

With all the concepts I've learned throughout my life coming from other people as well as through the observation and constant analysis on my own experiences and the experiences of other people, I've developed a model I call Life Strategy that tries to gather all these learnings into some elements and processes that allow all people, no matter their particular differences or the circumstances they're in, to understand better their own life and to give it the direction they desire with the decisions they make.

I'm not going to take credit for all the ideas that appear in this book. Most of them come from smarter people that have decided to focus on understanding specific areas and on doing the research and experiments to give validity to those ideas. Because one of my weaknesses is my capacity to remember specific facts and data such us the name of people or books, it is possible that I've forgotten the exact origin of some of the ideas I share in this book, however, at the end you can find a bibliography with some references that have helped me increase my understanding on many of these subjects.

Life Strategy is a universal way of living and is applicable to all people because it takes into account all those elements we all have in common that make us human beings as well as those things that makes us different and unique. This system allows us to group all the elements of human life so we can watch much more easily the state of our lives in each one of them and define which of them we need to pay more attention and on which we should learn more so we can have a more balanced development.

This book is divided in 4 chapter. In the first chapter I will talk about the fundamentals of Life Strategy which are the elements that make it up and the relationship they have with each other. I will talk about the purpose we should try to reach with this model, the basic principles that allows us to understand reality better, the resources we humans have, and the practical process through which we can apply all this model in our own life by keeping in mind all the previous elements.

In chapter 2, 3, and 4, I will talk in detail about each one of the 3 steps of the process of Life Strategy.

The first step talks about defining where we are and this consists on learning about ourselves, about what make us different, about the things we consider important and also about the different internal and external resources we have or need to get.

That knowledge is essential to be able to begin the second step that consists on defining our direction. About that step I will talk in chapter 3 and it is about setting goals in each area of our life. For this we must understand the process through which we define goals and also we must understand the way how each of the areas of life works and the way they interact with each other.

The third and last step of the process of Life Strategy is about execution. This process consists on defining the things we have to do to reach our goals and start taking action to see what results we get. This step is divided in other 3 sub-processes that are: planning, acting and reflexion and I will talk in detail about each one of them in chapter 4. This third step is where we move to reality all our goals and this is the step that allows us to manifest in the world all those things we value and that are a true source of well-being. for us.

By following these 3 steps throughout our whole lives we'll be able to guide our development and we'll be able to keep growing and reach each time higher levels of well-being.

The Epilogue is the last section of the book and in it we'll see again all this model called Life Strategy in a more concise way so we can unify all those concept I mentioned throughout the book and define how we are going to integrate them into our lives. In this Epilogue I will also talk about some obstacles we can find when trying to implement this model into our lives and I will finish by offering some final recommendations based on some of the biggest learnings I've acquired throughout my life and that I hope serve you to live a nicer life where you can enjoy more and suffer less.

I advise that you first do a quick reading of all the book so you can see what this model is about. After that first reading, I advise you to read again the fundamentals until you get a clear idea of what each one of those concepts mean and what they imply and then you can move to chapter 2 where you can find some exercises that will allow you to know yourself better. After you're satisfied with some of the answer you've given then you can start setting all the goals you want to achieve in your life based on all the concepts you will find in chapter 3. Lastly, you can read chapter 4 again so you start defining how you plan to execute each one of your short term goals.

As you acquire more experience you will notice the aspects that you need to learn more about so you can check those parts of the books that talk about them. This is a reference book that I advise to be constantly reviewing by focusing on those areas you feel you have weaknesses so you can become a more complete person without holes. It is also worth mentioning that with this book I just pretend to give an organization to all the elements that make up human life and therefore I couldn't talk about many of these concepts with the level of depth I'd want. There are many other books and resources that talk with more detail about the concepts I mentioned here and you can find some of those references at the end of this book in the Bibliography.

To end this introduction I just want to invite you to explore this model of seeing life and do everything you can to implement it so you can start feeling with much more control over your own life and start seeing changes that make you feel really good.

# Chapter 1. The Fundamentals

Life Strategy is a model that allows us to improve our understanding of human life and at the same time it gives us specific steps we can take to increase the control we have in life.

I developed this model using all the things I've learned about life throughout the years. I did this by researching about all the different aspects that make up human life and also by reflecting and analyzing constantly my own experience and the experience of other people.

The first thing was to determine which is the purpose we all have in life and try to make that purpose suitable to all people no matter their particular differences.

After defining this purpose the next step was to define the principles in which this model is based. These principles are the foundations that allows us to find meaning in life so that the decisions we make and the way we deal with the world is in harmony with reality. Having these principles always in our minds is the best way to avoid suffering in life.

Another important element that supports this model is the resources that are available to us. These resources are the things we use to move through life and to achieve each one of our goals and desires. Being conscious of these resources and knowing how each decision we make affects positively or negatively the level of each one of them will allow us to be more effective when we make decisions so we can achieve our goals faster and more easily.

Finally, and to make this model something applicable to all of us, I defined the process that allows us to manage our life so we know which roads to take based on everything we know about ourselves and the world.

From now on I'll start explaining with more detail each one of these elements and for this I'll start talking about the universal purpose we all humans have in life.

# The Purpose of Life

The question about the purpose of life is a question that has concerned almost all people since we humans have reason and consciousness. Some of the answers answers to this question came from spiritual guides and philosophers. These answers have been useful and in a lot of cases still are but they don't take into account the big differences that exists among people and for this reason they are suitable only to some very specific groups of people differentiated by their personality, location or personal beliefs.

After that, and thanks to the progress of science and the creation of new fields like Psychology, there have been more research on the answers to this question and we have been able to clear a lot of key concepts that can be helpful when it comes to defining a global answer.

Based in my study and my experience about this subject I can suggest an answer to this huge question which may appear simple at first but that includes a lot of the answers given in the past and that can help us as a guide to make many of the most important decisions we have in life.

My answer to this question is:

"The Purpose of Life is *Feeling Good.*"

I am sure this answer may sound simple but in a few moments I will explain what it really means *Feeling Good* and for that I will mention the 4 ways in which this sensation presents in human life and the way we can integrate each one of them in a balanced way so we guarantee that we can *Feel Good* most of the time.

Saying that feeling good is the purpose of life can also sound to a lot of people as a pretty selfish answer. We are used to hearing answers such as the purpose of life is to serve others, to reach enlightenment, to be obedient, to have kids, to live with honor and a lot more like those. The reason why Feeling Good is a simple answer but a the same time a very complete one is that one of the ways in which it manifests itself is "Satisfaction" and the way we experience satisfaction is by pursuing all those values that each person considers important and among those values we can find several of the things I just mentioned and a lot more.

Just as I said a few moments back, *Feeling Good* can show up in 4 different ways. The 4 ways in which we human can feel good are: pleasure, joy, happiness, and satisfaction. Each one of them are important in our lives and we must try to integrate them all but they don't have the same weight and we must know how to balance them appropriately so we can reach higher levels of *Feeling Good* in our lives.

Next I will talk about what each one of them means.

## Pleasure

Pleasure means feeling good physically. Some of the things that allows us to experience pleasure are: eating, physical contact with other people, the use of substances that affect our neurological centers of pleasure, the use of a good coat in bad weather, or the one I consider more meaningful, having sex.

Pleasure is essential in our lives. On the one hand, it is essential for our survival because it tells us that our body is fine, that means, that it's well fed, protected against the weather, and in a healthy state. On the other hand pleasure is also essential because it is one of the ways we realize that life is worth living and that can keep us motivated to keep moving and endure all those adversities that without a doubt we'll find on the way. Someone who can't experience pleasure will probably neglect his body until he loses his health or he may even find life very uninteresting and that could take away his will to live and to try to achieve things.

Pleasure has two big problems. The first one is that there are a lot of sources of pleasure that can be highly addictive and this can cause that we lose control of ourselves under different circumstances. Losing control of ourselves can make us get into a lot of troubles and create serious difficulties both in our lives and in the lives of other people and these difficulties can become an obstacle to *Feeling Good*. The second problem with pleasure is that we humans adapt very easily to a source of pleasure when we're constantly exposed to it and we stop enjoying it with the same intensity. When this happens is possible that each time we'll need a higher amount of those sources of pleasure to keep enjoying it and that can create an unbalance in our lives.

To manage the first problem appropriately we must avoid those sources of pleasure that has the potential of being highly addictive and that the consequences of falling in those addictions can be negative to our lives and the things we want to reach.

The way we handle the second issue is by enjoying the different sources of pleasure in a more restricted and balanced way so we don't get bored easily of any of them and we can keep enjoying them for much longer or even indefinitely.

## Joy

Joy means feeling good emotionally. We people usually feel joy under social contexts. Some of the biggest sources of joy in our lives can be when we meet someone new, when we share time with friends and family, or specially when we are we the person we like or love.

It is also possible to feel good when we are alone by remembering a good moment we spent with other people or even by reading books or watching television where we can interact in a passive way with the minds of other people.

Joy is also related to humor and recreation. A good strategy to add new sources of joy into our lives is to get into activities we are passionate about. Those activities could be some sort of hobby, watching events we enjoy, doing something artistic or practicing sports.

Searching joy in our lives is also very important but the problem is that these moments of joy rarely come alone.

A lot of our most joyful memories come from the time spent with other people but at the same time we can find that some of our most difficult and sad times can be related to those same people in case we lost them or had a conflict with them.

On the other side, and to offer an example, to be able to enjoy a hobby we usually need some level of skill in it and to develop that skill it may be necessary to go through a lot of practice full of effort and frustration that we may not find enjoyable at the time.

The best way to manage this phenomenon is by accepting it and being always aware that the moments of sadness and frustration we go through may be necessary to be able to enjoy those moments of joy and to decide previously that we are willing to pay that price for all the moments of joy that life can offer us.

The lives of most people are on a constant search of these two ways of *Feeling Good*, pleasure and joy. The problem with focusing on only these two sources of Feeling Good is that both are external and this causes that we don't have true control over the moment in which we can experience them. Because of this there will be times when we will enjoy big levels of these two ways of *Feeling Good* but there will also be other times when both ways will be away from our lives or where we may even be experiencing pain or sadness.

Since our purpose is *Feeling Good* most of the time, or even all the time, if we rely on only these two sensations to feel good there will be lots of moments where we're going to feel bad and have nothing to lean to. Here is where the other two ways of Feeling Good come in and their main characteristic is that the come from the inside and this makes them much more stable and constant. These ways of Feeling Good are happiness and satisfaction and I will talk about them next.

## Happiness

Happiness is the third way of *Feeling Good* and it means feeling good with the world. Happiness can be identified as an internal feeling that the world is a good place to live no matter what's happening or the circumstances in which we find ourselves.

The sensation of happiness is based on acceptance and appreciation.

Acceptance means accepting our present circumstances and the way the world works without giving it a valuation of good or bad, or in other words, accepting that things are what they are and that's it. To integrate acceptance into our lives it's important to develop the courage to see things as they truly are without pretending a world that could be nicer but that isn't real. Acceptance means accepting reality, and to know the reality we must be willing it to really see it no matter how pretty or ugly it may seem to us.

The other element on which happiness is sustained is appreciation. Appreciation is only achieved after we have managed to accept the reality of the world.

Being thankful means that no matter who we are or on what situation we are, there will always be something to be grateful about. The most fundamental thing is the fact that we are alive, that we have the opportunity to be born and to develop a life. Remembering and appreciating this simple fact can be reason enough to experience some grade of constant happiness. Besides this, almost all of us have a lot more reasons to be thankful: each one of our experiences, the resources we have, the people we've met, the potential of improvement, the possibility of achieving all kinds of goals, and many other things that can help us get constant happiness. The secret to integrate appreciation is to learn to identify all these things I just mentioned and try to remind ourselves constantly of them until this exercise becomes an unconscious habit.

Happiness doesn't have the same intensity as pleasure or joy but its big advantage is that it is more durable and it depends only on us. We could draw pleasure and joy as waves that sometimes go very high and other times go lower but they are constantly changing. Happiness, on the other hand, could be drawn as a flat line that once in a while can decrease its level in case of a huge deception but that we can manage to get it into a positive level and keep it there constantly if we are able to integrate acceptance and appreciation into our lives.

Happiness is based more on a feeling on tranquility and not so much in excitability as the two previous ways of feeling good. A good sign to know we have reached good levels of happiness is that we complain very little or even we stop complaining for the things that happen, we become less likely to get stressed out by certain situations and we are able to keep our calmness in difficult times. Happiness keep us emotionally protected from all the hard moments we may find in our lives.

People who manage to integrate these 3 ways of *Feeling Good* could without a doubt feel proud that they are living a good life and they will have reached a level of well-being unknown to a big portion of the world's population. Despite this, I suggest that they go a little bit further and fight to integrate the next way of *Feeling Good* so this way they can guarantee that most of the time they will feel good and that there will be very few things or events that can have the power to affect that sense of well-being.

## Satisfaction

Satisfaction is the last way of *Feeling Good* and when we talk of satisfaction we're talking about feeling good with ourselves. Feeling good with ourselves is a human need whether we want it or not. Each one of us was born with a series of values toward some aspects of life and if we are unaware of those impulses and we don't do what we think we should do to integrate those things into our lives, then we will have a feeling of emptiness that can't be hidden no matter how much pleasure, joy or happiness we may be experiencing.

This feeling of emptiness can be very mild but it's going to be there if we're not living accordingly to our main values. These values are called Core Values. We all have a list of things that are very important in our lives but in most cases we are not aware of those values because we've never taken the time to identify them and this can cause that we feel emptiness without knowing the reason.

These values can be things like family, freedom, friendship, service, creativity, honor, and many others that manifest in each person in different intensities and combinations. In the next chapter I will talk with more detail about the subject but for now it is worth mentioning that these core values are defined by our temperaments and by all those meaningful experiences we have in our lives.

We don't have the choice to pick which values we want to have and which not. Our only choice is between directing our efforts toward the achievement and maintenance of those values or simply to ignore them. Here is where it comes satisfaction. Satisfaction is not achieved by getting all the things related to our values but through all our actions, the things we do day by day that are directed toward getting and keeping those values.

When we know that something is important to us and we know what we must do to get it but we don't do it for any reason, be it fear, laziness, insecurity, lack of control or whatever, then this will make us feel bad with ourselves and we will feel that emptiness of which I talked previously. It may be that this emptiness won't be as strong as pain, sadness or anxiety, reason why a lot of people decides to ignore it and not pay attention to it, but if we have as our purpose to feel good most of the time, then it is necessary to pay attention to this emptiness and turn it into satisfaction through our daily actions.

Satisfaction is probably the hardest way of *Feeling Good* to get and the one that requires the most knowledge and skills to be able to experience it. Because of this a big part of this book will be focused on teaching you all the things you need to know so you can integrate it into your life.

Most people already know how to get pleasure and joy. Perhaps for different circumstances they're not able to experience them all they'd like but the way of getting them is not that complex. Happiness is also a little bit more simple to reach because is a purely internal process and in the third chapter I will talk about some specific techniques that will allow you to develop it. Satisfaction on the other hand is more complex. It requires to combine with harmony a big amount of elements such as our genetic configuration, the resources we have, our daily actions, the conditions that the world presents us, some internal obstacles we must overcome and a lot other factors. The idea is that with all the concepts that you learn throughout this book you will have the tool to define how you plan to get a high level of satisfaction in your life so you guarantee that you can feel good most of the time.

We have already identified that the purpose of Life Strategy is *Feeling Good* and that the 4 ways we can feel good are pleasure, joy, happiness and satisfaction. Now it's time to talk about the 5 principles on which this model called Life Strategy is based and that we must respect if we truly want to be successful applying this model into our lives.

# The Principles

The principles of Life Strategy are the bases with which we can make each one of our decisions and understand why things happen as they do. Having these principles always in our minds will allow us to find meaning to the world and the way it works and that will makes us more effective to move through it.

The 5 principles this model is based on are: rationality, uncertainty, responsibility, individuality and change. Latter I will talk about each one of them but one thing to keep in mind is that most suffering we humans experience comes from betraying or ignoring some of these principles. Therefore, if we want to live a life of practically no suffering then we must understand these principles and apply them in everything we do.

## Rationality

The principle of rationality tells us that our mind is our main tool to face the world and that all the decisions we make must be based on our best understanding of things.

There will always be the chance of making mistakes in anything we do but if those mistakes were made by ignoring consciously or unconsciously what our mind was telling us then the result will probably be that we'll feel bad with ourselves. Another negative effect of ignoring our minds is that we start to lose trust in ourselves and each time we become more dependent of the opinions and judgments of other people to decide what to do.

When we make mistakes but the decisions that led us to them were made based on the application of our ability to think and taking into account everything we knew at the time, then we will not feel bad for that mistake and we may even be glad because we learned something new and our ability to make better decisions in the future will be increased. This has the other effect of what we talked about previously that we will keep or even increase our confidence in ourselves and this will make us more effective.

Thinking effectively requires logic and that's why it is relatively important to develop that skill into our lives. We must try to think based on reality or in our best understanding of it. If something in the world for any reason doesn't make sense to us it means that some of our assumptions are wrong and we must try to correct them.

Emotions play a big part in our lives and we must try to be aware of them, listen to them and try to understand them. However, this doesn't mean that emotions are the best tool we have to make decisions. Decisions we make based only on our emotions without taking into account what our reason is telling us are the ones we regret most often. On the other hand, making decisions based only on our reason without listening to our emotions is also ignoring a very important part of our reality and the decisions we make won't be optimal. The best decisions are those in which we find harmony between what we think and what we feel and over these decisions, even if we end up being wrong, we will feel good.

## Uncertainty

The second principle is called "uncertainty". This principle tells us that we will never have all the information we need to make decisions and that there are a lot of external and internal factors out of our control that can affect the outcome of our goals.

The main thing we need to keep in mind with this principle is that we must accept it as a condition of reality and learn to be comfortable with it. We can't stop making decisions just because we don't know everything we need or because we're not certain of the results we'll get.

If we humans want to stay alive we have to keep moving all the time and the things that are hidden in the dark are always larger than those that we can see and because of this we need to develop the courage to face life without really knowing what's going to happen.

When we ignore the principle of uncertainty, we are thinking that we're always right and that things always have to come out as we desire, but if that is our attitude, then reality will be force to show us the opposite and that can cause us a lot of suffering.

Adopting the principle of uncertainty involves that we add two values into our life: courage and being humble.

We need courage to believe in ourselves and to risk doing things without knowing exactly what will happen and this implies that there is always the chance of getting hurt in some way. Courage is something that we can learn with practice but we must train it.

Being humble on the other side means accepting that we're not all powerful and that there are a lot of things we can do but that at the same time we depend on a lot of things out of our control. Sometimes those things will be on our side and other times they won't. Therefore, we must learn to accept whatever might happen without feeling bad for the results we get.

Uncertainty is one of the aspects that make life more interesting and fun. Not being sure what will happen allows us to be surprised and amazed in several occasions. Also it help us maintain a certain level of curiosity about the future and that can keep us motivated to keep learning, keep trying things and keep taking risks.

## Responsibility

The third principle of Life Strategy is responsibility. This principle tells us that *Feeling Good* is something that is totally under our own responsibility and that we can't blame anyone nor anything in case we feel bad.

This is because there are 4 ways of feeling good: pleasure, joy, happiness and satisfaction, and the last two ways depend entirely on us. Happiness depend on a few thought patterns and satisfaction depend on our actions, and both of these things are under our control.

It is our responsibility to develop these two ways of feeling good because they have the characteristic of letting us keep feeling good no matter the pain or sadness we have to face in several moments throughout our life.

There are a lot of external circumstances over which we have no control but those affect mainly pleasure and joy and that's the reason we can't depend only on those two for feeling good. If we feel bad it means that there is something we need to change either in the way we see the world or in our daily actions.

Learning to accept the responsibility we have over our own well-being. will give us a sense of incredible power that very few people will ever know exists. Knowing that we depend only on ourselves and that we can't blame our fathers, family, friends, couple or anyone for what we feel will free us from a lot of suffering.

Other thing to keep in mind with this principle is learning to accept that other people are also responsible for their own well-being. We must understand that even though there are things we can do to help or facilitate other people a change in how they feel, only they have the control to change their thoughts and actions if they really want to feel good. Getting this understanding will protect us from a lot of worries and will let us clear our mind so we can do the thing we can help with without letting ourselves be infected with the suffering of others.

## Individuality

Individuality is the fourth principle of Life Strategy. This principle says that all people have a unique configuration and have different resources throughout their lives.

This principle implies that one of our main goals in life must be learning about ourselves and analyzing objectively the resources we have. We all have a unique personality; we have strengths to do certain things and weaknesses to do others; we've had unique experiences and the mix of resources we have is also unique.

There is no person that is the same as another in the world and this imply that it is our responsibility to define which is the best road for us to follow without letting ourselves move blindly by the expectations and desires of others, the cultures that surround us or the teaching of a particular person. We must become critical of everything we learn so we can apply those insights into the peculiarities of our own lives.

Individuality also implies that we must accept that other people are different from us and the decisions they make can be good for them even if they're not for us. It means accepting those differences, tolerating them, and not criticizing or expressing unsolicited opinions over the lives of others because we simply don't know them well enough to know why the do what they do and why the live how they live. Accepting other people as they are is also extremely important to avoid suffering in life.

Just as we can realize that knowing ourselves is a very difficult task, we must also be humble to know that it is almost impossible to know others better than they know themselves. Therefore, we must not try to change them unless they agree with our intervention or even better they have asked us to help them change a particular aspect they don't feel satisfied with.

Individuality is other of the aspects that make life more interesting.

First, that we all are different will allow us to pursue those things we want to do and for which we're good at, while at the same time supporting ourselves on the strengths that other people have in areas different from ours.

Second, the differences among people are also interesting because they give us a unique sense of identity and give us the conviction that we are needed in the world and that there are things only we can do. If we were all exact clones then we'd be easily replaceable and I'm sure that will make us lose a lot of our motivation to do stuff and express ourselves through our actions.

The third and last aspect in which differences turn life more interesting is related with the curiosity we feel for exploring and knowing the world of other people. Trying to find things in common with others can get us closer to them and that can be a huge source of joy.

## Change

The last principle of Life Strategy is change. This principle tells us that every aspect of life is changing all the time and that it is our duty to accept those changes and try to be flexible enough to adapt to them.

Other people, the resources we have, the conditions the world put in front of us, and even we, are in a constant change and evolution.

The good thing about change is that while we remain alive we will always have something to keep ourselves busy with. No matter what we reach o the achievement we accumulate, there will always be something we have to do to keep adapting ourselves to the world and to all the possibilities it offers us.

Change is other of the things we have to accept to avoid suffering in live. It is true that to reach the things we want we must make a lot of effort and go through a lot of difficult times and because of that it's natural our desire to keep enjoying forever something we got but unfortunately the world doesn't work like that and if we expect things to be permanent then we will probably suffer unnecessarily when we lose them.

Change provoke that it will always be necessary to do something in the world. New creations to build, new expressions of art to design, new relationships to forge and new achievements to attain. This turns live into something very interesting that every step of the way is surprising us in new ways and is constantly inviting us to play by challenging us to see if we're able to adapt to the changes it puts in our way.

With this I have finished talking about the 5 principles of Life Strategy. We must keep these principles in our minds at all times, accept them, and use them as guides to understand reality and the why of the things that happen. When we internalize and turn these principles into an essential part of our philosophy of life then we'll discover that our levels of suffering will decrease substantially or even suffering can stop being a part of our lives.

# Resources

Resources are all the things we use to pursue each one of our goals and to carry out all the daily activities needed for our survival. When we manage our resources well we will be able to increase them and that will allow us to do more and bigger things and to do those things more efficiently.

The life quality we get depends mainly on how good we are managing the resources we have.

One of the reason for the huge progress we humans have had in comparison with other living species in our planet is the amount of resources we have accumulated throughout our history and also our unique ability to use our mind to figure out ways to use those same resources in new ways and with more efficiency. Other advantage we humans have is our ability to take into account our future needs and use our resources so we'll be able to satisfy those needs at the same time as we satisfy our present ones.

Talking about the different resources we humans have is essential because each one of the activities we do depends on those resources and I would even dare suggest that the act of living can be defined as the constant managing of resources for a purpose, which in our case is *Feeling Good*.

The single fact of being born already gives us some resources and as we grow those resources increase and develop in different measures depending on the things we do, our particular experiences and each one of the decisions we make.

The big difference in the resources people have can explain why the lives of two people are never the same and why we all must accept our own individuality and find out which are the most appropriate roads for us based on our unique combination of resources.

It is possible to learn at any time and no matter how old we are to develop and use more efficiently each one of our resources. However, the sooner we are conscious of our resources, the higher the chances of accumulating big amounts of them and that will increase the potential of the things we can do.

# Internal Resources

Our first resources are the internal resources and they're split between physical abilities and mental abilities.

## Physical abilities

Physical abilities are all the attributes of our body and the things we can do with it. Among physical abilities we can mention: health, appearance and physical dexterities.

### Health

The first of these attributes and the most fundamental is the capacity of our body to do all those processes such as breathing, pumping blood, processing food and all the others necessary to keep us alive and moving.

When we're young this capacity will probably be developed to its maximum level and there will be very little we need to do to keep it unless we were born with a disease or we've been in a serious accident. As we get older our body starts losing little by little its self-regulation and self-regeneration abilities and this causes that we start suffering from diseases that affect our levels of energy and our mobility. Here is where it becomes important to develop habits that allow us do delay that natural wear of our body so we can enjoy for much longer different aspects of life.

Health is the most important resource we have. If we lose

it or we have serious limitations in this area, it is very likely that the amount of things we can do will be seriously reduced or that we may even be unable to do several activities important for *Feeling Good*.

## Appearance

Appearance is other of the physical attributes we humans have. Personal appearance is determined by all those external attributes of our body and by the accessories we use. Among those attributes are the proportions of the different parts of our body, the shape of our face, our skin and hair color, among others. Also the clothing we use, make up, and any other accessory we put on can have an impact in the way we look and how others see us.

Appearance is very subjective and because of this each person has his own concept of what he considers attractive and what not. It is important to keep this in mind because there may be goals that are highly affected by it. For example, depending on our appearance we may or may not be attractive to someone we want to involve ourselves romantically. There are also some jobs that are exclusive to people that are considered of "good appearance" by a big enough group of people. Jobs such as modeling, some acting roles, and other jobs that require to be in front of many people usually have as a requirement that the people who do them have a good appearance.

Appearance is not a fixed attribute. As the years pass, appearance can chance positively or negatively. This depends on one hand on how lucky we are in our genetic pool and on the other on the action we take such as keeping our body in good shape, using clothing and accessories that improve our appearance or even using medical interventions to improve some aspect of our external appearance.

Depending on their goals people can give a high or low level of importance to this physical attribute and with this they will define the level of attention they need to give it.

**Physical Dexterities**

Physical dexterities are the things we can do with our body. Among those dexterities are: flexibility, muscular strength, cardiovascular resistance, and our speed and agility of movement. Other dexterities are height, balance, coordination, and our ability to use each one of our senses.

We can develop each one of those dexterities but there will be a limit based or our genes that will determine how far we can get.

The levels of dexterities we need will depend on our goals and the things we want to do. Playing in a sport at its higher levels require both good genes associated with some of those dexterities as well as a pretty demanding training. For example, playing basketball competitively in some leagues require a minimum height that is determined in big part by our genes and if we don't have it, it is possible we won't be able to pursue that goal.

# Mental Abilities

Besides our physical abilities, we humans have a big amount of mental abilities that make us unique and make us different from all other species. With these abilities we can overcome many of our physical limitations and achieve more complex and difficult things. Our mental abilities are: knowledge, emotions, reason, and creativity.

## Knowledge

Knowledge is the sum of all the information we have about how we and the world work. We humans have a big capacity for storing information, we could even say that in practical terms this capacity is unlimited. This allows us to gather information about all sorts of things and use that information to do many of our activities and reach our goals.

One advantage of acquiring knowledge is that the more we have the easier it will be to understand things of more complexity. At the same time, all the knowledge we have can be used by our reason and our imagination to generate new ideas and with them improve constantly in each area of life.

Even though we have a great capacity for storing information, we don't have the same ability to recover it, that means, to remember it. Remembering that information depends a lot on how we have stored it and on the techniques we use to recover it. Here is where it becomes important to focus when we are learning something so in the future it will be easier to access that stored knowledge.

## Emotions

Emotions are the biggest sources of energy we humans have to do stuff and the main cause of many of the things we do and the things we don't.

Daniel Goleman in his book emotional intelligence

proposes that the basic emotions are: joy, sadness, fear, anger, love, surprise, shame and aversion. There are also other emotions that can be a mix of the basic ones even though not everyone agree on which are basic emotions and which are manifestations of them.

Every single one of these emotions is important for our survival and for other aspects of our lives. Usually, the emotions we feel can be an important source of information to understand something about us or about the world. Therefore, it is very important that we listen to them and be conscious of them when we are experiencing them without denying or censoring them. By doing this we will learn something and we'll be able to decide if we want to act according to those emotions or if we should only accept it without letting it affect our actions.

For example, fear in a lot of cases can be useful because it may be telling us something important for our protection and security, but there are cases where the best thing to do is to act with courage no matter the fear we may be feeling. If we're not conscious that we're afraid, then fear may stop us without we even realizing it.

Learning to control our emotions appropriately, being conscious of them, listening to them, and changing them when they are not useful for our purposes is a big responsibility we humans have if we want to design a life where we can feel good most of the time.

**Reason**

Reason is the most important ability we humans have. We humans don't have many of the instincts animals have to satisfy their needs and this is because our needs increasing all the time and our environments are always changing.

While nature provided animals with a combination of instincts that allows them to survive, it gave us our ability to reason. This ability allows us to use our knowledge to figure out what we must do to survive and achieve our goals.

This ability for reasoning is in large part determined by our genes, but there are several things we can do to become more effective in its use.

The first thing is to acquire more knowledge. It is of no use to have a big capacity for reasoning, what is commonly called having a high IQ, if we don't have enough knowledge to apply that ability. The more information and data we have about the world the better the deductions and decisions we make.

The second thing we can do to increase our reasoning ability is to use it constantly to figure out solutions to our own problems. A lot of people become very dependent of others to solve their problems and this causes that their ability to think starts to atrophy and each time they lose trust in their own abilities to think. Getting used to trust our minds and propose solutions to our own problems is the best way to exercise our capacity for reason and feel more comfortable with its use.

## Creativity

Creativity is the ability we have to generate new ideas and knowledge. There are two ways to get those new ideas. The first is through our reason where from our knowledge we deduce new knowledge that allows us to understand something better or that allows us to do something more effectively.

The second way to generate new ideas is through our imagination. Our imagination can take us to worlds never seen and from there we can discover or generate new ideas or images that allows us to do something in a truly innovative way.

Creativity, just as reason, is an ability that can be improved through training. Generating new ideas also depends a lot on the amount of knowledge we have and on our ability to use our imagination.

Being creative requires courage because we're exploring things never explored before and we're doing things in a different way and this implies the risk of things not working out as expected. This is the reason why creative people in the world are relatively few. Most people wait for others to take risks to know what works so they can follow them. The big disadvantage of this is that most of the rewards are always for those who dare to explore first.

## Skills

Many of the things we want to do in life depend on much more than a single physical or mental ability. Most activities require a combination of several of these abilities and here is where we can talk about skills. A skill can be something like typing on a computer. To have this skill it is required certain dexterities such as finger agility and precision, visual and motor coordination, the knowledge about the position of each letter inside the keyboard, among other abilities.

It could be said that skills are the practical manifestations of our physical and mental abilities. Therefore it is better to focus on developing all these abilities from a particular skill we consider important for pursuing our goals instead of developing these abilities by themselves.

Defining which skills we need and developing them through the improvement of our abilities is in short how we people increase our internal resources and become more effective to face the world and all the obstacle it may present us.

# External Resources

External resources are those things the world gives us to live and do our activities. The amount of external resources is huge and there will always be something we can use. However, there are some categories in which we can group those resources so we can know them and manage them better. Those categories are: time, places, tools, money and other people.

## Time

Time is one of our main resources and we can analyze it from different dimensions.

On one hand we only have the time we remain alive. The duration of this time is very variable. Just as we can last a few years, there is also the possibility that we may reach 100 years or more and there is not a certain indicator to know that duration exactly. The amount of time we stay alive is affected by several factors. The first one is our health which is heavily influenced by our life habits but which is also affected by a lot of external circumstances out of our control. Aspects such as virus, accidents, genetic diseases, and many others, can destroy our health at any moment. Besides health, other factors such as the risks we take and even luck can have an impact in how much time we stay alive.

Our time alive is an important consideration when taking decisions but it is also important to take into account that even after our death the world will keep going and the lives of other people and beings may have been affected by the decisions we took so it is important to think about this when planning our lives.

We can also see time from a shorter perspective. Every minute, hour, day and week is available to us to do something. We can use that time well, that means, to move toward our purpose of *Feeling Good*, or we can waste it and use it for our own harm.

One of the characteristics of time is that once it passes we can't get it back. It's not worth obsessing to much about living every instant to the maximum but we must try to use most of our time alive in a productive, constructive, and above all, pleasant way.

In chapter 4 I will talk about more specific techniques we can use to become more productive when using our time so we can give a better use to this vital resource in our lives.

## Places

The second of the external resources provided by the world are places. Places are all those sites in which we can move, do our activities, store our tools, and so on. Some of those places may be provided by nature while others are designed and made by us. They can be sites such as houses, offices, recreational sites and many others.

Having access to some places will allow us to achieve some goals and do so some activities and because of this we must think about them as one of the many resources we need to manage carefully throughout our lives.

We can also think about places from the geographical point such as the countries, regions or cities we can live in or visit. Different places offer different opportunities and can make more easy or difficult the access to some of the resources we need to satisfy our different needs and desires.

Many times the place where we are is influenced by our jobs, our family or our culture, but in many cases deciding to move to a different place may be the right choice and it can give the push our life needs in relation with our different goals.

In short, places affect our comfort, the efficiency with which we can do things, the tools and resources we can get and even the people we can be with and it is because of this strong leverage it can have in our lives that we must think carefully about it.

## Tools

Tools are all those material things that offer us some utility to do some activity or to satisfy any need we have. Tools can be classified in three categories:

## Daily-life tools

Daily-life tools are the things we need to satisfy our most basic needs and can be things like food, clothes, shelter, furniture and all those things we need to do our day-to-day activities.

## Work tools

Work tools are the things we need to do something related to our job or to the way we obtain our income or other resources.

## Hobbies tools

Hobbies tools are those things we use for our recreation and enjoyment. These tools give us a more comfortable and interesting life in many ways.

Many of the things we have in life can belong to any or even several of those three categories. A shirt can protect us from cold but it can also be a work tool because it gives us the appearance we want to present and this can be very meaningful depending on the job we have.

A computer can be a work tool but also we can use it to entertain ourselves through games, media or to communicate with other people. It could even be a daily-life tool if we use it to manage several aspects of our life such as our personal finances.

Tools can multiply our productivity and this allow us to not be limited by our physical and mental abilities to do all our activities. This is one of the reason why it is so important to research what tools are available to do the things we want and to be systematic when getting them and using them so we can increase our efficiency and productivity.

## Money

Money can also be consider a tool but the thing that makes money special is that by itself it has no value, we usually can't use it to satisfy our needs directly. What makes money valuable is its universal acceptance that allows us to exchange certain amounts of it with other people in order to acquire the goods and services that will allow us to satisfy our needs.

Money is one of the most direct ways to have access to the tools and places we need for our purposes. Also through money we can hire the services of other people so they do an activity that we can't do for reasons of ability, time or desire, and this will free us to dedicate ourselves to the things we really want to do.

Because of the high importance of money in our lives and all the things it allows us to do, it is important to put some time into learning how to acquire it and manage it properly. In chapter 3 I will talk much more about money and how to think about our personal finances.

## Other people

The external resource that most leverage have in our life, both positive and negative, is other people. When we talk about others we are talking about our family, friends, work partners, acquaintances, and even people from the past or the present that we've never met but that we have gained access to them through things like books, videos or recordings.

First of all, other people are the biggest source we have to get knowledge. The different experiences other people have had has given them many lessons that we can use for our advantage to accelerate our learning process and move faster towards our goals.

Besides knowledge, other people also give us many of the goods and services we need and this takes away the need for us to learn about everything so we can dedicate ourselves to the things we do better and enjoy the most.

Other people are also the direct purpose of many of our goals and they may even be a source of every one of the ways we can feel good. Other people can give us pleasure and joy, help us find happiness and even allow us to feel satisfaction when our values are related with the constant interaction with other people in our lives.

Learning to manage all these relationships is essential if we want to have a good life of progress and growing. Some people are born with very good skills for relating with others while other people who find this much more difficult and they need to do a greater effort to learn to relate effectively.

## The Process

The part of Life Strategy that will connect all the previous elements and will turn this model into a really practical guide to know how to live our lives is the process.

The purpose of this process is to help us implement all 4 ways of *Feeling Good* into our lives in a harmonic and sustainable way. We already know that the 4 ways of *Feeling Good* are: pleasure, joy, happiness and satisfaction, and we know what each one of them implies and the advantages of focusing on the last two without forgetting or leaving aside the first two which are also very important for having a good life.

We reach this purpose by using our different resources. Those resources may be used in two ways. The first is by getting directly those things we need to feel good in any of its manifestations and the second is by using those resources to get more resources so we can pursue our other goals.

Using these resources requires that we make decisions and that we learn all we can about reality and about how the world works. One first step and a good foundation to improve our capacity for making decisions is integrating the 5 principles of Life Strategy and from there, and through our experience and the lessons we get, we can continue developing our own life philosophy.

In general terms this is the process implied in Life Strategy but the truth is that it is still very general and abstract and this doesn't tell us clearly how we can apply it exactly into our lives. This is the reason why this process is made up of 3 specific steps we must follow throughout all our life so it can become a practical model applicable to the lives of all human beings.

The names of the 3 steps of Life Strategy are: "Where are you?", "Where are you going?", and "What will you do?". Next,

I will talk briefly about each one of them and in the following chapters I will talk more thoroughly about these steps and the things we can do to implement them into our daily life.

## Step 1: Where are you?

The first step of Life Strategy is called "Where are you?". The objective of this step is to answer the best we can the following questions: who we are? what is important to us? what resources we have? and what can we do?

Answering these questions with precision will probably takes us all our life and we may even end our life without having found the definitive answer to all those questions. Despite this, this first step is something we must keep taking because the answers we have for those questions at any time are the foundation to make our decisions, choose where we are headed and figure out how we can get there.

To answer those question it's important to do 2 things. The first one is to study and learn as much as we can about subjects such as the differences among people, the different temperaments and their manifestations, the way values work in people, the attributes of personality, the strengths and weaknesses in people, and the external conditions the world may present that can become opportunities or obstacles depending on our particular goals.

After learning and acquiring at least a basic understanding on these subjects, the next step is to analyze ourselves, taking some time to observe ourselves as objectively as we can. We must try to understand why we like doing certain things and not others, why we're good for doing certain things, why we feel attracted to certain kind of people, among many other things. This is a step that can last for a lifetime but it is important to keep doing it little by little so we can keep moving forward and acquire the experience we need to get an even better understanding of ourselves.

Chapter 2 will be dedicated to talk exclusively about this step and explain you most of the concepts and techniques you need to understand to start putting it into practice.

## Step 2: Where are you going?

After having a little bit of clarity on the answers to the questions of the previous step, the next step is to use those answers to define where we're going. In other words, this step is about setting up goals.

There are infinity goals we can pursue, some of them will be things we may want to get throughout our lifetime while others are for our immediate future. We can have goals of long, medium and short-term, and many of those short-term goals may be steps we need to reach to be able to start working for our long-term goals.

The different goals we set for ourselves must have at least one of the following 5 purposes to be really valuable and productive for our lives:

**1.** Help us increase any of our internal or external resources.

**2.** Serve as a source of pleasure.

**3.** Serve as a source of joy.

4. Help us experience happiness.

5. Make us feel satisfaction.

There are many times where for different circumstances we can't do something to reach some of the 4 ways of *Feeling Good*, so we'll need to focus on goals related with increasing any of our resources.

In the life of people there are 9 areas: personal growth, health, work, finances, tools and places, romance, family, social relationships and recreation. Each one of those areas affects at least one of the ways of Feeling Good and this is the reason why we must learn about them and try to get a good balance among them.

All those areas are related to each other and what we do or obtain in one can affect what we can obtain in the others. Just as well as the shortcomings we have in any one of them can affect negatively the others. In the third chapter I will talk with more detail about this step, about the areas of life, and specially the things we need to keep in mind while setting all our goals.

## Step 3: What will you do?

Execution is the third step of this process and it consists on planning the specific actions we must take to reach all our short term goals and put those plans into practice.

Only through execution we get to feel good because knowing ourselves perfectly and having the best goals is of zero use unless we apply that knowledge into our reality and carry it forward through our daily actions.

Most people, by not having done the two previous steps, get busy simply surviving and taking care of the obligations put upon them by life or other people. The level of control they have over what happen in their lives is very low because they haven't taken the time to define what they want and see if what they're doing is in line or not with those wishes.

Execution becomes really valuable for us when it is in harmony with what we know about ourselves and the things we want to achieve.

This third step called What will you do? can be divided in 3 sub-steps which are: planning, acting and reflecting.

Planning consists in defining the specific actions we must take and the resources we need to reach each one of our short term goals.

After planning our next step is to put those plan into action. There are two ways we can execute those actions and they are: tasks and habits.

Tasks are all those actions that are inside our personal projects and our daily obligations and they're distinguish because they don't repeat often and usually they must be completed in certain order or at specific times.

Habits are all those actions we must take with certain regularity. They can be daily habits which are the most common but we can also find weekly, monthly and even annual habits.

There are some habits we need to develop only temporarily while we reach some goal, and there are others that we may wish to maintain throughout our life.

Both habits and tasks are needed in different circumstances and for different goals but habits have a big advantage over tasks. Habits, once they're set, stop depending so much on our willpower and become things we do almost automatically.

After taking action and getting some positive or negative results with relation to our goals we must proceed to the last step called reflecting. Reflecting consists on taking the time to analyze what happened and try to get some learning out of that experience. It is possible that things worked out as we expected but it is also very possible that we didn't get the results we wanted. When things don't come out as expected it's when we have the biggest chance of learning something important just as long as we take the time to reflect on that experience. That learning can be related to the way we executed our plans or it can be a deeper learning that take us to rethink some of our goals or even change something we believed about ourselves.

In chapter 4 I will talk again about this third step and I will give specific techniques that will allow us to become more productive and efficient while executing our plans.

In the following chapters I will talk about the 3 steps that make up the process of Life Strategy but before ending this chapter you will find a diagram that sorts out in a global and visual way all this model called Life Strategy and thanks to it you will be able to see all the elements that make it up and how they are related to each other.

# LIFE STRATEGY

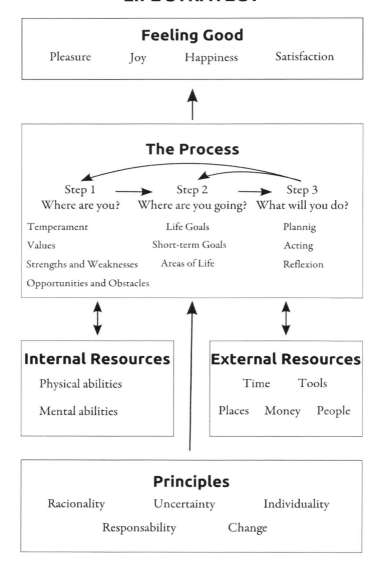

**Feeling Good**

Pleasure      Joy      Happiness      Satisfaction

**The Process**

Step 1          Step 2          Step 3
Where are you?   Where are you going?   What will you do?

Temperament          Life Goals          Plannig

Values          Short-term Goals          Acting

Strengths and Weaknesses      Areas of Life      Reflexion

Opportunities and Obstacles

**Internal Resources**

Physical abilities

Mental abilities

**External Resources**

Time      Tools

Places      Money      People

**Principles**

Racionality      Uncertainty      Individuality

Responsability          Change

# Chapter 2. Where are you?

In this chapter we'll talk about the first step of Life Strategy called "Where are you?". This step consists on acquiring a good knowledge about ourselves and about the things that make us unique and different. For this we must identify the things we consider the most important and also our current circumstances and the resources we have.

As I said in the first chapter, knowing ourselves is a process that takes a long time and that requires that we have many kinds of experiences. As we acquire more experiences we'll be able to obtain a more precise information about ourselves and about the world and this will allows us to use that knowledge more effectively while setting goals and planning how we're going to achieve them.

There are 4 basic categories in which we can group this knowledge about ourselves:

1.  Temperament

2.  Core Values

3.  Strengths and Weaknesses

**4.**   Opportunities and Obstacles

Each one of these categories can help us answer some of the question needed for discovering our own individuality, or in other words, what makes us different from other people. Since we're not all the same, the road each of one must follow to reach that purpose of *Feeling Good* must also be different.

# Temperament

The first concept I will talk about is temperament. Among the modern theories about temperament, one of the most popular and the one I agree the most with, is Dr. David Keirsey's theory proposed in his book Please Understand Me II published in 1998. Since the work made by Dr. Keirsey is very thorough, where he explains how his theory relates with many of the previous theories and also explains with detail all the characteristics of each temperament, in this section I will limit myself to only give a short summary of the main ideas of his theory and let you complement this information through his book and website.

According to Keirsey, temperament next to character are the two components of personality. Temperament is a configuration on inclinations while character is a configuration of habits. Temperament is our innate disposition to think, feel and act in certain ways while character are the habits we develop throughout our life when we interact with our environment. If our environment is beneficial then we will develop habits appropriate with our temperament, but if our environment is less friendly to our temperament then it's possible that it will much harder for us to develop a good character according to our temperament.

## The 4 temperaments

First of all, there are two great dimensions of human behavior in which we people differ: the way we communicate and the way we act.

Regarding the way we speak some people tend to be concrete; that means they talk more about things that can be seen or felt and also about present situations and other people. There are other people that prefer a more abstract communication; they talk about ideas, theories, possibilities, dreams, philosophies, beliefs, and all the things that can only be seen with our mind. According to Keirsey most people are concrete while only about 20 per cent of the population tends to be abstract.

The second dimensions has to do with the way we act. Some people are cooperative while others are utilitarians. Cooperative people tend to do things based on what is socially acceptable and moral, or in other words, what is considered right by society. On the other hand, utilitarian people give more importance to the results they can get over what other people might think. Utilitarians try to achieve their objective in the most effective and efficient way possible while cooperatives try to do the right thing.

Through a combination of these two dimensions we can obtain the 4 temperament. People who tend to be more concrete on their communication and utilitarians in how they do things Keirsey called them Artisans. People who are more concrete but their way of acting is cooperative are called Guardians. People who use abstract language and are utilitarians in how they act were called Rationals and those who prefer an abstract language and their way of acting is cooperative Keirsey called them Idealists.

Artisans are distinguished because they tend to excel in the performance of any of the arts: visual, scenic, politic, military and business. Among their main characteristics are that they tend to be fun, optimistic, focus on the present, risky, unconventional, generous, brave and spontaneous. They are good at using their bodies and their hand and this makes them good for using all types of tools and playing sports. Artisans tend to look for adventure, pleasure and stimulation. Dr. Keirsey estimates that between 30 and 35 per cent of the population are artisans.

Guardians are the temperament of those that work to keep our most important social institutions. They have the talent of managing goods and services and they use these skills for keeping everything working inside our families, communities, schools and businesses. They are workers, helpers, dependable, cautious, humble, and they care a lot about credentials and traditions. Guardians are about 40 to 45 per cent of the population.

Rationals are those who are good at solving problems related to any of the systems that compose our word such as organic, mechanical or social systems. Rationals like to analyze systems and work to make them better. They are pragmatic, skeptical, independent and determined. They are also distinguish for their ability to keep calm and for their desire for achievement and knowledge. Rationals are rare, only make up a 5 to 10 per cent of the population.

Idealists tend to be highly preoccupied with personal growth and development. They are constantly concerned about discovering who they are and improving all the time, and they are also good for helping others in these tasks. They like to work with others and usually have good abilities to help others, solve conflicts and inspire others to grow and reach their potential. They are enthusiastic, intuitive, loving, of good heart, ethical, kind, authentic and have a strong desire to create meaningful and harmonic relationships. Between 15 to 20 per cent of the population are idealists.

Each one of these temperaments can be manifested in 4 different types depending on features such as the level of extroversion, the tendency to be guided by logic or feeling and the need to do things more strictly or more spontaneously. To know each one of the 4 types in which each temperament is divided and to take the test to identify your temperament and your specific type I recommend that you visit Dr. Keirsey website: "http://www.keirsey.com" or read his book Please Understand Me II.

Identifying our temperament is essential because this affects the type of activities we like to do; the way we interact with other people; the language we use; the things we value; the way we see other people, the world and even time; the way we see ourselves; and the things we need to keep a good self-esteem. Temperament can affect the people we are attracted to and our capacity to create harmonic relationships with them, the kind of parents we tend to be and even the role we play as leaders. Understanding many of these things will allow us to design a life appropriate to our own peculiarities and will save us from a lot of trial and error trying to identify each one of these attributes in ourselves in an isolated way.

Now that you know very briefly what is temperament and its different manifestations we can proceed to talk about our values which are highly associated with our levels of satisfaction.

# Core Values

After understanding our temperament, the next step is to identify our core values. Core values are those things that are really important to us and because of this they're the things we need to feel satisfied.

As I said in chapter 1, satisfaction means feeling good with ourselves and we do this through the actions we take to obtain or maintain our core values. If the things we do are in line with our values then we will feel satisfied but if we are ignoring those values or are sacrificing them for something less important then we won't feel good with ourselves and our levels of satisfaction will decrease.

Some of our core values can come from our temperament and there are others that come from our culture or the different experiences we've had in life. It is also possible that some meaningful event can change one of our core values.

The requirement for feeling satisfied is not necessarily having the things we consider important in our lives but acting to get or keep those values. Satisfaction, even though it may be more durable than pleasure and joy, can also be lost if for some time we stop doing the things that make us feel good with ourselves.

## Everything has a price

A very important concept related to how core values work is accepting that everything we want to get or achieve in life has a price. It will always be necessary to sacrifice something to get something else that we consider more valuable. It is possible through a very good planning to reduce significantly the price we have to pay for something or in other works get it in a more efficient way. However, in most cases it is necessary to be conscious that we can't have everything in life and the decisions we make will have consequences and will stop us from pursuing other goals. We must take the time to define if what we're looking for really has the best probabilities of making us feel good in any of the 4 modalities and specially if what we're working towards could really be a source of satisfaction.

Accepting that everything has a price will free us and give us a lot of tranquility when making decisions and not obsess or stress ourselves for those things that become out of our reach. One of the reasons of the suffering of many people is that when they're in a situation that requires them to sacrifice something to achieve something that is more meaningful to them, for example their comfort, these people spend more time thinking about the things they're sacrificing instead of keeping their sight in what they can gain if they put up with that situation a little bit longer. Keeping our focus always on what we consider important and trying to ignore all those things that aren't and that we have to sacrifice will help us make more definitive decisions and to feel more tranquility with ourselves.

## The 33 groups of values

I will share with you a list I designed with the different values we can have. I designed this list by analyzing many other lists of values from different sources and condensing them in 33 groups of similar values so we can see with more clarity all the different values that exists and identify those that are really important to us.

This list is not perfect and if there is something you consider important but don't find it in this list then you can add it with no problem. Despite this, using this list can be a very good tool to start thinking about our core values and taking the first step toward identifying them. As we increase our experience we'll be able to do a more precise identification of our values which will help us make better decisions in life.

This list is divided in 33 groups of values and inside those groups there are 4 values that are related among them because they have similar meaning. The idea is first to define the groups we feel more identified with and then look for the word inside those groups that represents better what we feel is important. Further ahead I will talk about a more detail process to find our values but for now I'll leave you this list so you can observe it and analyze it.

### 33 Groups of Values

| | | | | |
|---|---|---|---|---|
| 1 | Friendship | Acceptance | Connection | Company |

| | | | | |
|---|---|---|---|---|
| 2 | Adventure | Risks | Exploration | Spontaneity |
| 3 | Beauty | Art | Elegance | Sensuality |
| 4 | Collaboration | Team Work | Unity | Synergy |
| 5 | Growth | Evolution | Learning | Achievement |
| 6 | Discipline | Focus | Persistence | Perseverance |
| 7 | Fun | Pleasure | Enthusiasm | Joy |
| 8 | Effectiveness | Efficiency | Pragmatism | Results |
| 9 | Excellence | Greatness | Perfection | Superiority |
| 10 | Artistic Expression | Creativity | Innovation | Originality |
| 11 | Family | Children | Offspring | Dynasty |
| 12 | Faith | Spirituality | Illusion | Hope |
| 13 | Generosity | Solidarity | Service | Charity |
| 14 | Skill | Dexterity | Competence | Flow |
| 15 | Honesty | Dependability | Integrity | Authenticity |
| 16 | Equality | Justice | Right | Equity |
| 17 | Impact | Change | Revolution | Transformation |
| 18 | Freedom | Independence | Autonomy | Self-Reliance |
| 19 | Leadership | Power | Domination | Control |
| 20 | Obedience | Authority | Respect | Devotion |
| 21 | Order | Cleanness | Purity | Hygiene |
| 22 | Concern | Understanding | Empathy | Affection |
| 23 | Prosperity | Wealth | Affluence | Comfort |
| 24 | Reason | Knowledge | Wisdom | Reality |
| 25 | Recognition | Fame | Appreciation | Status |

| 26 | Romance | Love | Sex | Intimacy |
| 27 | Health | Strength | Movement | Energy |
| 28 | Security | Protection | Caution | Care |
| 29 | Simplicity | Minimalism | Frugality | Humility |
| 30 | Loneliness | Privacy | Reserve | Silence |
| 31 | Hard Work | Responsibility | Commitment | Dedication |
| 32 | Tradition | Culture | Laws | Norms |
| 33 | Tranquility | Calm | Serenity | Inner Peace |

## Value System

We people are a little bit more complex than just having some core values and ignoring everything else and this is why we can classify all our different values in 4 categories depending on the level of importance they have for us:

1. Core values

2. Secondary values

3. Optional values

4. Disposable values

Core values are those of most importance for us and they're essential for our satisfaction. These are the values we can't sacrifice or ignore if our goal in life is to feel good in every sense. Inside this list of 33 groups we could say that between 3 and 7 of those groups are core values.

Secondary values are those that we consider important but

in case of having to choose between a core value and a secondary one, we would be willing to sacrifice the latter. It is possible that if from a very early age we make a good plan of our life we'll be able to integrate most of our core and secondary values. This is not necessary for reaching good levels of satisfaction but it can be a good challenge if what we want is to get the most out of life and enjoy it the most. Secondary values can be between 5 to 15 of those 33 groups.

The third group of values are the optional ones. These values are things that maybe we would like to have just as long as they don't demand a great effort or don't imply the sacrifice of more meaningful values for us. What distinguish these values is that in case we don't have them we won't experience anguish or anxiety. They can be useful to have a more interesting life but they're not required for our satisfaction.

The fourth and last group are all those disposable values that don't mean much to us and that we can easily sacrifice each time it's necessary.

The number of optional and disposable values can vary and they're the remaining after we've identified our core and secondary values.

The different combinations of how these values can present in our life are what I call our value system. The main use of having a value system defined is that it will serve us a great tool when making decisions in our lives because it will tell us what are the things that have more impact on our satisfaction and what are the things we can sacrifice or give up in case it is required for reaching our main goals.

As I said previously, our value system will be constantly evolving because as we live we'll get new experiences that will give us some insights that will allow us to identify better the impact all those different values have on our satisfaction.

## How to identify our values

The best source for discovering our values is our experience and the best method is reflecting. If we don't have much experience in many aspects of our life then we must try to guess or speculate with the little we know about ourselves about what we think are our core values. Then we should start doing things in the world that allow us to acquire the experience we need to check if what we thought was indeed right or if on the contrary we need to make some adjustments to our list of values.

Since our best method for identifying our values is reflecting on our experience, then what we have to do is ask ourselves a series of questions that will help us identify what are the things we consider the most important in our life and the things we have discovered are a true source of satisfaction for us every time we have them or every time we work to get them or keep them.

Next I will give a series of specific steps that can help you identify your core values and your own value system.

The first step is reviewing the list of values I showed you and try to understand globally what each of those 33 groups of values mean and the concepts inside of them. Doing this exercise will allow us to create a mental image that will help us recognize with more ease some of those values in ourselves when we ask the question I'll propose in the following steps. By not making this step it will be harder to find the exact word we need to identify something that we consider important in our life. In short, doing a review of all the values we may have will help us decrease the time we need for identify our own values.

The second step is answering the following questions that will help you analyze different aspects of your experience. These questions can be a good hint of the things that are important to you, the things you had based on to make important decisions in your life and the way you felt with the results you got. The questions are:

**1.** Which is the decision you feel the most proud of? Why do you feel proud of that decision? What were the consequences of making that decision?

**2.** What is the decision you regret the most? What did you lose because of that decision? What would you do different if you could take that decision again?

**3.** What are some of the activities that you've been interested throughout your life? What things you know how to do? What do those things have in common? What is what you like the most about those activities?

**4.** Who are the 3 people you admire the most in the world? What do you admire of those people? What do they have in common?

**5.** Who are the 3 people you despise the most? What distinguish those people? What do they have in common?

**6.** What are you most important current goals? Why do you want to achieve those goals? Would you be willing to sacrifice everything else for those goals? What would you not be willing to sacrifice?

**7.** What have been the times in your life when you've felt the best with yourself? What made you feel good with yourself at those times? What do those times have in common?

All those question will probably give you different answers but if you take your time to analyze them you will find that there are some things that remain constant and repeat themselves in several of those answer and probably among them you will find some of your core and secondary values.

The third step is to compare and associate some of the answer you've got from the previous questions with the list of 33 group of values until you manage to define a list of 5 to 7 groups of values that you consider have the highest level of importance to you.

Step four is choosing the word inside each one of those groups that best define what that value means to you. Having an exact word we can use to list our values will give us more mental clarity when making decisions.

The fifth and last step is to start testing your list of values in the real world by defining what goals you want to pursue and start working toward their achievement. Depending on the results you get you can analyze if having based yourself in those particular values was a good choice of if instead you should make some change to your value system.

This process of defining our core values and our value system is a process that takes years and that requires that we be willing to experiment constantly in all areas of our lives.

In short, our values are the ones that define the levels of satisfaction we feel at each moment in life. This makes it so important to put some time and effort into identify them and making this process one of our first goals in life because from there we will base ourselves to define the different roads we will follow and the personal history we want to create.

This first step of Life Strategy also requires that we identify the state of our internal and external resources which in practical terms translate into identifying our strengths and weaknesses and the opportunities and obstacles in our lives.

Our resources are also a very important guideline for making decisions and choosing the goals we want to pursue because different goals demand different kinds and amounts of resources to be achieved. Being able to define from the start if a goal is in or out of our reach will save us a lot of time and energy that we would have otherwise wasted on goals we would probably have failed at. Instead, we will be able to use our time more effectively in goals that can help us grow and experience some of the different ways of feeling good that are available.

## Strengths and Weaknesses

Strengths and weaknesses are related to our internal resources. Strengths are those resources we can use to achieve some of our goals while weaknesses are resources we lack that make more difficult the achievement of some of our goals. Our internal resources, as I said previously, are split by our physical abilities such as health, appearance and physical dexterities and by our mental abilities which are our knowledge, emotions, reason and creativity. Among those strengths and weaknesses we can also list all those skills that we consider relevant to the goals we have.

We all have a different combination of resources and that makes us unique from other people. Many of those differences come from our temperament, that means, that many of our internal resources are genetic. Despite this, depending on the use we give to those resources it is possible to develop them to good levels if we train them enough or if we don't pay enough attention to them they can also atrophy. This is the reason why it is important that we identify and do periodic evaluation of these resources. This will let us know what we have available to reach our short term goals and also it will help us develop strategies to improve our strengths and overcome some of our weaknesses.

Strengths and weaknesses can be defined in comparative terms. With this I mean that strengths are things we have in higher amounts that most people or things we can do with more ease than others. Weaknesses on the other hand are those things we have in less amount than other people or things that are more difficult for us than for others.

## Focusing on developing strengths or reducing weaknesses

One of the things we have to think carefully is if we want to focus exclusively on developing our strengths, reducing our weaknesses or doing both at the same time.

Each one of the previous strategies can be useful and we must use them at certain times but there are a few guidelines that might help us define what to do.

Since we all have some innate strengths in some areas it is advisable to focus initially on knowing those strengths and use them to achieve those goals associated with them. Once we use those strengths to reach some goals we will increase our resources so we can pursue other types of goals. Having well defined strengths and supporting ourselves mostly in them is a pretty efficient strategy because reducing our weaknesses is something that requires a great deal of effort and because we can support on others and each one of us can focus on doing the things we do best.

By using this strategy we'll be able to achieve many things but probably we'll get to a point where we have some very important goals for us that depend on those areas where we have weaknesses. At this point we must decide if those goals are really worth pursuing, and if they are, then we must start working to overcome our weaknesses.

Overcoming weaknesses as I just said can be a process that requires a lot of effort but it can also give us many benefits. One of them is that weaknesses limit us in many way and by reducing them we will have many more options available in life in relationship to the goals we can pursue as well as the way of achieving them. Other advantage of reducing our weaknesses is that we will depend much less on other people for doing some things and this helps us because even though other people are some of our greatest sources of joy in many cases, there are also many cases where they become huge sources of stress and the reason why we lose our tranquility so often.

In short, the strategy I recommend to follow is to focus initially on using our strengths to the max to achieve some goals with them. After this, and when we consider it necessary, we can start focusing on reducing our weakness until they don't stop us anymore from getting the things we want, and then we can keep focusing on developing both aspects in a balanced way by increasing our strengths little by little and reducing our weaknesses in the same way.

## How to develop strengths and reduce weaknesses

There are many ways how we develop strengths and reduce weaknesses and this depends on the resources we're talking about.

With respect to our physical abilities, health can be improve by certain habits such as exercise, diet, rest and also through more direct methods such as medical interventions or drugs. Our appearance can also be improved by exercise, diet, hygiene habits and personal care, and through the clothing and accessories we use. Our different physical dexterities are improved mainly through practice and constant training.

Regarding our mental abilities, knowledge is acquire in several ways, the first one being through direct or indirect instruction. That means, when a teacher give us those knowledge face to face or through some mediums like books, recording, videos or any other way. The second way we acquire knowledge is through our own experience and the experience of others. For this we need to analyze and reflect on those experiences and try to extract important lessons we can apply in our own lives. The last way to acquire knowledge is building it from our previous knowledge with the help of our reason and creativity.

The second of our mental abilities are our emotions. Developing our emotions means that we are able to feel them appropriately and we can recognize when we feel them and control our actions so we can express those emotion in the most positive and constructive way without letting them own us. All emotions have their purpose and utility, even those we think are negative such as anger or fear. Learning how we can use those emotions for our own well-being is how we manage to turn those emotions into true strengths we can use to get the things we want.

Our third mental ability is our reason. This ability is influenced in a big measure by our genetic composition but there are many things we can do to use it to its max. The first thing is to acquire more knowledge because knowledge is the material our reason uses for working and the more knowledge we have, the more complex and correct our deductions will be. The other thing we can do is to use it often to solve the problems of our own life or do exercises or simulations that allow us to train our ability to reason and give us the confidence to use it later in more meaningful situations.

Our last mental ability is our creativity. Same as reason, some people have naturally higher levels of creativity than others but this aspect is also flexible and can be taken to higher levels through constant practice and the use of techniques developed to get us used to think creatively. One of the aspects of creativity is that it is not enough just to think creatively but it is also important to have enough courage to apply those creative ideas in the real world. Only through this we will be able to find out if our creativity and our ideas can really have the impact we expect and if that's not the case, then we must keep improving them and experimenting.

Lastly, the way we develop our skills are through practice and experimentation. The more we use our abilities in one activity the higher the chances of improving our skill to do it and that will let us turn that skill into a strength that makes us competitive.

## How to discover our strengths and weaknesses

The way we discover our strengths and weaknesses is relatively easy. The first thing is to analyze our internal resources, both our physical and mental attributes, and observe in which of their components we present strengths or weaknesses and in what measure. Regarding skills we must analyze first each one of the areas of our life and determine which are the skills we consider we should have and determine how we are regarding those skills. Since the number of possible skills is practically unlimited, it is not worth to list all those things we can't do but focus only on those that have true relevancy to our lives.

# Opportunities and Obstacles

Opportunities and obstacles represent the state of our

external resources in relation to the things we want to do. Also, they are all those conditions or situations that the world presents us that can facilitate or make more difficult the achievement of our goals.

The more we use the opportunities that are available to us and the better we are with dealing with the obstacles we find in our way, the higher will our progress in life be.

Regarding external resources, opportunities and obstacles are related to time, places, tools, money and everything related with the other people in our lives.

Same as with skills, each one of those resources only become opportunities and obstacles when we compare them with the things we want to achieve. For example, for money to be an opportunity or an obstacle it doesn't matter how much we have but what we want to do with it. If what we have is enough to get the things we want then it will be an opportunity even though to someone else that same amount of money may be very little and not enough to do what they want. Then for them that money will be an obstacle they must overcome. It is the same thing with each one of the other external resources, we always have to compare them with the requisites needed for doing the things we want and check if those things we want are really associated with our well-being by offering us satisfaction or any other of the ways of *Feeling Good*.

Opportunities and obstacles are also associated with many circumstances we may find in life. There will be times when those circumstances may be beneficial for us and push us more than we had planned. In other circumstances they may obstruct the achievement of our goals or even keep us from doing many of the things we wanted to do.

Some of those circumstances, both positive and negative, can be things like inheritances, someone we met, the change of value of one of our properties, a disease we or someone close to us caught, or even the death of someone meaningful in our lives. Most of the time those situations are out of our control and we must accept them and try to adapt to them as soon as possible.

The regularity in which those circumstances may present is also very variable. There will be times in our life when we may not find any meaningful opportunity and obstacle and everything will go with some tranquility and just as planned. Other times those opportunities and obstacles can present really rapidly. Sometimes we may find ourselves in front of one opportunity after the other and other times there may be so many obstacles at the same time that we will think life is punishing us for something.

All of these circumstances are normal and may present themselves through our lifetime. The best thing we can do is to be aware of them when they present themselves and use them or handle them the best way we can.

## How to use opportunities and handle obstacles

On one side there are the opportunities related with our external resources and those resources are things we can start increasing even before we need them. Usually the best opportunities in life are unexpected things that require that we have some resources to be able to take advantage of them and if we don't, then we'll lose that chance. This is the reason why it is important from a very early age to have as a goal to put attention to each one of our external resources so we can be prepare when we need them.

Time is a fixed resource so what we can do is try to use it better through some productivity techniques and avoid doing many things that don't add much to our life and well-being. One tactic we can use to free some of our time is to delegate to other people those activities that should be done but in which we don't want to spend our time. There are many recreational activities that are low quality and can even harm our health if they become habits, and these activities rob us from a lot of time. If we try to remove them then we fill free a big chunk of our time to use it in more valuable things.

One example of how through time we can use opportunities is when we want to make a trip and we find there are some really cheap flight tickets but only if we travel is some specific dates. If we have good control over our time and the freedom to use it as we find convenient, then it will be possible to take advantage of that trip, but if we are full of obligations on those days then that opportunity will be gone.

One of the more meaningful ways of earning time is trying to retire from our jobs as soon as possible. Retiring means that we no longer have the need to work for money to satisfy our basic needs and that we can use our time in those projects, jobs or activities we are most passionate about.

Sites and places are others of our external resources. One way to increase our opportunities related with those resources is by moving to a new city or country that can presents us with better advantages in relationship to the things we want to do. This option has made it possible for a lot of people to reach their goals which would have been impossible if they had stayed in their home town. Different sites offer different advantages and we must analyze this well so we can define where we can be better and see if it's really possible to move to those places.

We can also increase our opportunities related with these resources by gaining access to different sites and places such as houses, offices, training or recreational facilities, etc. The more places we have to do our activities the higher the chances of increasing our internal and external resources.

Other of our external resources are our tools. Tools have a big impact on the speed we can do our different activities and in many cases limit the things we can do. Having the right tools can also help us take advantage of a good opportunity that comes our way.

We must do two things with tools for them to be really useful: the first is to acquire them or get access to them and the second is to use them effectively. Having a top-of-the-line camera or computer won't do us any good if we don't know how to use them at that level. Here is where it becomes important to be efficient while acquiring our tools. This means not spending additional money on features or models of some products that we'll never need. If we acquire our tools keeping in mind our needs and the things we want to use them for then we'll be able to save some money and that money we save can be used to get other tools we need for different activities.

Money is a very valuable resource that affects the access to many other resources and that's why managing it well is such an essential part in everyone's life. Through money we acquire the places and tools we need, we can go to other places permanently or temporarily, we can relate to people of different social context and even with money we can free some of our time.

The way we acquire money is through our work and through its efficient use which means controlling our expenses and investing our money on things that allow us to earn more money without our direct and constant intervention.

Other people are also some of our biggest sources of opportunities and obstacles in life and that's the reason learning to relate to others is something we must learn as soon as possible.

On the one hand there is the quantity of people we know and who know us and on the other is the quality of the people closest to us. The better those people are the bigger will be the things we would be able to do and the less the worries or obstacles we can find because of the problems they could get themselves into.

To improve both the quantity and quality of the people in our lives it is required that we develop certain social skills to be able to communicate and interact with other people and to have a criteria to define what person we let into our life in a meaningful way and which we don't.

Having good levels on each of these resources can help us do and achieve many of the things we desire and so this is the first way of increasing our resources and reducing our possible obstacles. The other way of handling opportunities is by being prepared for them when they show up. The way we realize if something is or not an opportunity is by being clear about what we want to achieve and how we plan to achieve it. When we have these two aspects clear in our minds it is going to be easier to define if a situation that presents itself has any relationship or not with some of our goals and if it does, be able to know if that situation will facilitate or obstruct its achievement.

In reality, the only options we have when it comes to opportunities is to take advantage of them or to let them go and the options we have against obstacle are to overcome them or let ourselves be stopped by them. We don't know when an opportunity or an obstacle may present itself in our lives and neither how big it will be and that's why it is important to be aware and prepared through all our different resources and also be very clear about our goals and plans so we can recognize those situation faster and use them in the best way possible.

With this subject I have finished talking about the first step of life strategy called "Where are you?". In this step we learned about our temperament, our core values and the value system, about our strengths and weaknesses and about the opportunities and obstacles. It is important to identify each one of these aspects in ourselves and continue increasing our understanding of them as we live. To define precisely many of this aspect it is required to have some information that can only be obtained by executing the following steps, however, starting to think about these concepts is a requisite for doing a good job on step 2 which is called "Where are you going?". And that step consists on setting all our goals in the different areas of life.

# Chapter 3. Where are you going?

The second step of Life Strategy is called "Where are you going?", and it consists on defining our direction, or in other words, setting all our goals. What makes this a complex process is that there are different areas in life that are interrelated and each one of them helps in some way so we can feel good. It is for these reasons that we must be aware of these factors so we can define better deadlines of our goals and at the same time define priorities that allows us to do all this process with more harmony.

Another important aspect to be aware of is trying to get our goals in line with our different values, specially our core and secondary values. In addition, we must take into account our internal and external resources and also the opportunities and obstacles that we may encounter in different moments, so those goals to really have the potential to make us feel good and the odds of achieving them are in our favor.

Throughout this chapter I will talk about two subjects. First I will talk about each one of the areas of life. Inside these areas I will talk about their effect on making us feel good, the relationship they have with our resources, the relationship they have with the other areas and the different aspects that make them up. This first part will probably be the largest part of the whole book because I won't limit myself to only defining these areas but I will also share with you some of the practical learnings I've acquired through my research and experience that will allow you to understand better how these areas work and that way you will be able to make better decisions in each one of them.

In the second part of this chapter I'll explain the process we can follow to set our goals and the different aspects we must keep in mind when doing it.

# The 9 Areas of Life

Our life is divided in 9 areas: personal growth, health, work, finances, tools and places, romance, family, social relationships and recreation. The origin of these areas comes from the model "Wheel of Life" of the book "Co-Active Coaching" written by Laura Whitworth and other authors. In these model they talked about 8 areas but I decided to split in two the area of "friends and family" and I called these new areas "social relationships" and "family". I did this so there is a better separation in our goals so we have more clarity while setting them.

Each one of these areas gives us things that allows to feel good and also all these areas are related to one another. This implies that we must achieve some goals in some of them to be able to do the things we want in the others. Next I will talk about each one of these areas so they serve us as a model to define all our goals in life.

# Personal Growth

Personal growth is everything related to the way we manage our minds and emotions. This is one of the areas of more impact in life because having shortcomings in it won't allow us to perform effectively in our daily activities and this will make it more complicated to achieve our goals. This area has a huge effect on making us feel good, in each one of our internal and external resources, and the strengths we develop in this area are going to influence all the other areas.

Inside this area we can set goals concerning things like: happiness, character, self-control and self-awareness, time management, learning, emotions and spirituality.

## Happiness

Happiness is a state of tranquility and mental peace where we arrive when we feel good with the world. Happiness is the third form of Feeling Good and the reason why it's also included in this area is that the process to achieve happiness is internal. Probably you've heard that we don't need anything nor anyone to be happy and that is correct. We may need these things to experience pleasure, joy or satisfaction, but happiness comes mainly from our way of thinking and some techniques of doing it.

My concept of happiness is related with the tranquility pursued by the Stoics in the way expressed in the book "A Guide to the Good Life" of William Irvine. This book talks about several techniques to achieve tranquility through acceptance and appreciation which are the two elements needed to achieve happiness as I mention in chapter 1.

It is mentioned there that "the easiest way for us to achieve happiness is learning to want the things we already have". The specific technique the stoics recommended to achieve this goal is called Negative Visualization. This technique consists on spending time picturing that we have lost the things we value and picturing the bad things that can happen to us. The goal of this is to learn to not give for certain the things we have so we can enjoy them more while we can.

The reason why this technique is very effective and why we must practice it constantly throughout our life is because we humans are "insatiable", just as it is said in the book: "After working hard to get what we want, we lose interest in the object of our desire. Instead of feeling satisfied, we feel bored, and in answer to this boredom we keep forming new and each time bigger desires". This phenomenon is called Hedonistic Adaptation and it makes us enjoy life less. Practicing Negative Visualization where we consciously imagine we lose the things we have, we regain our appreciation for these things and with this appreciation we can regain our capacity for enjoying the world.

The second technique recommended on that book that can help us gain happiness is called Fatalism. The fatalism the stoics recommend is a fatalism when it comes to the past and the present. This fatalism consists on keeping in mind the belief that our actions don't have any effect on the past and therefore we must avoid spending time and energy imagining how the past could be different. This doesn't mean that we stop thinking about the past because there surely are lots of learning we can get from it, but what it means is that we don't torture ourselves for what happened and also stop desiring that things would've been different or the situations we find ourselves in would be different.

These two mental techniques can help us increase our capacity for appreciation and acceptance which are essential requisites to be able to experience happiness and the tranquility that defines it. In case we notice that we're not as happy as we'd like, we must try to integrate these techniques and many others that appear in the book I mentioned.

## Character

Character is one of the personal characteristics that better define a person who has achieved a high level of maturity. Character makes people really effective to face any type of situation they may encounter in life and also lead and inspire others to do great things.

Character is composed of several qualities and many people have different opinions on what those qualities may be. One of the best lists I found was the one proposed by Jim Rohn in his audio program "Build an Unshakable Character". In this program Jim talked about 12 qualities or "pillar": courage, integrity and honesty, perseverance, wisdom, responsibility, humor, flexibility, patience, confidence, physical health, achievements, and living well at the top. In this moment I'm not going to define each one of those characteristics because it is very likely that you already know what they mean and there will be other sections in this book where I may talk about some of them. I suggest that you acquire Jim Rohn's program or one of many other resources that talk about each one of these qualities.

What concerns us at the time is that it is important to have each one of these 12 qualities of character. If by analyzing ourselves we notice that we are lacking in any one of them then we can set goals in order to improve it and turn it into a true pillar of our character.

A good character opens up doors in life. Other people will give us more opportunities when they notice that our character is unshakable because they feel they can trust us, and this is very important in many situations and allows us to avoid many kinds of conflicts. Character is our number one tool to have more success in each one of our goals and this makes it so important to develop it as early as possible. I would even consider that developing a good character should be one of the first goal any person set in life because from there the possibilities of what can be achieving can be seriously expanded.

## Self-awareness and self-control

Self-awareness is a skill that allows us to observe ourselves and see what we're doing in the moment. Self-control is other skill we can develop that depends on self-awareness. Self-control is the capacity we have to correct our actions or to avoid doing things based on what we consider we should or shouldn't do.

Many times in life we let ourselves be carried away by our desire, emotions, fear, or many other things, and we do things that are counter-productive for what we want and consider important. Self-control is the ability to stop ourselves just before doing something we consider we shouldn't do, and also the ability to stop doing something we shouldn't be doing. Another way in which self-control can manifest is when because of fear or anxiety we don't do something that is important to achieve our goals, and with self-control we can regain the courage we were lacking to take action and start moving toward those goals. Both of these skills can be increased in ourselves through training and constant practice and having a good level in them will help us a lot in achieving the things we want. If we notice shortcoming in these two skills then we must set goals to develop them and turn them into strengths.

## Time Management

Time management is other skill that affects how productive we can be. We all have exactly the same time. Each day has 24 hours for all but we will see some people that in those 24 hours get a lot done while others don't. The difference between these two types of people is the skill they have for managing time. Since this topic is highly related with the third step of Life Strategy, then I will leave it until that chapter to talk about many of the different techniques we can use to improve our time management and make sure that each day we make some progress toward each one of the things we want in life.

## Learning

Learning consists in our ability to acquire new knowledge and skills. Knowledge are the facts and information we have in our mind while skills are the practical things we can do with the things we know.

In most cultures, kids from a very early age are put into

an educational system so they can start learning the knowledge and the skills they need to know and face the world. On general, most of these systems are badly designed or have many limitations that causes that the knowledge and skills people get are very few or not very valuable to face the real world.

Besides the education systems, there are many ways of learning and that's why it is important for every person to get responsible for his own education. Education can be acquire through experience which is one of the most effective ways of learning many things. Others ways of learning are games or simulated circumstances that allows us to learn in a safe environment things that would be very risky to practice in reality because of their risks.

Since there are so many subjects and skills that are available for learning, it is important that people follow their interests and curiosities and explore all the things that call their attention as long as they have the time for it. On the other side, having someone as a guide or mentor can be very useful because they can tell us about some important things we must learn that may not be that interesting to us but that are required for achieving the things we want.

Learning is a lifelong process and through it we can keep growing as people. Having always among our personal growth goals some related with acquiring new knowledge and skills can guarantee that we won't stall in life and that can allows us to keep being competent and competitive for many years.

## Emotions

Handling our emotions should be another of our personal

growth goals. Managing our emotions doesn't mean controlling them excessively, repressing or never expressing them. What it means is learning to be aware when we are under a strong emotional state, trying to identify the cause of that state and acting in the way we think is convenient.

As I said previously, among the basic emotions we can find: joy, sadness, fear, anger, love, surprise, shame and disgust, and many of the other emotions are mixes or different intensities of these basic ones.

Emotions are a very important source of knowledge and are capable of reaching conclusions and complex decisions that are outside of our rational mind because of the huge amount of factors they take into account. Many times through a hunch we can arrive to many good decisions, but one condition for this is that we are aware of how we feel and that we have acquire enough right information related to those decisions so our brain can generate the conclusions we need and then tell us about them in the form of hunches.

Just as emotions are very useful in some cases and allows us to truly enjoy life, in other cases they can become our worst enemies and makes us get into a lot of troubles or keep us from doing many of the things we need to do to achieve our goals. This is also the reason why we must include among our goals learning to manage all these harmful emotions so they don't become an obstacle in our lives.

## Spirituality

Spirituality is a complex concept that means different things for different people and that's why I'm not going to approach it directly. For some people spirituality can mean the adherence to a religion and its rituals, while for others, spirituality is more of a state of high consciousness achieved through practices like meditation. There are other people that can associate spirituality with the connection with nature and there may be many different ways of expressing spirituality than the ones I mentioned. Since this is such a relative subject for people, but a very meaningful one to many and associated to the core values of many people, then it is required that each person defines what spirituality means to them and develop the goals associated with achieving the levels of it that each one wants to have.

# Health

Health is a very important area of life because it affects all the others and because it really limits us when we lack it. Health is highly associated with pleasure since activities such us eating and exercising are good sources for experiencing it. And at the same time having good health in general will make us feel well physically.

In addition to being an area of life, in the first chapter we saw that health is also a resource because through it we get both the physical and mental energy we need to do practically any activity in life. There will be some moments where because of a disease or an accident our health may have a serious setback and we must focus exclusively on it no matter what other goals we may have at the moment. If we don't take care of our health it is possible that we may not live all the years that would have been possible with better habits and because of that we will lose the opportunity to experience many interesting things in life.

To enjoy good health it is necessary to pay attention to diet, exercise, resting and sleeping, stress, supplements, diseases, appearance and hygiene.

## Diet

Diet is related to everything we introduce in our bodies. Our body is a factory that performs very complex physical and chemical operations and its main source of energy to do all this is the food we eat. The things we eat have a direct impact on our appearance, on the possible disease we may acquire, on our levels of physical and mental energy, among many other aspects. This makes it a requisite that we take care of our diet so we can keep ourselves healthy for many years, specially when we get old.

There are many experts in the world who research the effects of all kinds of foods and substances in our body and all the time they're making discoveries that we can implement in our lives.

Among the things we need to keeping mind when planning our diet are not only the things we eat but also how often we eat them and in what quantities. This in important because these two last factors can have big effects, both positive and negative, in our health.

## Exercise

Exercise is another of the essential elements to keep our

health because it allows us to keep in optimal conditions the different systems in our body. Among the systems affected by exercise are: our osseous, muscular, respiratory, cardiovascular and even our immune system.

Exercise can also help us increase our energy levels to do stuff. It may seem counter-intuitive and we may even think that doing daily exercise can get us more tired but in many cases with regular exercise we can increase our energy levels throughout the day.

Regarding exercise there are also many experts that dedicate their lives to research and design exercise programs for many different goals and circumstances. I recommend that you find out which of those programs is right for you and start implementing it in your own life.

## Sleeping

Sleeping is also very important to keep a good health and it consists mainly on how much time we sleep and the quality of that time. It is generally accepted that the human body needs between 7 and 8 hours of daily sleep in order to recover and maintain good energy levels and the ideal is that those hours are continuous and at night.

There are many other strategies for sleeping but they are harder to manage and only adapt well to certain lifestyles.

Quality dream is characterized by a good amount of silence and darkness. These things can be simulated through ear plugs or sleeping masks in case our environment isn't the best.

## Stress

Stress is a mental state that can have negative effects in our bodies and our health if we don't control it. Stress is cause by many different problems in life that make us feel worry and anxious. This doesn't let us think clearly and it keeps us in a negative mind state.

Stress is also related with diseases because it lowers our immunological response and that makes us vulnerable to all kinds of illnesses such us cancer, diabetics, viruses and many others.

One of the strategies to control our levels of stress is to apply the 5 principles of Life strategy. These principles will protect us from many situations that could cause us suffering and anxiety and they will allow us to maintain positive mind state. Relaxation is other technique that can help us reduce our levels of stress and it has even been used on a clinical level to help manage symptoms of some chronic diseases.

## Supplements

Supplements are all those things we consume to alter some process in our body or to complement some chemical deficiency. Many supplements are related to drugs that are designed to treat several diseases or negative alteration, and they can help our body regain a normal functioning level. Many drugs have side effects that can be negative to our health and that is the reason why we must not abuse them and only use them when necessary, leaving our body regulate itself in the other times. There are supplements or substances that can help us increase our performance in different activities and keep high energy levels. It is also important to know them and research their side effects.

## Diseases

Diseases are things that affect negatively our body in some way. They can cause our levels of health to drop temporarily or permanently. Some of the causes of those diseases can be accidents, our life habits, some genetic component or something in the environment like a virus or bacteria, among others.

Through diet, exercise, rest, stress management and supplements, it is possible to avoid or control some diseases so we must try to do our best to prevent them and don't let them get into our lives unnecessarily. On the other hand, there are many things that are outside our control that can cause us a disease and all we have left is to look for a way to overcome it.

Many times in life, when we lose our health because of a disease, getting it back takes automatically the number one priority for us and even for the people closest to us. It is important to keep this in mind because if we have very strict and demanding plans in other areas of life, and we don't consider some setbacks we may face such as a sudden drop in our health, then we will surely fail at those goals which will force us to make correction, reset them, or even in some case, quit them.

## Appearance and hygiene

Physical appearance and hygiene can be included in this area of health. Appearance is related to the image we want to project and how attractive we can be to other people, and this can be useful is some situations depending on our goals and the things we consider important. Appearance is affected by our genetic configuration but each one of the elements of health can also affect it positively or negatively.

Hygiene has to do with the care and constant maintenance we give to our body. Just to give some examples, inside hygiene we can talk about the care we give to our hair, nails, teeth, skin, etc.

Regarding this area we must analyze how is our appearance and hygiene and compare them to the things we want to achieve so we can define if we need to improve in any of these areas and set specific goals to do it.

# Work

Work is a very important area in life because after sleeping, it is one of the activities in which we spend the most time. Because of this is important that we design a life where work becomes a real source of satisfaction and at the same time where it help us achieve all the other goals we have in our lives.

Work is any activity that we do to produce a change in the world or in other people, or to increase any of our resources. One of the resources most associated with work is money but an activity doesn't necessarily have to be paid in order to be consider work. There are many other ways work can benefits us. On the one hand we may be doing it to have an impact we consider meaningful and which is related to our values. On the other hand it can gives us resources such as contacts, knowledge or skills, that can be of great use to achieve some of our other goals.

Work also has a big effect on the other areas of life. Depending on the job we have our health can be affected in some way. It also impacts our finances because it is one of the main sources of income for most people, and with this it also affects the tools and places we may have access to.

Our work also have a big impact on our social relationships. Through work we can meet our best friends or even our romantic partner. In addition, when we have kids it is usually important to create a balance between the time we spend with them and the time we spend working and in other activities so we don't impact any of them negatively.

Next, I will talk about the different elements we must keep in mind when setting our work goals.

## Reasons for working

The first thing we must identify is that there are several reasons why we can do a job and it is required to know them and be conscious of them so we distribute our different lines of work in the best way. The three reasons for working are:

1. For money

2. For passion

3. To have an impact

## Working for money

Receiving some income for any activity we do is not a

requirement for that activity to be considered work. The reason why many people associate work mainly with money is because they're still at the point where work is their only source of income. As we'll see in the next section, there are other ways to generate income, the main one being investments, or as Robert Kiyosaki says in his book Rich Dad Poor Dad "the rich make their money work for them".

Despite this, money is still a very important consideration and there are several things to keep in mind if we want to acquire it through work. If we work for somebody else through a direct job or by providing our personal services, then our income is going to be limited by the skill and knowledge we have and the time we spend doing that job. The more unique and specialized our knowledge and skills are, and if they are exactly what the person or organization that is hiring us need, then the higher will be our income. If the things we can do can be done by any other person then our income will be lower because we will be competing with many more people and there will be some people that will be willing to do the same as us and for less money.

Other aspect that affects our income is time. The more time we spend doing some work the bigger our income will be. The limit with this is that we all only have 24 hours everyday and we can only spend a small part of that time working and this limits the amount of money we can earn in case this is our only source of income.

Income received by this type of work is called salary or honorariums. This depends on the type of relationship we have with the person that hired us to do some activity. If we have a job relationship where we must obey some schedules and go on a daily basis to a specific place then we will probably be employees and the money we received will be called salary.

When we provide our personal services to several organizations or people but we maintain some control over our time and the way we do our job then we will probably be self-employed and the income we received for our services will be called honorariums.

When doing independent work, that means, when we decide the goal of our job and what we expect to achieve through it, then we stop talking about being employees or self-employees and we will turn into people who earn their income not through a salary or honorariums, but through the profits we make depending on how efficient we are doing our work.

People who do independent work don't have a guarantee amount of income they can receive. In some works they might not received any monetary income or they may even lose money while doing it. There may be other works where they can earn huge amounts of money that would be impossible to earn through a salary or honorariums.

The way independent people earn their income is by creating products and services other people are willing to pay for in order to satisfy some of their needs. If the income that the independent worker gets is bigger that what he spent to produce those services or products then he will have a profit. There are other cases where the producer of goods and services spends more money that he received from his clients and that will generate for him a loss. There are many reason why this might happen: inefficient processes, not selling enough quantity to cover his fixed costs, some unforeseen event that makes him have an extra expense or many others. Not all independent work is motivated by profit. We may decide for several reasons to do something or produce something that benefits others or ourselves knowing beforehand that we won't get any income for that work, and in that case that work may still be valid and meaningful.

The decisions over getting our income through a job or through independent work depends on many factors such as the resources we have, our skills to do some activities and our skill to offer them to others in an effective manner, and also it depends a lot on our values and the needs we have for independence and self-direction. Despite that, these two ways of working are not exclusive and we can do both at the same time depending on the situation we're in.

## Working for passion

Doing a job we don't like or that we're not passionate about just for money should occur only when we are starting our work life or on those times we face a major setback. Most people when they think about work, they think about jobs they don't like and that's the reason they see work as an obligation that doesn't please them and they split their lives between the time they spend working and the time they spend doing activities they enjoy.

When we make our work be something that really makes us feel good, then that work stops being an obligation and turns into one more of the activities we use to enjoy life and express our values to the world.

When planning our work life, the idea is that we move as quickly as possible to a form of work we are passionate about. The way to find this type of work is by experimenting and testing many different activities to identify those in which we feel better and also acquiring the credentials we need in order to perform them.

In most cases, and when we are just starting, it will be necessary to work just to earn the money we need to survive, acquire the things we need and increase our financial resources. Many of those jobs may be activities we really don't like since they may be stressful or very demanding physically, mentally or emotionally. Despite this, we must do them because of our need and if we really want to get out of them and move to other forms of work more associated with what we really want to do, then what I suggest is having clear that we are only doing it momentarily and using that time very well to accumulate the highest amount of resources possible so we can plan our transition to more enjoyable forms of work.

## Working for impact

Something that can give true meaning to the works we do even though they may not be very enjoyable or are not a big source of income, is the impact we expect to have when we do them.

Having an impact in the world can manifest in different dimensions, from impacting the whole population through some public politics to satisfying the need of only one person or even of other living beings or the environment in general.

The size of the impact is not what gives meaning to our

job but the effort we put into them based on the resources and opportunities we have available at any given time in our lives. Many times we can generate a bigger change by focusing on helping in a meaningful way only one person instead of trying to help millions but in a more superficial way. Different types of people are in different positions that allow them to define better the scale in which they can have the most impact and a big part of turning a job into something very meaningful is learning to identify that scale. In case circumstances change, then we must simply adjust that scale by either making our are of impact bigger or smaller so we can keep being as effective as possible.

Every single one of the 3 reasons for working is important and the ideal is to have different lines of work to satisfy them. We could even try to integrate all 3 in the same job and that will make that activity into a very meaningful part in our lives.

## Independence

There are two ways we can do our work: one is by supporting other organizations or people achieve the goals and visions they set and the other is by defining ourselves the impact we want to have and working either on our own or with a group of people to materialize that impact.

The decision over designing our work independently or by supporting others depends on several factors.

The first of those factors are our core values. Some of us have among our core values the value of independence and because of this we will be able to get more satisfaction from our work if we design it so we can make the decision on what we want to do in the world and the reasons for doing it. Many people, I would even say most, don't have such a high need for independence or are not very comfortable taking high level decisions and for these people a support job is what gives them the most satisfaction and where they can have the most impact.

The second factor that affects the decision we make are the resources we have. If we're just starting and we don't have enough resources such as money, social contacts, knowledge or skills, then we will probably have to start in a support job that allows us to get those resources. Some people are going to feel better continuing their career in this type of work while others are going to try to get the resources they need as fast as possible so they can get independent and start working under their own direction.

In conclusion, these decisions depends of how good we know ourselves and the modality we think will give us the highest amount of satisfaction depending on our personal goals and values.

## Specialization

The advantage we have of living in a society surrounded by all kinds of people is that when it comes to work, each one of us can focus and specialize in doing the things we do best and enjoy the most, while at the same time benefiting ourselves from the work of other people. This in economy is called division of labor, and it's one of the main principles to achieve an efficient economy with a good growing potential.

The subject of specialization is related with independence because when we decide to focus on support work, then we will be able to specialized in really concrete things, and the more specialized we are the more valuable and useful we will be to the people or the organizations that want to hire our services.

When we decide that we prefer an independent type of work, specialization keeps being important but we will have to learn and acquire skills on a lot of subjects that will make our levels of specialization much lower. Since people who decide to follow independent work have to make the decision over which direction to go, and they have to work with other people who can help them in that road, most of the times they have to become generalist and learn a little about many subjects. This will help them get a clearer understanding on how things work so they can communicate much better with others and use more effectively the services of other people who have higher levels of specialization in certain areas.

## Credentials

Having credentials is necessary to perform many types of jobs. Credentials are the things that tell other people that we can do some sort of job or it tells them with some level of trust that we have certain skills and we can use them.

Credentials can take many forms. The most common are the ones we get through degrees or certificates when we complete a cycle of formal education and we can call these Formal Credentials. When we finish school, university, or even an advance degree, we will receive a document that validates that we have finished that process and received the instruction on a particular subject. These types of credentials are very important when we decide we want to do support work and having them can translate into a big increase in our salary or honorariums. Different people and organizations give different importance to those credential because many times that a person has that piece of paper doesn't guarantee that they can perform the job in a competitive manner. In some cases, the law requires some certification or even permission from some authority in order to perform some jobs. For example, in most countries these type of credentials are required to work in medicine or law.

Acquiring formal credentials can be expensive in both time and money and we must analyze very well if it is worth pursuing those credentials because many times our current educational systems are more interested in certifying the higher amount of people even in cases where people don't have enough knowledge and skills to perform some activity.

There are other types of credentials that can also be very useful to prove the things we can do. When we have managed to use our skills to do something competitive in the world and we have evidence of it, then we will be able to show other people that we indeed have those skills and that will give us more credibility. All the achievements we've had and all the things we've created, can be a good credential to show other people or organizations that want to hire us in case we're looking for support work, or in case our work is independent, we can show those credentials to our clients to give them confidence that the products or services we are offering them can really satisfy their needs.

If our focus from the beginning is independent work, then

formal credentials won't be as important because our clients won't be as interested in those credential but they will give more importance to the trust we generate in them through our achievement and reputation.

No matter what type of credentials we require, it is very important and it can give us great advantages to keep increasing both the quantity and the quality of those credentials. This will increase the opportunities presented to us and it will allow the world to have more trust in us and that can help us benefit ourselves much more from our work and have a bigger impact.

# Finances

This area is about the way we acquire and manage money. A good handling of our money can give us a huge growth in many areas while a poor one can become one of the main sources of complications and problems in our lives.

Money by itself has very little effect on helping us feel good, but when we use that money in harmony with our core values and the things we consider important or required to enjoy life, then that money can become a big foundation for our well-being.

The knowledge on how to manage money is rarely acquired by people despite its big impact in all our lives. This can be because the cultures or our educational systems don't teach that knowledge, because a lack of curiosity or simply because we don't know that knowledge exists. There are several principles that if we apply in our lives can help us gain mastery over our finances and enjoy all the advantages that this implies.

Good money management concerns several aspects. First is the way we acquire it and the way we spend it. Aside from that is the way we use that money as a source of leverage that can really facilitate many aspects of our lives or create very serious difficulties. In the following sections I will talk about each one of these aspects: income, expenses, saving, debt, investing and security.

## Income

Income has to with all the ways we acquire our money. The amount of money we earn is important but it's not the only consideration. The way we acquire our money is also very important and we must keep it in mind while planning this aspect of our lives.

Money can be acquire in several ways. The first of them is through presents from other people or through luck. When we're little kids, probably most of our money comes from our parents or the people who take care of use. Other manifestations of this type of income are things like donations, inheritances, prizes, lotteries, or any type of gambling.

As we grow we start acquiring some physical and mental skills that allows us to perform certain jobs that can give us some income. Our work becomes then the second way of acquiring money and we already talked a little about it in the previous section.

A third way of acquiring money is using the money we have available and putting it in investments that can give us additional income without our constant intervention.

The fourth way of generating income is when through our work we create something like a product, business, piece of art, or any other creation, and once created, these things have the potential to keep earning us money even if we stop working. A good example are the royalties we receive when we publish a book or launch a new record. This income can also presents in the form of dividends from a business once we stop working full time on them.

The problem with the first way of earning income, that means presents, is that we have very little control or in many cases no control at all over it. We depend entirely on luck and on the good will of other people and the resources they have. It is for this reason that depending exclusively on this type of income once we reach our adult life becomes very risky and inefficient.

Work is the option most of us have to acquire money when we're just starting and don't have any other capital. The works we do depend on our mental and physical dexterities and the credentials we have. The bigger those dexterities and the bigger our credentials, the higher will be the chances that we find jobs that give us a higher amount of money in less time, and in some cases, even with less effort.

As I said in the previous section, those works can be of support or independent. Different people have different preferences over which type of work they want to do and if they can do it depending on their particular circumstances. While there are some people who only have available support work, there are others who only have independent work available,, and still others who can choose between the two. One basic way of independent work is commerce, where people acquire some product so they can sell it later for a bigger price and gain a profit.

Relying exclusively on our work to generate income is also very risky because at any time and for many circumstances we can lose that job and be left with nothing. This implies that we have to look for another job, and this can be an easy or complex process depending on many factors, among them: luck. It is also possible for us to get a disease or have an accident that keep us from working and that means that our income from this aspect can disappear and we will be depending on the will of other people or on luck in order to acquire some money to survive.

Here is where the last two ways of acquiring money come, be it by putting our money on some investment or creating things that allow us to generate passive income. The ideal is that we try to integrate as soon as possible one of these two sources of income because they will allow us to stop being limited by the time we have available for working or for the luck and will of other people.

Acquiring these two types of income can be a complex process and there are many ways to get them. Depending on our particular circumstances and on our skills, there will be different methods available to us for getting these types of income. The things in which we can invest or the things we can create will depend on our interest, the places we are, the people we know, and the resources we have. It is usually required to try several things until finding those that allows us to obtain the levels of income we want.

Ideally, we should try to integrate all 4 ways of getting income into our lives. Over the first one we don't have much control but on those occasions we receive money that way, be thankful and use that money for our advantage. The other three ways of acquiring money are under our control and developing them depends on the decisions we make throughout our lives and the things we decide to focus on.

## Expenses

Earning money is important, but something that truly defines a good management of our personal finances is the way we spend it and how we use it.

We people need money to do many things. The first of those things is to satisfy our basic needs. Needs such as food, shelter, clothing, health, and transportation, are basic things we need to survive and do our daily activities. Even though these are basic needs, there are many ways we can satisfy them. We can do it in the most simple way by using the things that nature give us for free, or we can do it in a really luxury and expensive way by eating the most exotic foods prepared by the best chefs, dressing in really fancy clothes, living in huge palaces, and so on. This means that the amount of money we spend on this item can vary hugely, from practically nothing to real fortunes.

Aside from our basic needs, other of the things we can spend our money is acquiring tools. Those tools can have two destinies, the first are the tools we need to do our work and the second are the tools we need to enjoy our hobbies and to enjoy life in general.

When we plan to acquire some tool we will find that there

are many options to choose from. Tools come in many different tiers and all of them have different functions, are made from different materials, and their construction can make them of higher or lower quality and that will give them a different duration. Each one of these aspects affects the price of those tools or products and that's why we must define very well which are the needs we pretend to fulfill with that tool in order to define if we really need it, and if we do, which of all the options is the one that adapts the best to our requirements. Being systematic while acquiring tools will allow us to manage our money more efficiently and then use the money we save to make investments or put it to other uses we consider valuable.

Regarding tools, it is not always required to buy them if we just intent to use them for one time or very rarely. We can borrow the tool from other person or we can rent it, this way we will be managing our money more efficiently.

Another of our possible expenses are all those activities we do for our own enjoyment, for our growth or for work. There are many recreational activities in which we can spend our money. Activities like concerts, traveling, any type of show, social reunions, among many others. There are also activities we do for our growth, things like formal education, conferences, seminars, etc. Lastly, it is possible that some of the works we do, instead of giving us income, require that we spend money in order to perform them. This could be because things didn't come out as we planned or because we decided that we wanted to do that type of work for any other benefit or because it was associated with our values. Each one of those things can generate extra expenses in our lives.

The last way how we spend our money are through other people, when we give or donate them the money directly, or when we pay to satisfy some of their basic needs, buy them tools or pay for the activities they do. This type of expense is usually associated with family. We usually take care of the expenses of our kids whey they're small and in some cases even in their adult age. It is also possible to do it with other members of our family, be it our parents, siblings, romantic partner, or any other person we're helping. This can also be a very valuable use of our money, specially when are core values are related to things like family, friendship or even solidarity. When we're single and we have no kids, the expenses in this area probably won't be as high and this can be an advantage so we can use some of that money to invest it and keep growing in that early part of life.

We people spend our money on any of the 4 previous ways. The amount of money we spend depend on our needs, our habits, and our tastes. One of the principles to keep in mind is not letting that the money we spend on these items be higher that the money we earn. If we respect this principle we'll be able to save and that can increase our sources of income and allows us to increase our expenses in the future in case we want to.

## Saving

When we spend less than we earn then we'll be able to save. Saving is the foundation for growing financially and to achieve each time higher levels of income and expenses in a sustainable and responsible way. The higher the percentage of money we save from the money we earn, the faster we'll be able to reach many of our goals such as the acquisition of new tools, the acquisition of investments that allows us to reduce the time we spend working for money, or even it will allow us to retire and that can turn work into something optional.

The key with saving is our self-control. We must manage our expenses in a very responsible and efficient way. We should try to spend money only on the things that are really valuable to our lives and always trying to keep our expenses below our income. Developing this capacity for self-control is a goal that most people should set as soon as possible because its effects on many other aspects of life is very meaningful.

## Debt

The opposite of saving is debt. In reality there are two types of debts, one being good debts and other bad debts as Robert Kiyosaki says.

When our expenses become bigger than our income then we will have to borrow money to pay for them and in that case we are talking about bad debts. This type of debt is the one that don't let us grow, and if we don't manage it carefully, it can become one of the main sources of stress in our lives.

The other type of debt can help us grow and because of this it can be consider good debt. These are the debts we use to acquire investments that allow us to generate additional income. When we borrow money we usually have to pay some interest depending on how long we take to pay them and also on other factors. If we only acquire debt for investments that allow us to earn more than those interests, then those debts will be positive to our lives.

Debt management is another essential part of our personal finances. As a first step we must try to eliminate any kind of bad debt in case we have them, and once we're free of those debts, define if we want to invest only with the money we save or use also money coming from good debts. Both strategies are valid but depending on the investment and the type of situation we find ourselves, we must analyze which is more convenient.

## Investments

When we implement saving in our lives we'll be able to start accumulating money and that will allow us to maintain a reserve. We can use that money in two ways. The first one is using it for our different expenses. This is a valid use and in some cases necessary, but the other use we can give to the money we've saved and that will have a more positive impact in our finances is investing it.

Investing consists on making our money work for ourselves so it can generate more money. This can be done in several ways, for example, by acquiring properties to rent or by acquiring things that have the potential of increasing in value so we can sale them later to generate a profit.

In formal terms, the most common investments are things related to real state which can be properties such as houses, offices, warehouses or pieces of land. These properties have the potential of generating income both through their rents as well as increasing their value in order to gain capital gains. We can also invest in any business directly or indirectly through the stock market so we can obtain income from dividends and also when our stocks increase their prices. Any thing we can acquire that we can rent or that has the potential of increasing its value can be consider an investment.

Every investment requires at least some management and monitoring, and this means that a minimal work from our part will always be necessary. Good management can usually be the most important factor to turn a bad investment into a good one, or vice versa. Because of a bad administration, a good investment can become a real source of loses.

Regarding investments it is also important to talk about risk. It is never guarantee that we will obtain the profits we expect. There will always be the possibility of things not going as planned and our earning can be less than we expected or we may even get loses. That risk is always going to be present when investing so we must learn to not freak out and keep our tranquility in those moments when the results we get are not as expected.

As with everything, learning to invest requires knowledge, practice and experience. Anything we invest requires that we understand how it works if we sincerely expect to obtain some profit from it. There will be times when we can trust other people to invest our money but we must be very careful since no one is going to care so much about our own resources as ourselves.

Investments give us freedom just as long as they're managed by other people most of the time or that the time they require from us be minimal. If we have to be looking after an investment all the time then that won't be a real investment that generate us passive income but a self-imposed type of work.

The power of investments comes from not being limited to time as ourselves. If we manage them properly, it is possible to have control over a big amount of investments at the same time and that will allow us to grow much faster and increase more and more our financial resources. The process of investing is slow at the beginning and requires a lot of effort but as our investments start to grow, they start getting traction and each time it will be easier to keep growing and reaching level of income that would have been impossible to obtain from our work alone.

## Security

Regarding the proper management of our personal finances, it is also important to talk about security. There are many situations we can find in life that can create a huge damage to our finances. Situations such as losing our jobs, a big unexpected expense, a business not going as planned, or even a natural catastrophe which could have affected or destroyed some of our properties or investments. All of those things can occur and it is important to think about strategies that allow us to be less exposed to them and lower the impact they have so we can recover more easily.

There are many strategies to protect against those risks. On the first place, to avoid that losing a job or a disease affects us gravely, it is important to incorporate other sources of income into our lives such as investments or things we've created with our work. Another important aspect to lower the impact is to have good flexibility in our expenses so we can reduce them to a minimum in case we lose some of our income level for any reason.

When it comes to natural catastrophes, there are many insurances that can protect us against them. For example, if we have a property such as a house, then it will be possible to acquire an insurance in case of a fire, earthquake or any other natural event. Acquiring those insurances is not free and that's why we need to analyze if we should really acquire them considering both the cost of the insurance and the probabilities of those events really happening.

There will be times when we have an unforeseen expense. For example, we or someone close to us can get seriously ill or suffer an accident and that can require us to spend big amounts of money on medical care and even surgeries, and this can represent a major setback in our finances. It is also possible that an essential tool for our work or for our daily life breaks, gets lost or stolen, and we may need to replace it immediately which will generate an expense we didn't have in our budget.

There are several ways how we may manage these situations. The first one is by keeping a reserve of money through saving so we can face those expenses in case they occur. Another strategy is to maintain open credit in case we need to borrow money in an instant and under good conditions that allows us to pay that debt in a comfortable way. When we don't have easy access to credit and we don't have any savings, then we will be force to make drastic choices like selling some of the things we have for a price really below its true value, borrowing money from other people under very abusive circumstances, or even, we may be forced to do jobs we wouldn't have done if it weren't for the emergency caused by that unexpected expense.

Keeping in mind the subject of security while managing

our personal finances is very important to be able to feel really calm and to know we're prepare to face many types of situations.

Setting goals in each one of these areas of our personal finances is very important. Having goals related to how we earn and spend our money, with the quantity of the money we save, with the debts we get ourselves into, with the investments we acquire, and with the different strategies that allows us to face some unforeseen events, are all important elements of our personal finances which is a big source of resources and opportunities for many of the things we want to do in life.

# Tools and Places

Tools and places are two of our external resources. In the first chapter I talked briefly about them and now I will talk about both of these resources in a more detailed way.

Tools and places are one of the main advantages we have over animals and it is one of the main reasons why we can do many different types of activities and have so much impact even with all our physical limitations that make us inferior in many aspects to other creatures.

Both tools and places can help us do things we need to feel good. By themselves they can be a source of pleasure and they can also help us do activities that give us pleasure and joy. They don't affect happiness that much but we can appreciate the things we have and that can increase our happiness levels.

Tools and places have a big effect in satisfaction because they allow us to do many things we need to achieve the goals that are associated with our core values.

There are several types of tools and places and there are different ways we can access them. Next I will talk about all these aspects so we know what things we need to keep in mind when setting the goals associated with these resources.

In total, there are 3 types of tools we need in life: daily-life tools, work tools and hobbies tools. There are also some tools that can have several of these functions depending on how we use them.

## Daily-life tools

Daily life tools are those things we need to satisfy our basic needs. These tools can help us satisfy needs such as hunger, shelter, transportation, communication, maintenance and rest.

Among these tools is our furniture and the appliances we have in our houses like for example: beds, chairs and everything we need to prepare and consume our foods. Transportation vehicles such as bicycles, bikes, cars, planes, and communication devices like phones and the Internet, belong also to this category. We need several of these things to carry on with our daily lives and to satisfy the needs we need to survive.

As I said in the previous section where I talked about expenses, there are many way we can satisfy those needs. The most basic is using our body to do many activities and using the raw elements that nature provides us. When we do this we'll notice that the less tools we use to do some activity the higher the effort it will require from us and the longer we'll take to do it. Here is where it becomes a good strategy to try to get or even build tools that help us do each one of these activities in a more efficient way so we can save time and energy to pursue the other projects or activities we want.

## Work tools

The other type of tools are our work tools. These tools are the ones we need to increase any of our resources or to create the impact we desire in the world or in other people. Improving our work tools can also help us increase our productivity and that will make us more competitive for society in general and other people.

When it comes to defining what tools we need to do our job, we must analyze very carefully our real needs and the things we plan to do with those tools. Having this clear on our minds will allow us to choose those tools that are going to be really useful to do the things we want without limiting us and at the same time without getting into unnecessary costs.

Regarding work tools, the idea is to replace them only when they stop working and can't be fixed, or when the new tools we plan to acquire really give us a huge increase of productivity.

## Hobby tools

We call hobbies to all the activities we do that aren't related to our job or to satisfying our basic needs. We do these activities for our own enjoyment or comfort. We can do these activities on our own or with other people and in many cases, they can be the greatest sources of joy we experience in life.

Some examples of these activities are things like sports, the production or enjoyment of any form of art such as music, dancing, theater, visual arts, literature, among others. They can also be social gatherings or any thing we do to entertain ourselves.

Many of these activities require some tools. Some of those tools may be optional but others are essential to do those activities. For example, if we want to play the piano, one essential tool we need is the piano, which could go from a simple electronic toy keyboard to a big grand piano. There may be other tools that could be useful but not absolutely required: things like piano exercise books, amplifiers, earphones or any other type of accessory.

Since the amount of hobbies we can have could be really high, that means that we must be very careful when acquiring tools for them. The first thing we must do is getting those tools we need to satisfy our basic needs and our work needs in the level we desire. After having what is needed and essential in these two categories, then we can start getting the tools we need for our different hobbies. The reason for this is that both our everyday tools as well as our work tools can really help us grow and progress, while our hobbies tools are usually good for enjoying the moment but they don't have that big of an impact in our future. If we focus exclusively on getting these type of resources then we may risk getting stuck financially. One of the reason many people have problems managing their expenses is that they spend more than they should in these type of tools and because of that their finances are not very healthy.

The amount of money we spend on these tools should

depend on our level of commitment to each one of our hobbies. We can assign more money to those activities we are the most committed, and be careful of spending too much on things we seldom do and that are not as meaningful to our well-being.

## Sites and places

We can also put all our goals related to the places we want to live or work inside this area. It may be that we want to move to those places, or it can be that we are already at those places and we must do some things that allows us to stay in them.

We can have access to different opportunities and resources depending on the places we are. This makes that looking for a new place to live or work be the best thing we can do depending on our goals. Moving to a new place can be a complex process and in many situation it depends a lot on the luck we have and the opportunities we have available. A change of place can also be a good strategy in case we want to give our life a new beginning. We'll be able to change some of the activities and the people that surround us, and that can help us as a motivation to do new things and to keep growing in case we feel we are in a rut.

Real state properties are also included in this area of our lives. Different properties can give us different comforts and they can be required for acquiring and storing certain types of tools. When we have a big house it will be possible to get many big-sized tools that we wouldn't have be able to get if our home would have been smaller. Places where we can work, study or recreate ourselves are other important resource we should keep in mind. The higher the number of places we have access to, the more activities we will be able to do and this could be important when pursuing some goals.

## How to acquire tools and places

There are many different ways we can acquire the tools and places we need. Some of them imply that we spend some money while others may be free or cost us something different than money.

The first way to acquire any type of tool or place is buying them with our money. In many cases this will be the best option since we will have complete control over the things we acquire and that can give us more flexibility when using them. This option is the best when we plan to use them very often and for a relatively long time.

The second way of acquiring tools and places is by renting them. The big advantage of this way of accessing these resources is that we need less money to be able to use them and that can help us access things that because of their price would be very difficult for us to buy. Renting instead of buying can be useful when we only think on using a tool or place for a very short time, when we don't plan on using them that often, or when we simply don't have the money to buy them.

The last way of accessing the tools and places we need is through our social relationships and the exchanges we do with other people in a commercial or friendly way. It is possible to develop a good network of people that can kindly lend us some of their tools in case we need them. It is also possible to create reciprocal relationships with other people where we put at their disposal the tools and places we have and they do the same for us. This last method can be very useful when we have very little money and can help us move forward in the early stages of our development.

## How to get rid of tools and places

It is also important to think about how we plan to get rid of the things we don't need anymore. We can do this by selling those things, renting them, giving them away or simply throwing them away. Here is where it comes important to put attention to the real value of things before buying them and analyzing how quickly they lose their value after we buy them. This can be a decisive factor when choosing tools since maybe getting a more expensive one will allow us to sell it later and regain some of its value. If we would have chosen a cheaper one, then it is probable that after we stop using it no one else would be interesting and we would be force to throw it away and with that losing everything we paid for it.

Other thing I suggest is getting used to getting rid of the things we don't need as fast as possible so we can maybe recover some of the value we pay for them and at the same time benefit other people who may still find those things valuable.

# Romance

Romance is an area of life that has one of the biggest effect on the way it makes us feel since through it we can experience some of the highest expressions of pleasure, joy and satisfaction we may feel in life.

Romance is a very complex area in life since it involves high levels of intimacy with other people and that can be the source of many conflicts caused by problems of communication or personal differences that can make us feel stressed and concerned.

The area of romance implies several aspects that make it a little more complex but because of the huge impact it can have on the way we feel, it is important that we learn to manage this area in the best way possible and put ourselves goals that allow us to get from this area as many positive experiences as possible.

Romance can be a double edge sword because it can give us some of our bigger satisfactions in life but it can also complicate our lives very seriously and be the origin of many of our main problems and sufferings.

Regarding romance it is important to understand several feelings such as lust, love, attachment, and subjects such as sex, dating, commitment, marriage and even breaking up.

## Lust, love and attachment

Dr. Helen Fishers says that there are three brain mechanism associated with the search for a romantic partner and these are lust, romantic love and attachment. She says that many times they can be confused but they're not the same and they can present by themselves or with the others at the same time.

Lust is a process in which a person starts to interest us romantically and sexually. The reason for this interest can come from an infinite number of causes. Some of them may be biological or genetic that make us respond to certain physical traits and also to certain types of personality. The interest for other person can also be born from our past experiences, the relationships we've had with our parents, our self-esteem, and many other circumstances that are not always easy to identify but that can suddenly spark our interest for another person to the point that we spend a big part of our time thinking about them.

This desire is rarely a rational process. We don't have control over which person we feel attracted to and which we don't. We may also feel sexually attracted to several people at the same time.

Something to keep in mind with lust is that we may feel attracted for the things we perceive and not necessarily for the real characteristics the other person have. It is possible that we may be idealizing the other person by putting them qualities they don't really have and that may be affecting our levels of attraction. Other thing to keep in mind with lust and attraction is that just as it can appear suddenly for another person, it can also disappear the same way for many different reasons. Lust is usually the starting point when starting a romantic and passionate relationship with some else, but by itself it's not enough to make that a lasting and constructive relationship for us, or in other words, a relationship that can gives us real pleasure, joy and satisfaction. If our goal at any moment is not to have a lasting relationship then lust alone can be enough, but if our goal is to be in a relationship with the characteristics I just mentioned, then there will be another important requisite called love.

Romantic love is another feeling that in most cases is based on high levels of attraction but it has higher levels of maturity where, besides being just a feeling, it is also a way of acting and thinking about the other person and it is affected more by reason. Love implies a decision to act in certain ways where we care for the well-being. of the other person and we learn to accept in a more unconditional way many of their qualities and defects. When we love another person and they also love us back, then we'll usually take them into account when making many of our decisions and that can really affect the shape our life takes as well as the things we can do.

Love is based on decisions, the decisions to act in certain ways, the decision to express ourselves in certain ways and also the decision to give the other person a higher level of important in our lives. This in most cases is not easy to do because it depends not only on what we do, but also on what the other person does and the decisions they take regarding us.

The third brain mechanism associated with this subject is called attachment. This is what we feel for someone we have been for a very long time and with whom we have experienced many things. Dr. Fisher says that the reason for this attachment is so we learn to tolerate the other person long enough to be able to raise kids with them and that it can also be useful to keep two people together for a very long time.

Experiencing lust, love and attachment, can be one of the biggest sources of joy we may have in life and it is therefore important to try to integrate them into our lives.

## Sex

Sex is one of the experiences that can give us the most physical pleasure in life. By itself, sex can be a true source of pleasure, but when it is joint by feelings of love, it can also become one of the greatest sources of joy and satisfaction.

Most of us have a strong sexual need coming from our genetic configurations as well as from the culture in which we move. Having physical contact with a person we feel attracted, and reaching climax through ejaculation or orgasm, are great experiences we need in life and they make of life a more fun and interesting experience. That is why we must learn to include this aspect into our lives in the way we consider most convenient.

Sex is also the main characteristic that differentiate romantic relationships from other relationships such as friendships or the relationships we have with our family. Through sex it is possible to reach a level of intimacy with other person that would be very difficult to reach just by talking or sharing other types of activities.

One of the main risks is that sex is also the way we have kids and this is something that implies a big level of responsibility and it can seriously affect our lives. In case we don't desire kids because we don't think that the time or the person we're with is not the right one, or simply because we don't plan to have kids, then we need to take all the preventive measure we can to avoid a pregnancy, but also having present that in many cases it's impossible to completely remove the risk of it happening. The way we implement sex in our lives depends a lot on what we think about this risk and also about our other goals. Other risk associated with sex is that we may get some sort of disease. There are some diseases that can be cured by simply taking some pill while there are others that can even kill us. This is another risk we must be aware of so we learn to use the different resources we currently have to protect ourselves.

## Dating

When we're attract to someone else, usually our first encounters with them would be through dating. Dating means spending time with other person talking and sharing any type of activities with the goal of getting to know them and maybe starting a romantic relationship. When there's a minimal level of interest from both parts then a first date can happen and from that moment the interest level in any or both people can grow, decrease or even disappear depending on the interactions and that will define what will happen in the future.

Since attraction doesn't really tells us anything really trustworthy from the other person, it is through dating that we really get to know who the other person is and if we feel good when we're with them. Dating can also be a great source of joy and it is the way we spend the most time with the person we're interested in when starting a relationship. Even in those circumstances when a relationship moves to higher levels of commitment and familiarity, keep going out on dates can really help maintain the passion and romance.

## Commitment

When two people discover that they feel good together and there are high levels of attraction or even love between them, then it is possible that with time those two people decide to commit to each other and decide to make their relationship exclusive where they will stop seeing and dating other people romantically and where they will involve the other person in many other aspects of their lives.

This commitment is not absolutely necessary for having a romantic relationship with someone else. A relationship can be very enjoyable even if it just stays in spending time through dating and having casual sex. Commitment is a stage that can affect both positively and negatively some relationships. In some cases it may destroy the relationship when two people are not really compatible or when their love doesn't have good foundations. It may also be possible for commitment to be a requisite so two people can stay together. Deciding if committing or not to another person depends a lot on every specific circumstance, on the differences of the people involved, what they want for their lives and what they're willing to give or share.

## Marriage

Marriage is a formality that many people use to make the commitment they have for each other official. Since marriage is such a cultural aspect, it may be possible that people for many different types of pressures or expectations, decide to get married without giving it the proper consideration.

Getting married has certain legal effects that can be risky in case the relationship doesn't work out. There are financial risks and usually the person who has more properties, resources, and income, can face big loses.

Deciding to get married is a very important decision that needs to be properly considered by both parts. We should also be conscious that being married is not an absolute condition for enjoying a healthy and committed relationship that provides big doses of pleasure, happiness, and satisfaction for the parties involved.

Since marriage requires a higher level of intimacy, commitment, and interdependence, it is require that there is a certain level of compatibility between the two people so there can be some harmony in the relationship. The compatibility that is required is not so much of the particular tastes or personality, but more about the core values they have and the way they think about aspects that are very important in a marriage such us the decision to have kids and how to raise them, how to manage money, ideological values, and so on. Many of the differences in personality can be complementary and they allow the couple to work as a team where both make the effort to reach the things that are important for them.

Something that is seen in many marriages and long-term relationships is the evolution of the feelings of attraction and love through time. When a relationship is just starting there is a strong attraction which is the source of passion in the relationship. As time goes on, those levels of attraction start diminishing. Some experts say that the duration of those high levels of attraction last for two years average. As time passes and depending on the things that happen in the relationship and the experiences they have, it is possible for the feeling of love to keep growing more and more. It may not become as intense as the initial levels of attraction but it is much more stable and this gives it the potential to grow also to very high levels with time.

Marriage has some psychological effects, both positive and

negative, that can affect the relationship and its dynamics. On the one hand, getting married to someone can give us a sense of belonging and acceptance that can help us feel good even when we're going to some tough times. A negative effect of marriage is that sometimes people stop trying to keep attractive to their partner and they start taking less care both on their appearance and the things they do. It is possible that they start to think that the other person should accept them no matter what they do and this attitude can transform or even destroy many relationships. Another aspect regarding marriage is that when people decide to live together, the familiarity between them grows so much that the relationship may turn into a simple management of resources or daily activities and the things that gave the relationship so much pleasure, joy and satisfaction could be left aside.

## Break-ups

Romantic relationships can end no matter what stage they are and this implies the separation of the people involved. It is possible that this occur even before the first date or even after being married for 50 years or more. That a relationship ends doesn't necessarily means that it failed. A relationship could have been worthy no matter how long it lasted just as long as both people enjoyed most of the time they spent together and those people have benefited from the relationship which implies that the relationship hasn't been destructive or harmful for any of the parts involved.

Many times the reason for the separation can be communication problems that aren't solved in time. Other times break-ups occur because the people involved have very different values or want different things for their future. There are times when two people can feel good in the relationship but for some particular circumstance in the life of one of them they can be force to break up temporarily or permanently.

Break ups in most cases are hard emotionally since losing from our lives someone who at some time was very important for us is a painful process. Depending on the relationship and the reason for breaking up this pain and sadness can vary in magnitude and it make take different times to heal.

# Family

Family is another area of life. This area has a big impact throughout all our lives. On the one hand, as we're growing up and we depend on our family for our survival, from them comes many of the opportunities that we have access as well as the culture we develop and our way of thinking. Those aspects I just mentioned can also be influenced by our own decisions, but in most cases and for most people, family is a determinant factor in them.

For many people the family they grew with are their parents and in some cases their siblings. This is the traditional family that have been seen through history, but in many cases the composition of this family can change and the heads of the family could be the grandparents, uncles or aunts, or even foster parents. There are also some people that have been raised by their older siblings or that from a very early age they had to raise by themselves for certain circumstances in their lives. Each one of these compositions can have some positive and negative effect in people. It can affect their psychological composition as well as the things they do in their adult life.

# Children

As we grow, the natural process is that we start separating from the people who raise us and we start depending less and less on them as time passes.

At this point, or maybe a little later, some people decide to start their own family by getting a partner and having children. The future of the romantic relationship can end in the early stages or it can go on until the death of one of them, but once one have children, the relationship with those children, be it good or bad, usually lasts for life.

First of all, our children can be a true source of joy and satisfaction in our lives. Children can also affect many of the decisions we take in each area of our lives since having them has a strong psychological impact that can make us change many things in our character and personality and it may even modify some of our core values.

Having children implies a requirement of some of our resources such as money and time and that can keep us from getting some of the other goals we have in life or it can make more difficult their achievement. Once we are financially responsible for another person then we must become more careful in the way we manage our money. Sometimes we may need to reduce our expenses associated with recreation and in many cases we become more conservative.

Another aspect to keep in mind with children is that we can help them grow by giving them some of the resources they need to develop but at the end of the day they are independent people that can choose any road they want to follow and this can sometimes become a big source of stress and concern for the parents. It is important to accept that what we can do as parents is very limited and the biggest impact we have in our children is only in the first years of their lives. We must do this so we learn to maintain some tranquility no matter the road our children decide to take.

Since having kids is an event of such a huge impact, we must try to be as clear as possible on our goals regarding this aspect and think about them very strategically. Defining if we want to have kids or not is not an easy decision to make because all the pros and cons it implies and because a future event can make us rethink that decision. Other decision we must try to make consciously is looking the best time to have kids keeping in mind all the other goals we have in our lives, the state of our current resources and the things we may need if we have children. If we decide that we don't want children or we decide to leave it for later, then we must look for strategies that allow us to diminish the probability of it happening in an unexpected way so we can plan and execute our different life goals much more strategically.

## Close family

Our close family are those members that are related to us by blood or by law and with whom we interact frequently and they take part in many of the activities we do or have a big weight in the decisions we make. We usually feel closer to the family we grow with. Since our family are not people we chose to have in our lives, then we may observe that in some cases we may be very much like them and share their way of thinking, but in other cases we can feel like strangers that don't have a lot of common with them and this causes that we're not able to relate with high levels of intimacy with them.

Keeping good relationships with our close family is very important because family can be our only support in case things don't work out as we planned and we suffer a big setback in life. Having this support, and at the same time being a support for other members of our family, is a big need we humans have because the world is not always as kind as we wish and because we may make many mistakes and the only ones who would be willing to give us a second chance would be the members of our close family. The only case where taking distance from our close family would be a better strategy is when the relationships among them are very troubled and the behavior of some of those member are really self-destructive or their behavior with us is harmful and with bad-ill.

Family has many other positive aspects. On the one hand they can be our biggest source of joy and the time we spend with them can be the moments we remember more kindly throughout our life. Family gatherings and parties on some special occasions can be some of the best moments we have in our life and that's why we must take advantage of them while we still can.

The goals we can set regarding our close family can be deciding how close we want to be to them, the quality of the relationship we want to have with the different members of our family and deciding the specific things we must do to create and maintain those types of relationships.

## Further family

There are many members of our family that for many reasons don't play an active part in our lives and therefore they don't have such a meaningful impact in it. It is possible that we may see them once a year or even more rarely. This doesn't mean that we must completely forget about them or that trying to keep at least kind and positive relationship with them is not important. Some member of our further family can in some moment help us in a very meaningful way and they may even be willing to offer us opportunities that no one else would. The other thing is that we don't know who those members may be and that's the reason we should try to keep positive relationships with them in the few occasions we meet.

By speaking of children and our different family members, we learn what are the different considerations we must keep in mind when making decisions in this area. The goals we define regarding our family must also take into account the other areas of our lives, the things we want to get from them and the resources we have at our disposal.

# Social Relationships

We can group all the relationships we have with people outside our family or our romantic partners in this area called social relationships. Inside this area we can add all those relationships we have with friends, acquaintances, partners, contacts, teachers, mentors, pupils or followers.

These relationships really affect our life since they are one of the resources we can use. For example, some of our connections can be every important or even essential to be successful in many of the projects we have and also through many of these relationships we can experience or learn to experience any of the ways of feeling good: pleasure, joy, happiness and satisfaction.

## Friends

Friends are close people in our lives with whom we share many activities and intimate things and because of this they get to see how we really are without those masks we usually wear in front of other people in our lives. Through our friends we can live moments full of joy and they can also help us overcome difficult times in our lives.

Having a good group of friends is important because on the one hand we humans are social beings and in each of us there is that need to share time with others and feel accepted in certain contexts. On the other hand, friendships are important because they are of great help to reach many of the things we want and to see through an external and trustworthy source if what we do and the way others see us is in harmony what what we think of ourselves and our actions. We people have a blind spot when looking at ourselves so there are certain aspects of ourselves that we wouldn't be able to know if it weren't through the eyes and the perception of other people we can trust. Getting to know these aspects will allow us to make changes in ourselves that we wouldn't have realized were necessary without the help of those external sources.

# Connections

Since social relationships work as networks where each person knows others and those at the same time know different people, then it is possible to create a bast amount of connections and access many people that we would have thought unreachable. Each person has a social circle made up of family members, friends or simple acquaintances. The big advantages of social relationships is that we can access the people inside the social circles of the people we know and therefore the possible connections we can make becomes almost unlimited.

One important reason to keep in mind all these connections is that we're all different in many ways. We have different internal and external resources; we have access to different opportunities and also our values and our personalities are different. In many cases, and for most of the goals we can set in any area of life, we will need other people to execute them. We will need the resources they have, the opportunities they can offer us, or many other things. If we have access to those people then the chances of being successful in many of our goals will increase.

Having access to other people and taking advantage of these social networks requires that we also become valuable members of those networks. That means that through our resources, strengths, the things we know and the things we can do, we'll be perceived by others as valuable connections and this way they will be more open to get to know us, help us, or even introduce us to other members of their social groups.

Because these different connections have so much impact and we don't know when we might need them, it is necessary that we put ourselves goals to develop them the best we can and turn them into one of the many resources we count on to reach our purposes.

## Mentors and guides

Life is complex and trying to learn all we need through experience and trial and error is a very slow, inefficient and in some cases painful strategy. This is the reason why throughout history there has always been people who pass the knowledge and learnings they have acquired to other people so they can accelerate their growing process.

The figure in charge of providing knowledge and guiding the experience of others to help them grow faster can take many forms and names. We could talk about teachers, mentors, coaches, counselors, guides, authors and experts, among many others. All these people through different mediums and methods have as their goal helping others grow faster than they could on their own and helping them learn the things they need to know about the world. This process is one of the many causes why we humans develop so quickly.

It doesn't matter what phase we're in life, there will always be cases when we can play the role of apprentice and in others the role of mentors. To be guides or mentors we don't need to be the number one expert of the world about something. The single fact of having more experience than other person in any particular area or having knowledge about doing something will let us guide other people to reach similar levels of performance in that area.

Since getting mentors or guides can speed up our

development we must keep this point in mind when setting our social life goals. We must also be conscious that we can also be mentors on some issues for other people.

# Recreation

The last area of life is recreation. This area involves all those activities we do for our own enjoyment. They are activities that are associated with some of the 4 ways of Feeling Good, in other words, if they don't make us feel good in some way they're not recreation. One characteristic of recreation is that they are activities more of consumption than production. In general, they are things in which we spend time, money or energy but not necessarily for gaining something or increasing our resources but more as a way to feel good.

There is an unlimited number of recreation activities in which we can spend time so it is necessary that we give it a little though to decide which of them have the greatest potential of making us feel good so we can distribute more efficiently our time and other resources among them. Something to keep in mind is that there will always be interesting things we could be doing and knowing that we are missing them can cause us anxiety. The key to handle this issue is to accept we're not able to enjoy everything the world have to offer and try that the things we choose to spend our time on really have the potential to improve our life quality and the way in which we enjoy it.

## Passive and active recreation

Before talking about the specific things we can do to

entertain ourselves, it is important to talk about the difference between passive recreational activities and active ones.

When we speak about passive recreation we are talking about all those consumption activities where the effort we have to make is very low or even none. They are activities like watching television, listening to music, reading literature, seeing art, going to sport events or drinking alcohol, among others. This type of activities are very useful when we just want to relax from a hard day at work or other stressful situation. Doing this type of activities once in a while is good but one problem of turning them into our main source of recreation is that usually these activities have a negative impact on our health – both physical and mental – because that passivity make us more lazy to do other things and some of our different dexterities can start to atrophy. Another disadvantage of these type of activities is that the potential they have to help us experience satisfaction or joy is much lower than other forms of active recreation.

Active recreational activities are all those where we have to make a physical or mental effort to do them. Activities like sports, playing music, writing, painting, dancing, walking through nature, among many others, are activities that require a little bit more effort which can cause that they are not as pleasurable as passive activities of pure consumption, but they have a bigger potential of giving us joy and satisfaction. They even have the side effect of increasing our physical and mental dexterities.

A good strategy for getting the most our of this area is trying that most of our recreational activities are active ones and the few passive activities we do are for relaxing or in cases where we feel really tire physically or mentally. We can also try to do these activities with other people so they have a higher potential of giving us higher levels of joy.

## Travels

One of the forms of recreation that has the more positive effect in our life is traveling. Travelings allows us to remove ourselves of our day to day life and see other places, share with different people and discover new ways of living life and doing things. The world is huge in comparison to our size as humans, and because of this, even if want to and spend our whole lives getting to know it, the amount of places we could ever visit is very limited. This doesn't mean that our effort to know all we can is not valuable. Inside many people there is a strong need for exploration that can be fulfilled through travels and this can be an important source of satisfaction. Besides, travels can give us different perspectives to rethink the way we face many situations in life and they can help us understand the impact that we can have in other cultures as well as the impact other cultures have on us. This makes us more conscious of how dependent we are from one another so we appreciate more all our differences.

There are many types of travels we can do, some of them can be planned to the last detail while others can be of adventure where along the way we decide what we want to do next. There are travels we can do on our own or with others. Travels to know the most beautiful places of the world and travels that can also open up our eyes by showing us that not everything is nice and shining. Some people can even decide to become nomads where they spend more time traveling that on a fixed place.

## Arts

Art is also a very complete way of recreation and it offer several benefits. Among the different arts we can mention theater, dance, painting, drawing, sculpting, singing, music, and many more.

In art we can play the role of consumer and spectator where we appreciate and entertain ourselves with the artistic expressions of other people. We can also play the role of producers where we are the ones who express through it. Both of these are valid forms of entertainment, and when we became producers of art we can also become consumers at the same time when we appreciate what others do to learn from them.

To produce art we must develop several physical and mental dexterities and in many cases we must develop our creativity. This process can become demanding since developing new skills requires big effort, making mistakes and correcting them constantly.

The satisfaction of producing art comes when we improve and become able to do things we couldn't do before. It can also come when we see that the things we've created are appreciated by other people.

## Sports

Sport is other form of recreation where we can play the role both of participants and spectators. When we participate in a sport the aspect that it's worked the most is the physical one, but to perform competitively in some sports it may also be necessary to develop many other skills such as team work, the ability to keep focus, and the capacity of managing our emotions so they don't interfere with our performance.

Being sport spectators can also be a very gratifying experience in many cases because we tent to identify with some teams or players and watching them fight to achieve victory or overcome their limits can produce certain emotions that can make our life more interesting.

## Social gatherings

Getting together with other people and sharing time with them can also be a high quality recreational activity. We are social beings and sharing time with other people is an activity that can give us satisfaction and joy. Just as having conflicts with other people put us in a bad emotional state, working together with others, helping them in the things we can or simply having fun with them can be a good strategy to increase our levels of joy and to feel much better emotionally.

When programming social gatherings we can try to take advantage of all those situations that are considered special in different cultures and get together with people in dates such as birthdays, christmas and other celebrations. We can also play a more active part in this process and program all type of activities more frequently and invite other people to join them.

The ideas with the goals we set in the area of recreation is to define the activities we want to do by keeping in mind our resources, our interests, and trying that those activities really have the potential to make us feel good, or even better, that they could also increase some of our skills or resources.

# How to Set Goals

Now that we know the different areas of life and the types of goals related with each one of them, it is time to talk about the process how we can set our goals.

Setting goals is a constant process that requires good planning skills and where we must keep in mind everything we know about ourselves, our resources, and also the knowledge we have about the different areas of life and about the world.

The reason why this is a constant process is that all these factors are constantly changing. As the years pass we learn more things about each one of these subjects and this allows us to improve and adjust our goals to make them more effective to feel good. Our resources also fluctuate constantly where sometimes they increase and in others they diminish and we must be conscious of these changes so we can adjusts our goals.

## What are goals?

There are 3 characteristics that distinguish goals from dreams, desires and ideals.

The first characteristic of goal is the intention. It is not enough to just say that we would like to achieve something but we must also internally commit to figure out how we're going to achieve those goals and do the things we need to get them.

Very often, we listen to people say they'd like to get something in their lives but for the way they say it it's easy to realize that those are just dreams to them and that they don't really have the intention to achieve those things. This could be because they haven't thought about what pursuing that goal implies, that they internally feel they don't have the resources or that simply they think they don't deserve it. Because of any of these reasons they lack the conviction when they talk about what they want. When we set a goal we must have the conviction that we will do everything in our power to turn it into a reality and that we won't let it stay only on our imagination.

The second characteristic of goal is that they have a deadline. I will talk more about deadlines in a while but something worth mentioning is that one of the ways how intention is manifested in goals is when they have a clear deadline to be achieved. This deadline can vary depending on our current situation and the resources we have. It is possible that there are some things that we can't pursue or achieve in the short term and therefore we must wait and prepare ourselves for when we have the chance of pursuing them. Having a deadline is very important to plan the actions we must take more effectively and not waste time unnecessarily.

The third and last characteristic of goals is that they are measurable. This mean that there are some indexes that allows us to define if we have achieved a goal or not and at the same time it allows us to measure our progress. Having unclear goals is one of the main reason why the goals we set don't have the power to keep us motivated and why it becomes much harder or even impossible to define the things we have to do to achieve them.

# The 2 types of goals

In Life Strategy there are only two types of goals worth pursuing. The first are the goals that make us feel good through pleasure, joy, happiness or satisfaction, and the second are those goals that allows us to increase our resources so we can ultimately pursue the first type of goals. If what we want to do don't have the potential of making us feel good or of helping us increase our resources then it won't probably be worth doing.

When we're beginning our life or when we become serious in applying Life Strategy we'll find that most of our short term goals are from the second type, that means, goals that allow us to increase our resources. This is because goals are build one upon the other and to achieve more ambitious goals it will be required to go through many intermediary phases and goals.

Both types of goals have the power to keep us motivated. While in the first the motivation is more direct, in the second type we must remind ourselves that the reason for pursuing them is that they are a requisite to be able to do those things that really make us feel good.

As our life advances, we'll be able to dedicate more time to pursuing those goals that can make us feel good because we'll have many of the resources we need to do it.

# How to define goals

As I said previously, there are several things we need to keep in mind while defining goals.

The first are our core values. The first goals we should set are those related to our core values so they can help us experience satisfaction. This is because satisfaction is the way of *Feeling Good* that have the most impact in us since it helps us maintain a good state even in those times when we are not enjoying the other ways of *Feeling Good*.

Once we define which of our goals are related with our core values we can proceed to set all the other goals related to the first three ways of feeling good. After having these long term goals our next step is to analyze the things we need to reach them, in other words, analyze what resources we need and which are the intermediate goals required to achieve them.

## Short and long term goals

When we define goals the ideal is to first set our long term goals and from there start defining our shorter term goals that can be more specific manifestations of those long term goals or that can be intermediary steps we need to achieve to be able to pursue those goals.

I call Life Goals to the longest term goals we can think of. Those goals are the maximum things we can imagine we want to achieve in each area of life. The size of those goals is limited only by our imagination; by what we think is achievable; by our valuation of who we are, what we have and what we can ever have; and above all, by the relationship those goals have to each other.

The truth is that in life we can't have it all, if we are going to pursue some paths we will have to forget about many others. This makes the process of setting our goals a process of selection in which we have to give up many different things so that the things we choose do really have to potential of giving us the life we desire.

These life goals are also constantly evolving so it is necessary to review them constantly. Reviewing these goals constantly is important to keep present at all times what are our true purposes and this way check if what we're doing is really associated with those purposes. It is also important to review them constantly so we can make the corrections we find necessary based on the different learnings we get from our experience.

Having well defined life goals is one important first step but by themselves they don't have enough power to guide our day to day activities. Here is where it comes the importance of defining shorter term goals like goals of a few months, one year, or a maximum of 2 years. These short term goals have a bigger effect on our productivity but the secret for them to be really valuable and avoid spending time doing things of no use is to verify that those goals are really associated with our long term goals.

Getting a good balance on the goals we set, both inside each area of our life as well as between each one of those areas, requires a thoroughly process of planning since those goals will get into conflict with each other in case they require the same resources. The way we solve these conflicts is by giving up some of our goals or adjusting them so they become more viable. This adjustment of goals can be done by setting different deadlines or by decreasing their scope. Having conflict-free and well defined goals will give us mental clarity so we can focus almost all our efforts in the execution of those goals and this will increase the likelihood of achieving them.

## How to prioritize goals

We can have a huge number of different goals in each area of our life and a very important decision we have to make is giving them the right priority so we know in which ones to focus our main efforts and resources. This also helps us in case we find some problem or obstacle that keep us from pursuing some goal because it gives us some standards to know which one of them we can sacrifice.

Other concept that affects the priority we give our goals is the leverage they can offer us. There are some goals that because of the area of life they belong, they have the potential to ease or complicate the achievement of other goals in the future. The areas of life that I consider offer the most positive leverage are: personal growth, work, finances, romance and social relationships.

Reaching good levels of success in each one of those areas will open us doors to achieve other goals in the other areas much more easily. Personal growth affects everything we do and how effective we are and therefore their effect on any type of goal we decide to pursue is evident. Work also allows us to get money as well as increase all the other resources that are essential for pursuing our goals. Through a good management of our personal finances we will be able to acquire enough money to get the things we need and do some activities that allow us to achieve many types of goals in almost all areas. Romance has a huge effect in how it make us feel and it can give us a lot of motivation to pursue some of our most ambitious goals. Lastly, social relationships are an important source of both resources and opportunities and that's why managing well this part of our life can give us many advantages along the road.

## Balance

When we talk about setting goals a concept that appears frequently is that of balance. We can see balance from two different perspectives.

The first way we can see balance is in the sense of working constantly to achieve similar levels of development in each area of life. The second way to see it is by working to achieve similar levels on the four ways of feeling good, that means, that we can enjoy pleasure, joy, happiness and satisfaction in similar amounts or intensities.

Under my experience and what I've seen in the lives of other people, I propose that a more effective strategy is to focus on a few goals at the same time, put the most effort we can in them so we can achieve them as quickly as possible. Then, once we reach them, focus on others to keep repeating this process. In the short term we may be living an unbalanced life where we are focusing too much in some areas and very little in others. But when we observe our life long term in periods of 5, 10 or more years, we'll see that in general we will have good levels of achievement in all areas of life which would have been much more difficult to get if we had spent our last years working on each one of our goals at the same time but without giving enough dedication to any of them.

To end this chapter, goals are the ones that give us the direction we must take at each moment and to define them it is necessary to keep in mind several aspects related to ourselves such as the things we consider important (our values) and the resources we have. Also the quality of our goals depends a lot on the things we know about the world and about how each area of life works. All this knowledge is acquire little by little so the goals we set at the beginning can change, in some cases progressively an in others they can be radically transformed. The only way we will know if those goals need to be reviewed is by not letting them stay on only dreams or ideals and by starting to take action as quickly as possible to verify with the world and with reality the real viability of those goals. In case we see we need to correct them, then we should step back, do the necessary changes and get back to action. The execution of our goals becomes then step 3 of Life Strategy and about this I will talk on the next chapter.

# Chapter 4. What will you do?

The third and last step of Life Strategy is called "What will you do?". The objective of this step is to define the things we must do to achieve each one of our short-term goals, start executing those plans and see what results we get so we can make corrections in case it's necessary.

It is through this step that we manage to test in reality each one of our goals and this way express our core values by using all the resources we have. The two previous steps are essential to enjoy a life that make us feel good in every aspect but these steps by themselves are worthless unless they're joined by the actions that test them with reality.

We are born with many voids and deficiencies. We have voids in the way we think, in our resources, in our knowledge and in our dexterities. Each one of those voids can make us judge reality badly and make decisions that make us fail and not get the things we want. This is something totally natural for us humans and the process through which we start filling those voids little by little is through constant execution. Despite this, the fact of acting by itself is not enough. We only manage to fill those voids when the way we act is directed by some purposes, some principles and specially some intentions.

When we decide to do something because we want to achieve a goal and we use everything we know until that moment to define the goal, execute it, and we find that things didn't work out as we expected, then there is going to be a big possibility of filling some of those voids and that will let us be more effective the next time we try.

We face two big obstacles when doing this step. These obstacles are our minds and our emotions. Sometimes our minds play dirty and try to distract us or direct us to things that are less stressful to keep us from doing the things we need to progress in our goals. The reasons why our minds do this can be of every kind and it affects us all in different times of our lives. This is why it is necessary to train ourselves so we can manage this phenomenon more effectively.

Regarding our emotions, they also have a huge impact on the things we do. Emotions such as fear or anxiety can paralyze us because in life we don't have anything guaranteed and we don't know if we'll have success on the things we want to do. There will always be a risk in anything we do and our emotions can react excessively in front of those risks and keep us from acting as we should and this causes us to not be effective when getting one or several of our goals. Depending on our personality we react in different way to those risks. Some people are more adventurous or even like and pursue risks while there are others that are much more cautious and avoid taking risks at all cost. Each one of us is in some point inside those two extremes and we tend to be either more risky or careful. That is a natural configuration of us humans and we should respect it to some degree in order to feel comfortable and calm with ourselves. But at the same time we must learn to be flexible so that we become more risky or cautious depending on each particular situation, and the way we learn to know when to be either is by the wisdom we get from the world and the way it works.

There are other emotions such as desire or love that can make us actively pursue things that can move us away from our true goals and the things we consider important. Those desires in some way make us blind and don't let us see the negative effects that pursuing something have for our well-being and the possibility we have to feel good.

Since we humans face these two obstacles when executing the actions we need to reach our goals, then it becomes necessary to look for strategies that let us overcome or manage these obstacles in the most effective way. We can group those strategies in two modalities. The first one are tasks and the other are habits or routines. Each one of these modalities have their characteristics, uses and techniques to apply them in our lives. In the next sections I'll talk about all these aspects of tasks and habits but before talking about them I'll talk about the process through which we define what tasks and habits we should do and that process is called planning.

# Planning

After defining our short-term goals, that means, those goals that have a deadline of no more than one or two years, the next step is to plan specifically the actions we must take to reach those goals and see if we have enough resources to achieve them. In this step we define what tasks and habits we have to perform, the deadlines to do those activities, the order in which we should do them and the different resources we need.

This planning can show us that the goals we set are not viable and can't be completed in the time we have defined and this make it necessary for us to review them and change their deadline if possible, or if not, decide to focus on other goals.

If after planning we discover that the actions we should take are possible and we have or can get the resources we need to achieve those goals, then the next step will be to start executing those plans

Many people usually arrive to this point. They define what they want and set a plan to get it but they never start taking action, be it for lack of discipline; laziness; fear of failure, rejection or even success; or simply for lack of courage. This happen to all of us in many of our plans and this is why it is important to learn to overcome these obstacles so we can really start executing our plans and get the progress we want in the real world.

## Projects

The way we plan the achievement of all those goals that are relatively complex because of the amount of actions or resources they require is through projects.

There are many goals we can set that require very little steps to be completed and therefore their level of planning is not as high. On the other side there are goals that are much more complex and require that we think very well about all the tasks, habits, and resources we need to complete them and organize all those factors in a more systematic way.

Some simple goals can be those related with acquiring or buying a tool, getting used to sleeping 8 hours a day, flossing before going to sleep, among others. The planning of these goals is relatively simple and it is possible to know very well what we need to do to execute them without planning them in detail.

There are other goals that are not as simple, like for example writing a book, gaining financial independence, organizing a trip to other country, among many others. Those goals require that we sit to think about all the things we need to achieve them and organize those thoughts in clear projects. The ideal is that those projects are in writing and the basic points it should include are:

**1.** The main objective which is the goal we want to achieve.

**2.** The reasons why we want to achieve that goal so we can keep ourselves motivated.

**3.** The list of activities we should do where we include both tasks and habits. Inside this point we can also define the times we have for doing those actions so we can see if it is possible to achieve that goal in the desired time.

**4.** A list of all the resources we need such as money, knowledge, dexterities, tools, places, and the collaboration of other people. Inside this point it is important to think how we're going to get those resources we lack and that are essential for achieving our goal.

The previous are the basic points that every project should have but depending on the complexity of our goal it could be necessary to define other aspects such as specific objectives, budgets, and indicators that allow us to measure our progress at different times.

Many times we don't have all the information we need to define a complete project from the beginning and in these cases we must at least define what we need to get started and as we execute we'll add the details missing.

Being able to execute effectively a plan depends on factors such as the amount of resources we have, the time we have available to do it, the people involved and the skills they have, and other external factors such as competition and luck.

One recommendation regarding projects is that we don't try to work on more that five projects a the same time. A range of 3 to 5 projects at the same time will allow us to focus appropriately in each one of them and give them our best effort so the chances of having success in its execution increase.

## Efficiency

Efficiency is a term usually used in the area of management and it can be defined as the relationship among the resources needed or used to achieve some goal and the results we get. The less resources we use to achieve some goal the more efficient we will be and this is important because our resources are limited.

All our resources such as time, money, skills, physical energy and mental capacity have their limits and we can use them only in some projects and some tasks at the same time. This implies that if we're not very efficient when using those resources then the amount of activities we'll be able to do will be less and therefore the things we manage to get in our lives will also be less.

Efficiency depends on many aspects. The tools we have affect directly the efficiency of the processes in which we use them. Better tools allows us to do the same thing in less time, at lower cost and in many cases with less physical effort from our part. That is the reason why investing in better tools can be a good strategy to be able to do more things in our life and have more achievements.

Efficiency is also affected by our skills and by our capacity to use the tools we have. If we improve our knowledge about how something works or practice a skill for long enough, then it will be possible to reach higher levels of performance on those activities and therefore we will become more efficient when doing them.

One more way how we can increase the efficiency is by distributing the work among many people so each one can focus on those things he does better and this way a project can be finished in less time than it would take a single person.

Trying to be efficient when planning the achievement of our goals will allow us to get them with less resources and then we could use the rest of our resources to pursue other projects.

# Tasks

Many of the actions we must take to progress in any goal are things that we only have to do for one time and in general they will let us do other actions later. This type of actions are called tasks and can vary hugely in terms of complexity. There are some tasks that can take us only a few minutes while others can require the execution of many sub-tasks and to complete them it would be necessary the support and collaboration of many people.

Stephen R. Covey in his book "The 7 habits of highly effective people" talks about learning to distinguish between the importance and the urgency of tasks and he advises us to focus on those tasks that are important because it is through them that we achieve our most meaningful goals. There is a big amount of important things that we must do but because they're not urgent we postpone them and this causes that we don't get the progress we want in each area of life.

## Energy

The first thing we need to be able to execute the tasks we have inside our different plans and projects is energy. If we let ourselves be overcome by laziness then we probably won't be able to succeed on those difficult tasks that are part of every project.

Usually the way we gain energy is by trying to keep all the different ways of *Feeling Good* in some acceptable levels and the other thing we can do is to act in small and low-complexity things so we start to get some traction and feel each time more motivated to approach more complex tasks.

Health also has a very important effect on our energy levels and this affects directly the discipline we have to do our different tasks and habits. Health is composed of several aspects and having even only one of them in poor levels can be cause enough for suffering a big loss of energy that can keep us from acting effectively. For this reason it is necessary to put attention to all those aspects being the main ones: exercise, diet and rest. When we do exercise our levels of physical energy increases and we feel more motivated to do stuff during the day. Just like that, when we sleep more than we should, instead of waking up with more energy, we wake up with more laziness and it takes more work to do productive stuff.

Many times when we are failing when executing some of our goals or habits, it is probable that we become too hard on ourselves and accuse ourselves of lacking strong will. The truth is that in many cases the cause of that low energy level can be found on our physiological part which can be improved if we pay enough attention to each one of the elements that make up health.

## Results

We won't always get the results we want in many of the things we decide to do. The causes of those little failures can be many. We ourselves could have been the cause if we see that we didn't try hard enough or didn't have the courage to do some of the things we had to do. Other cause can be that we didn't have enough knowledge to perform those tasks correctly and because of that things didn't work out as expected. In that case we must try to learn through experience what knowledge we were lacking and try to acquire it for the next time we face a similar task.

There are other causes that are simply out of our control and therefore we must accept calmly that things didn't go as we wanted and decide if we want to keep trying or if we are going to dedicate ourselves to a different task. Among those external causes we can find the performance of other people, some unexpected events that affected our plans in a meaningful way, or simply bad luck.

Since we can't be sure of always getting the results we expect in each one of our goals, we must try to understand that probably all those projects made up of many sub-tasks won't go exactly as planned. It is possible that we take longer than we planned, that we need more resources than was on our budget, or that even something happens that keep us from completing those plans.

The ideal is to do the process of planning as thoroughly as possible so we consider all the possible obstacles we could face and define strategies that let us handle them in case they present. At the same time we should also learn to keep calm and try to extract the bigger benefit and learning from those unsuccessful projects so we don't lose motivation to dedicate ourselves to new projects.

## Lists of things to do

One way of managing each project so we see what things we have to do and in what order is with lists of things to do.

These lists can be done on paper or ideally they could be done with some software that allows us to manage them much faster by having access to them from many different places and devices.

We can create a list for every one of our current projects

and we can manage those lists in two ways depending on the type of tasks. There are some tasks that should be completed in certain order and until we're not done with one we can't move on to the next. These tasks have no specific deadlines but since they depend on others we must organize them into our to-do-list in the order in which we need to complete them by putting on top the ones we need to complete first. As we start completing the top task, we cross it out or remove it from the list, and then we see what task follows and we start working on it. Using lists this way will allows us to know at any moment what is the next task we should do and this way we can avoid feeling overwhelmed by all the things we have left to do.

The other type of tasks of which our projects can be composed of are scheduled tasks. They can be events like meetings, special occasions, times when we should handle some paperwork or times when we have to deliver some work. The ideal is that we separate these tasks from the ones that we need to do in order. We can also order these lists by date so at any moment we know what are the things we need to do on the following days.

To make these lists really valuable in our lives we need to be constantly updating them by adding new tasks and by deleting those we've already completed. The process of crossing out a task has an important psychological effect that in many cases can make us feel good and it becomes a source of satisfaction and pride for ourselves because we are proving that we're being effective when doing the things we need to do to achieve our goals.

## Priorities

Since we can have several projects at the same time besides all the loose tasks we have related to our more simple goals and to the different obligations and activities of daily life, it becomes necessary to learn to give the right priority to those tasks and decide on which of them we are going to work at any time and to which give our highest efforts.

One first step is to do those things that are urgent such as commitments we have with other people or things that have a close deadline. If there are tasks that are urgent is because they are necessary and we should do them but this doesn't mean that these are the most valuable tasks we could be spending our time in. The origin of many of these tasks and urgent commitments can be other people and what those tasks will really benefit are the goals of other people and not necessarily our own.

Little by little we should start organizing our activities so we spend less on urgent tasks that don't help directly the achievement of our goals and dedicate that time to the other tasks we think are more important for us.

After getting rid of those urgent tasks, we should start giving priority to those activities and those moments reserved for our habits, both those that we're developing as well as those we already have.

The additional time we have left is the time we have available to do all those task that we have inside each one of our to-do lists. Usually we must give more importance to those tasks related to our most important goals. After them we can pass to the other tasks until we complete what we wanted to do for the day.

Between tasks or at the end of our daily journey, we can also dedicate some time for recreation and entertainment where we do things for our own enjoyment. In some days those moments can be of just a few minutes while in others we can dedicate several hours or even the whole day to those activities that are also important for living an enjoyable life that makes us feel good.

## Reduction and elimination

One of the keys for having more time in our life to dedicate to the things we consider really important and that can have a positive effect on the way we feel is reducing little by little those activities of low value that can be urgent or necessary but that don't really help us move on with our life. Spending long hours on jobs we don't enjoy or that are not leaving us enough resources to do other important things is one of the activities we should try to free ourselves from as soon as possible. Other low values activities can be going to meetings or social events that don't have that big of an impact for us, spending a big part of our time on passive-recreation, or sleeping more than enough. It is necessary to check constantly how we're spending our time so each time we can reduce more and more the number of low-value activities we identify in our lives.

The quality of life is measure in the way we spend our time. If we spend our time doing things that make us feel good or that really help us advance in our goals, then we could say that we are living a good life. If, on the contrary, our time is spend on obligation to obligation and the little time we have left we spend it by distracting ourselves through low-value or harmful activities, then it is very probable that we are living a bad life and that will reflect on a darker future with more problems.

# Habits

Habits are those activities or actions we do in a repetitive way or with certain consistency. The habits that are done frequently, that means, those we do at least once a week to those we do everyday, are usually called routines and these are really important for the achievement of many goals. These routines are also important because they give us an identity characterized by some patterns of behavior.

There are other habits that can be done more sporadically like once a month. One example of those habits can be things like cutting our hair or paying our bills. We can also have habits that are done once a year: especial events like birthdays, anniversaries, or any other specific holiday from our culture.

The habits we should pay the most attention to are our daily and weekly habits. By being activities we do more frequently it is possible to turn them in almost automatic things that don't depend so much on our will or emotional states.

Our willpower is pretty limited and is consumed very rapidly. Since it is limited we can't depend only on it to do all the things we have to do so we must reserve it for those activities that are new or that require a big physical or emotional effort. Here is where it becomes important to turn many of our activities into daily or weekly habits so we can preserve our willpower.

There are many aspects related to habits on a neurological level. When we do certain activities in a repetitive way we start creating brain connections that let us do those activities in a faster and more consistent way. We create brain connections that guide our actions and our movements almost automatically. Some daily routines such as showering or brushing our teeth are so automatic and we've been doing them for so long that probably we're not conscious of each one of the movements we do but if we'd record ourselves in a video we could see that we almost always shower the same way and the movements we do are almost always the same. This is because of the neurological connections we've developed through the constant repetition of these activities.

The problem is that just as we develop brain connections for the things we need to do, we also develop them for thinks we do to distract ourselves or activities that are harmful to us in some way. This is the reason why after we have become addicted to some activity or substance that keep us from the things we want to achieve, stop doing those activities becomes really hard and it requires almost exclusive dedication in order to break those connections and turn them into more productive ones.

## How to develop habits

To develop habits we must follow a series of steps and recommendations. First we must be very clear on why we want to develop that specific habit or routine. One of the most important ways to keep ourselves motivated as we develop a habit and not quit at the middle of the process is by knowing really well why we want to do it. For the habits we want to develop to be really important they need to be related to some of the goals we want to achieve and at the same time those goals must help us feel good in some way or increase our resources. By meeting this requirement we will have a very important first step to be able to keep doing the effort to develop a habit when things get hard.

The other point is accepting that we can't try to develop all our habits at the same time. If a habit we're developing is something that requires a great deal of effort or time such as begin going to the gym, or a habit related to our job or with developing some skill, then the best thing to do is to focus only on those habits until we have them established in our lives. When we have that habit set, which implies that we have created the required brain connections so we don't depend so much on our willpower, then in that moment we can decide which other habit we want to develop and do the same process.

There are other habits that are more simple such as flossing every night, or calling someone close to us frequently, and they only take us a few minutes each day and in this case we could try to develop several of these habits at the same time. Despite this, we shouldn't try to develop more that three habits at the same time so this way we guarantee that those habits become a part of our daily routine without of a big conscious effort to do them.

Other aspect to keep in mind when developing habits is that we must try to keep high levels of consistency especially at the beginning of the process. This means that if we want to develop a daily habit we must do our best effort so that in the first month we don't fail a single time in that activity and also it means that we try to do them on similar situations such as at the same time, in the same place and with the same tools. That consistency is the one that will allow our minds to figure out the patterns so it learns to handle that habit unconsciously and we can them focus our willpower in other activities. If for any reason there was a day in which we couldn't do the habit, then we need to analyze why and don't allow ourselves to fail the next day. When we fail once while we're setting a goal it is still easy to get back on the process but when we fail two times in a row, failing a third time won't be that hard and it is possible that we leave aside our goal and start distracting ourselves with less important things.

There are certain tools that can help us develop habits and one of them are alarms. Having a device that let us know the time when we should do some activity is a great resource to let our mind rest and focus on what is doing without having to keep a mental agenda with all the things we have to do at all times. Trusting only on our minds becomes a very inefficient process with a high rate of failure since the moment we have a problem or find ourselves in a very stressful situation we will probably forget that we were developing a habit and stop doing it.

These alarms can be specially important while we develop a habit. Once we've been doing something for several months very consistently then the alarm may stop being necessary since that activity is already something automatic and natural in our lives.

As a last recommendation when developing habits, it is very important that you try to start as soon as possible and if it is necessary in a gradual way. Many times there are new routines we want to develop to progress in some of our goals, routines such as exercising, practicing some musical instrument, writing, doing some sport, or many others, and we don't start because we feel that we're missing something like a tool or any other thing of no real importance, and that gives us an excuse to not do anything and keep postponing those habits. What we should do is act as soon as possible. If we still don't have the right clothing, or the most comfortable shoes, or if we can only dedicate 10 to 15 minutes each day to that activity, it doesn't matter, we must try to do it as soon as possible. As we start doing some activity a lot of those little logistical problems disappear quickly. Regarding rhythm, it is advisable to start slow and putting ourselves small goals at first will help us become more motivated and that will let us overcome that initial inertia and from there we can gradually increase our daily goals until getting that activity to our desired level.

## Vices

Vices are all those negative habits or routines that are an obstacle to achieve our goals and that in many cases can make us feel bad or make us lose many of our physical or mental dexterities in a temporal or permanent way if we abuse those activities. Since vices have a negative effect on our lives, in case we have them, one of our main purposes should be to diminish them or even to remove them completely.

When we have serious vices it is commonly a good strategy to focus on eliminating those habits before trying to develop other positive habits.

There are many strategies we can use to eliminate different

types of vices and I will talk about them next.

There are certain types of vices that are related with the consumption of substances that cause a chemical reaction in our body that make us feel pleasure but that can also have the effect of being addictive or making our bodies react badly if we diminish or eliminate the consumption of those substances. When the levels of addiction to some of these substances becomes very high it may become very difficult for us to be able to overcome those addictions on our own and when this is the case the best thing we can do is to look for professional help that can help us eliminate those addictions and give us tools that lower the chances of we falling back to them.

There are other vices that are related to specific activities that require the access to some place or a tool to do them. For example, in some cases watching television could become a vice that could be giving us problems in our lives. Other vices of this type could be spending too much time playing video-games, listening to music, eating, surfing the web or many other ways of passive recreation. Many of these activities are not bad by themselves but when we do them in excess and we're not able to control the time we spend doing them, then in that moment it could become a problem that we should try to overcome.

A good strategy to handle this type of vices is by eliminating or restricting the access we have to the tools or places that allow us to do them. If what we want is to stop seeing television, what we can do is to sell it so even if we want to watch we can't do it or be in the need to do something of more effort like going to the house of some friend to do that activity. If we want to stop eating unhealthy food then the first thing we should do is to stop buying that type of food when we go to the market so when we have cravings for them we go to the kitchen and realize we don't have any. If we want to stop playing video-games, then we can uninstall them or give them away so our access to them becomes limited. This type of habits are relatively easy to control since through a simple change of our environment we can really decrease the access we have to them and with this we won't have to depend so much on our willpower to avoid those temptations.

The last type of vices are those related to activities or people whose access is a necessity and therefore we depend entirely on our willpower to control ourselves to avoid doing them. They can be vices such as spending too much time with people that are harmful for our lives or using internet or social networks in excess. They can become difficult to avoid because for our work or our other obligations we need to access these tools constantly. These vices are harder to eliminate and once we've done it, it can still be hard not to fall back on them. The strategy to handle this type of vices is to fill our lives with more positive habits so we don't have the time nor the mental need to look for those vices to distract ourselves.

## How to keep habits

Keeping habits requires a process of constant supervision. It requires that frequently, at least once a week, we sit and analyze if we've been doing the habits we've established. We can do this analysis with a list we have on a piece of paper or some software that tells us all the habits we have and the times when we do them. If we find that we've stopped doing some of our habits then we need to analyze if those habits are necessary for our current goals and in case they are, try to get them back into our lives as soon as possible. Regaining a lost habit usually requires less time and effort than when one is trying to develop it for the first time. If we decide that some of our habits have stopped being useful for our goals or for the things we want to achieve, or that simply there are more important things in which we should be using our time, then it may become necessary to remove that habit from our lives and decide if we want to replace it for other habits or dedicate ourselves to the execution of other tasks that we have in our to-do lists.

## Patience

Patience is the most important virtue when it comes to developing habits and removing vices. Developing a habit doesn't happen overnight. Usually it requires months of constant effort and dedication to turn one activity into something that we do automatically or without too much help from our willpower. Just like that, eliminating a habit we've had for years is not something that happens instantly. For these reasons patience becomes so important, because without it we couldn't wait for so long to start seeing the results of our efforts.

If we lose patience we will possibly try to develop more habits than we can handle at the same time or try really hard in some of them and that can be counter-productive since the chances of failing can increase and that can have a negative effect on our motivation to continue. Since in each area of our lives we have many goals and inside those areas we can find that we have many habits, it is possible for the list of habits we have to develop to be really big. Logically we can't develop them all at once, and possibly it will take several years or even decades to develop each one of them and here is where we usually become impatient and try to get progress from each one of our goals as quickly as possible and what we do with this is to lower our effectiveness.

# Reflexion

After executing the tasks and habits we have inside our plans the next step is to reflect on what happened. Reflexion is the stage that really allows us to grow and become more effective to do things in the world.

The way reflexion works is that every time we do the previous steps and get to the process of execution we will see in the real world the result of our thinking, goals and actions, and we will be able to check if the thinks we though in the beginning apply to reality or not.

If our judgment was correct and our skills and resources were the right ones, then we'll have success in our goals and that can let us experience some of the ways of *Feeling Good* and at the same time it can help us increase our resources.

If things didn't come out as planned or as we wanted, then that could have been caused by several situations.

The first thing that could have gone wrong was the way we executed our plans. Maybe we didn't have the right skills, or we didn't consider a critical detail when doing our project and because of it we failed. Maybe we weren't disciplined enough in executing the plan or maybe an external circumstance got in the way and kept us from doing what we wanted. If any of these was the case, then there will possibly be some learning we can get from that experience that can help us in future situations.

Maybe we acquired some competence in some skill and we will be able to do it much better next time. Maybe we learned something about the world that will allow us to keep it mind the next time we design a project. Or maybe we learned that under some circumstances we are not as productive or we have some psychological obstacles that we must overcome to improve our execution capabilities. We could also have learned about certain risks that can present in any project and therefore we will be able to develop strategies that allows us to minimize the impact of those risks in the future.

The second type of learning we could have gotten could be associated with a mistake we made when setting our goals. Maybe the deadlines we set were not really viable, or maybe something we though would make us feel good didn't. Maybe we put ourselves many goals for a short period of time and for trying to distribute our efforts in all of them we didn't manage to be effective in some of them, or maybe it was all the contrary and we put ourselves very few goals and we had a lot of time left that we could have used to get some progress in our other goals.

From these mistakes we can acquire knowledge that allows us to understand better each area of life and know the potential impact they can have in the way we feel by keeping in mind our different values. We could have also have learned about the quantity of goals we are able to handle easily so we can progress at a good rate.

The third type of learning, and maybe the deeper, is that regarding what we know about ourselves and about our resources. We could have learned that some values we considered important and that we thought had the power to give us satisfaction didn't really have that power or that there are other values that could be more meaningful in our life than those.

Through the execution we could have also realize many things that allow us to modify our value system by moving some of them up or down in their level of importance. As we adjust our value system we will be able to choose goals that are more compatible with who we really are and therefore those goal will have a bigger impact in our well-being.

Besides having learned some things about our values we could have acquired some important knowledge about our different resources. We could have realized that we have some strengths or certain skills to do different types of activities much more easily than other people or at the same time we could have realized that we have some internal limitations that make it harder for us to achieve some type of goals and because of that we must become more careful in getting involved in activities that require a great deal of those areas in which we are not as strong.

We could also have learned about opportunities the world offers us and that we could use by setting short-term goals that allows us to take advantage of them. Just like that, the world is not full of roses and we could have realized that there are some external conditions that can become obstacles to achieve our goals and therefore we must look for strategies that allows us to overcome those obstacles without letting ourselves be stopped by them.

The reason why these are called deeper learnings is because

those learning imply reviewing step 2 and 3 of Life Strategy and that means that our goals should change to adapt to our new value system and the resources we have and therefore the actions we must do to achieve those goals should also change.

In general terms this is what this process called reflexion implies but there are several more concepts we should understand to do this process with more tranquility and effectiveness.

## Everything is an experiment

One good strategy is to learn to see everything we do as an experiment. Some times those experiments will succeed and we will get the things we want but other times those experiments will fail and we will have to analyze why they failed so we can try again.

Adopting this perspective to everything we do will free us from a lot of stress and frustration when things go wrong and we'll be able to recover more quickly, analyze the things that happened with more objectivity, and acquire learnings that will make us more effective in the future.

Another advantage of seeing everything as an experiment is that we take off the pressure of having to be always right. We no longer have to be afraid of making mistakes and we will stop seeing those mistakes as catastrophes we should be ashamed of. Freeing our mind from all these forms of self-pressure is a great way to do our tasks and habits with much more tranquility and that usually have a good effect on our performance. When we push ourselves too much or we try to do something with too much self-consciousness, it is much easier for us to make mistakes and that our body or mind won't answer with the flow and the effectiveness required.

We will also learn to measure risks better because by accepting that things are an experiment and can go wrong, then we will try to protect ourselves from those risks and this way the times we get hurt physically, emotionally or mentally will be seriously reduced. When we believe that the only choice we have is winning then it is possible that we take unnecessary risks that cause a great damage to our live and our future in case things don't work as expected.

## Detachment to results

The effect that starting to see everything as an experiment is that little by little we give less importance to the results we get and we will start focusing much more in the process which is also essential for our satisfaction. As I mentioned previously, satisfaction is the fourth way of *Feeling Good* and we get it with the actions we do day by day that are directed to achieving or maintaining our core values. This means that the process is what matters the most when it comes to experiencing satisfaction and that we have manage to integrate or not a value into our life is just a side benefit that can help us feel a little bit better.

Detachment from results will also teach us to not judge other people for what they have achieved or for the things they have. If we are going to judge them it must be for the way they are living their lives, for the discipline they have, for how clear they have their values and for the way the goals they have set for themselves are associated with those values. Just as we are in a process of constant learning where through our experience we improve each one of these aspects other people are in the same process and since it is too difficult to know where they come from or what is it that they're trying to achieve, it is almost impossible to judge if their actual condition reflects something that we should judge about them.

Regarding this subject we should also have respect and humility to accept that the goals we set for ourselves are based on who we are, the things we want, our strengths, weaknesses, opportunities and obstacles. That we choose more ambitious goals than other people in some areas doesn't mean that we are better than them or that our goals are smaller than other people's is not reason either to feel bad with ourselves. We all do the best we can with what we have available and what we consider important and this without a doubt is the cause of the infinity of roads that we people choose in live.

## When to reflect

The moment when we can get the most valuable learnings is when we finish an execution process where we could have gotten what we wanted or where things didn't go as expected. In those times it is possible to analyze a great deal of factors and dynamics that can give us learnings we can use to improve each one of the processes related with steps 1, 2 and 3 of Life Strategy. When reflecting it is good to look for a calm time and place where we can sit or lay down to think about everything that happened and after some good analysis identify the learnings we consider valuable. Other way to think is to go walk on nature or a place where the noise levels are minimal so we can focus on our thoughts and we can have important insights that help us grow and become more effective. Those insights can also be of use for other people in case we decide to teach them.

## Starting again

To finish this chapter it is worth mentioning that the process of reflection implies a process of starting again and it is through this process that our life becomes a constant cycle where these 3 steps of Life Strategy are always evolving and adapting better to our reality. It is possible that we don't have to start from zero but it is necessary to use in all the steps the things we learn and that we keep trying to get the results we want in each area of our lives. Through this process our life will start to take more and more the shape as we see it in our minds and how we think it should be and this is important so we achieve our true purpose of designing a life where we can feel good in everyone of its manifestations most of the time.

# Epilogue

Adopting Life Strategy as our model to understand life can help us get a better control and understand better how each one of its elements works. Thanks to this understanding we'll be able to make better decisions in our life and that will allow us to enjoy it more while we have it.

This model allows us to include most of the elements that make up human life so our understanding of how life works increases and that helps us get the most out of it. Even though most of us already have some of this knowledge, it's necessary a model that allows us to give it the organization and the order to all these concepts to understand how they interact with each other and how we can use them to make our life more complete and interesting.

This model also works to diagnose and identify the areas where we have problems so we can define the reasons why we're feeling bad and do the corrections we think necessary on the different aspects of our lives.

Life Strategy also has the characteristic of being universal. This means that each one of its elements and its processes can be applied to all people no matter their particular differences, their ideologies, their philosophies, or their resources. It is something that all people can use to live their lives in a more systematic way based on who they really are. For this reason giving advise about the roads people should follow is usually a waste of time since it's more effective that everyone make their own decision about what they want in their own life because they're the ones that can know themselves and their particular circumstances the best.

Throughout these chapters we learned about each one of the elements that make up human life.

We discovered that our main purpose is to Feel Good and that *Feeling Good* can be manifested in four different ways. The four ways we can feel good are pleasure with means feeling good physically, joy with means feeling good emotionally, happiness which means feeling good with the world and satisfaction which means feeling good with ourselves.

Each one of those ways of feeling good have their advantages and disadvantages and we learned that all four are necessary but that if we want to feel good most of the time we should give a little more priority to acquiring happiness and satisfaction since they're the most permanent ways of feeling good and they can fill the emptiness in those times when we can't enjoy pleasure or joy.

We learned that to avoid suffering in life we have to accept and be conscious of some principles that help us understand better how the world works and this way we will be in more harmony with it. These principles are rationality, uncertainty, responsibility, individuality and change.

We also learned about the different resources we humans have at our disposal. These internal and external resources determine many of the things we can do and they're also in constant evolution where through our actions and decisions we can increase them or deplete them and that implies that we have to update our goals constantly.

Lastly, through chapters 2 to 4, we explored the 3 steps that make up the process of Life Strategy.

The first step talked about gaining clarity about who we are and our current state. We learned what temperament is and how it affects our way of life. We also discovered what are core values and the big importance they have because of their relationship with satisfaction. We learned how to define our value system and how useful it can be when it comes to making decisions over the roads we want to pursue in life and the roads we're willing to sacrifice. That chapter also talks about the need to analyze our strengths, weakness, opportunities and obstacles and the way those aspects are related with our different resources and the way they affect the different goals we can set in life.

We learned that the purpose of step 2 is to define the direction we want to take in each area of our lives and the way to do this is by setting goals. We learned about the process how we define goals and the things we should keep in mind so that the goals we set can be really achievable and be really compatible among them.

Since life is divided is several areas we determined that a good way to organize all our life goals is by dividing them in those areas and about each one of them I explained the elements that make them up and how each one of those areas can affect the way we feel, our resources, and the effect they have on other areas.

We learned that in total there are 9 areas which are: personal growth, health, work, finances, tools and places, romance, family, social relationships and recreation. We got some practical knowledge about how each one of those areas works so we can make better decisions inside each one of them and we also understood that that knowledge is just a starting point that each one of us should complement with our own experience.

In chapter 4 we talked about the third and last step of Life Strategy that consists on executing our goals and this step is made up of three sub-processes: planning, acting and reflexion.

Planning consists on defining specifically what we have to do and the resources we need to reach each one of our short-term goals. The things we have to do can be presented in the way of tasks or habits and we learned about the strategies and specific considerations that we should keep in mind when implementing both of them. Lastly be talked about the last sub-process inside this step which is called reflexion. We learned that reflexion is essential for our growth and that if we want to become more effective in the way we face the world it's necessary that we reflect after we finish an execution process to analyze why things came out as they did and see what learning we can get to improve any of the previous steps.

# Likely obstacles

It is possible that we find several obstacles when we first try to implement this model in our lives.

The first of them is that we lack understanding on many of the concepts that make up Life Strategy. My goal with this book was not to explain in detail many of the concepts that I mention but offer an organization that allows us to understand their importance and their relationship with human life. Each one of those concepts requires many books to explain them with clarity and that's why it's important that each one of us try to deepen our knowledge of them through other books or resources and also through our own experience so we understand better what they mean and what they really imply. At the end of this book I will list some of the books that have allowed me to understand many of these concepts but without a doubt it is necessary that you complement this information with many other sources.

The second obstacle with which we can find ourselves is that we're not used to thinking about all these details in our own lives and because of that we may see this process as overwhelming and we won't know where to start. The truth is that most of us are used to analyze and make opinions on the lives of other people but in front of our own life we maintain many blind spots. It is important that we start little by little. First with step 1 we observe ourselves to analyze our temperament, our values, our resources and our particular situations. This process takes some time while we understand all of these concepts and we compare them with the observations we do in our own lives. After having a minimal understanding of these aspects we can proceed to set our goals more systematically. After identifying the things we want to achieve in the short-term it's necessary that we start executing and then through the experience we get improve all the previous steps. It is important to accept that this process is not done in a short time, it is a process that last for a lifetime and therefore we should be patient and try to improve the way we do it so we can enjoy all the progress we get along the way.

A third obstacle are the distractions that we have gathered throughout our daily life. By not having designed our life in a more systematic way it's possible that our life is full of distractions that can be manifested on all type of activities, people, things or commitments that we have gathered but that don't make us feel good nor help us achieve the things we want. Freeing ourselves from those distractions can take time and is something that we do gradually. As we start implementing positive changes in our lives then those distractions will start diminishing one by one until we reach a level where we spend most of our time in a truly meaningful way for us.

Each one of those obstacles can make it harder or even keep us from implementing this model called Life Strategy and therefore we must be conscious of them so we can manage them more effectively.

## Final Recommendations

To finish I would like to share with you 10 important lessons I've acquired through my experience and also through other people that I think can help you experience and have a more enjoyable life full of opportunities to develop yourself and all your ideals.

# 1. Learn from the experience of others

Despite getting a lot of important knowledge and insights from the process of reflexion that we can use to grow and improve in each one of the steps of Life Strategy, the truth is that we can also do some cheating and dedicate some of our time to study the reflexions done by other people through history, and use that knowledge in our life to make it richer without the need to go through all the painful experiences to obtain those learning that are at our disposal with simply opening a book.

Thanks to the experiences and learnings of other people we can advance much more quickly and at a very early age we can achieve many things that not many people would have been able to achieve some centuries before even if they'd lived more than 100 years. That is the power that has supporting ourselves on the shoulders of those that came before us so we can reach each time higher things in the world.

# 2. Develop resilience

Develop the skill to recover rapidly from any negative event that can happen in your life no matter how big it is. The way you do this is by developing flexibility in each area of your life so that you can respond with more freedom to a higher number of possible situations.

Resilience is a concept that is just starting to be used with more frequency in the fields of modern psychology and it's seen as the capacity to recover from catastrophic events. People who have good levels of resilience are less likely to fall into negative emotional states such us depression or anxiety. Other way we can develop resilience is by putting ourselves voluntarily in difficult but controlled situations that allows us to get familiar with those events and be able to respond with more skill in case one event of those characteristics shows up in our lives.

# 3. Protect yourself through happiness and satisfaction

In life not everything always happen as we expect it. There are times when we can't reach some of our goals permanently and we lose that potential. It may also be possible that we lose a very important person from our lives and that can become a true source of sadness and pain. It is normal to feel bad in front of those situations and if we're people who want to experiment all we can in life then we must accept that the loss of important things in our life is something that will surely happen and accept that that's the price we have to pay to live our life to the maximum.

The best way we have to face these loses in life and not let them lower our emotional states or our well-being too much is by learning to really integrate happiness and satisfaction. As I said previously, we get happiness by accepting and appreciating the things that happen and satisfaction is experienced when we act based on the knowledge and skills we have at any time and trying to always be in harmony with our core values. Since these two ways of feeling good are more related to ourselves than to the things that happen outside, it's possible that when things that causes us pain or sadness happen – which will surely do – then they won't hit us as hard and we'll be able to maintain some minimal levels of well-being that will allow us to recover quickly.

# 4. Learn to ignore criticism

Everyone's life is different because we all have a unique combination of temperament, values, resources, experiences, goals and desires. Learning about each one of those things about ourselves is really hard and therefore expecting that other people know us more that we know ourselves is impossible. It is for this reason that we should not let the criticisms that other people make of our lives acquire any importance. The only case where those criticisms may be valuable and when we should hear them is when they're about a very particular aspect of our life and the person it comes from is someone who has valuable experience on that aspect and is someone we respect and trust.

In most cases, criticisms are more motivated by the fears, insecurities and prejudices of other people than by their true desire to help us grow and help us get the things that are really important to us. This is the reason why it's a good idea to learn to not listen to these external criticism and keep doing what we think is right based on our best understanding of the world and of ourselves.

# 5. Be careful with the word failure

The word failure is really complex because it has the power to make us feel bad if we don't use it correctly. The wrong way of using this word is to define those events that didn't go as we expected even though we made our best effort with the resources and the knowledge we had. As I said in the section of reflexion, we must learn to see everything as an experiment where we should focus more on the process and on doing our best effort than on the results we get. If we live this way we'll always be growing even though many times things won't work out as we want it.

The moments the word failure have real meaning is when we talk about those goals we gave up even though they were still important to us and through a little bit more effort it would have been possible to achieve them. There are some goals that because of the circumstances they become almost impossible to achieve. For example, we could have had an accident or caught a disease that keep us from competing at the highest levels of some sport, or a specific person of our life can leave for any reason and therefore the goals we have associated with that person stop being viable. Despite this, the proportion of these types of goals is very low compared with all those goals that we can keep pursuing as long as we keep making the effort and keep trying to increase our resources and our ability to execute.

## 6. Take care of your reputation

Just a moment ago I recommended that you stop giving importance to the criticisms of other people since those opinions don't consider many things in your life, but right now I'm also advising that you take care of your reputation which is highly associated with your character and your integrity. It doesn't matter that a lot of people disagree with what you do, what it's really important is that what you do is related with your values and what you think is right. If you do things this way you will be proving your integrity, and even though other people don't like the things you do, they will still trust you because they know that you're living based on your own code and that will give you a good reputation which is very important because it gives you access to many opportunities throughout your life.

## 7. Learn to say "I don't know"

It is not necessary to know everything in life. There are many things that we can't still understand or explain and in most cases we don't need to do it. Many things don't have any relationship with what we want with our lives and unless we have a high curiosity to learn or discover something, we shouldn't try to learn it all and specially we shouldn't pretend in front of other people that we know something we really don't.

Each of us can specialize in certain types of knowledge or skills and we can rely on one another in case we need some of those things we don't have. This allows us to learn and understand those things that really interest us and that have relation with what we want to do.

## 8. Listen to your instinct

Reason is a very powerful tool when taking decisions but we must know when to use it and when to listen to our instinct. The problem reason have is that there are many decisions that we must make but over which we don't have enough knowledge and we'll never have it so we must choose among several options without having a really logical reason to do it. Any of those options could be right and the way we make the decision is by listening to our instinct. Our mind is composed both from a conscious as well as an unconscious part. The unconscious is huge and it holds a lot of data about all sort of things that would be impossible to store on our conscious mind. That is the reason why our unconscious is able to make mental operations where it take into account a lot of factors and this way it can reach conclusions over which decision to make and then it passes those conclusions to us in the form of instincts or hunches.

Learning to listen to those instincts can help us make decisions that can provide us with the highest levels of well-being in those cases where we are confused on which road to follow.

## 9. Don't give yourself so much importance

Even though our main purpose in Life Strategy is to feel good, this doesn't mean that we should focus on only us and give ourselves a higher level of importance than to everything else. We people life inside a system made up of many other people, living beings and many different things. If you compare our magnitude and our impact inside those systems we will see that we are very tiny creatures. Yes, it is possible to have a big impact in some people and circumstances, but from a global perspective, that impact will still be small. We must learn to see ourselves from this perspective so this way we don't get so stressed about our defects and the difficult circumstances in our lives. Stop giving ourselves so much importance will makes us more free to enjoy many things in our lives and to risk doing the things we really want to do and focus on having the impact we want to have on some particular areas.

## 10. Have fun

To finish I just want to mention that life should be a fun experience. There is no reason to stress more than enough, or to worry and let ourselves fall into states of depression. If we apply the principles of Life Strategy, its different concepts and some of the recommendations I just gave you, then it will become much easier to move through life with more flow where the obstacles become just challenges to be overcome and where success is a celebration of who we are and of our way of living life. Enjoying life, trying to get the most out of it and convey that energy to those around us can be the best way to turn this world in a much nicer and interesting place to life.

# References

- Allen, David. (2015). Getting Things Done: The Art of Stress-Free Productivity.

- Bevelin, Peter. (2005). Seeking Wisdom: From Darwin to Munger.

- Branden, Nathaniel. (2008). The Psychology of Romantic Love: Romantic Love in an Anti-Romantic Age.

- Branden, Nathaniel. (1981). The Psychology of Self-Esteem.

- Colvin, Geoff. (2010). Talent is Overrated: What Really Separates World-Class Performers from Everybody Else.

- Covey, Stephen. (1990). The 7 Habits of Highly Effective People: Powerful Lessons in Personal Change.

- Goleman, Daniel. (2013). Focus: The Hidden Driver of Excellence.

- Goleman, Daniel. (1995). Emotional Intelligence.

- Keirsey, David. (1998). Please Understand Me II: Temperament, Character, Intelligence.

- Kiyosaki, Robert. y Lechter, Sharon. (2000). Rich Dad, Poor Dad.

- Haidt, Jonathan. (2006). The Happiness Hypothesis: Finding Modern Truth in Ancient Wisdom.

- Irvine, William. (2008). A Guide to the Good Life: The Ancient Art of Stoic Joy.

- Loehr, Jim. y Schwartz, Tony. (2005). The Power of Full Engagement: Managing Energy, Not Time, Is the Key to High Performance and Personal Renewal.

- Marshall, Sebastian. (2011). Ikigai.

- Sivers, Derek. (2011). Anything You Want. 40 Lessons for a New Kind of Entrepreneur.

- Tynan. (2014). Superhuman By Habit: A Guide to Becoming the Best Possible Version of Yourself, One Tiny Habit at a Time.

- Whitworth, Laura y Kimsey-House, Karen. (2007). Co-Active Coaching: New Skills for Coaching People Toward Success in Work and, Life. 2nd Edition.

22239814R00115

Printed in Great Britain
by Amazon